Depravity

Depravity
A Narrative of 16 Serial Killers

Harvey Rosenfeld

DEPRAVITY
A NARRATIVE OF 16 SERIAL KILLERS

Copyright © 2009 Harvey Rosenfeld.

All rights reserved. No part of this book may be used or reproduced by any means, graphic, electronic, or mechanical, including photocopying, recording, taping or by any information storage retrieval system without the written permission of the author except in the case of brief quotations embodied in critical articles and reviews.

iUniverse books may be ordered through booksellers or by contacting:

iUniverse
1663 Liberty Drive
Bloomington, IN 47403
www.iuniverse.com
844-349-9409

Because of the dynamic nature of the Internet, any web addresses or links contained in this book may have changed since publication and may no longer be valid. The views expressed in this work are solely those of the author and do not necessarily reflect the views of the publisher, and the publisher hereby disclaims any responsibility for them.

Any people depicted in stock imagery provided by Getty Images are models, and such images are being used for illustrative purposes only.
Certain stock imagery © Getty Images.

ISBN: 978-1-4401-2847-9 (sc)
ISBN: 978-1-4401-2845-5 (hc)
ISBN: 978-1-4401-2846-2 (e)

Print information available on the last page.

iUniverse rev. date: 12/07/2021

We express gratitude to our son, Robbie, for completing the technical preparations of the book with great professionalism; to the staff of the Birnbaum Library at Pace University; and to Mrs. Anna Shepper for her translation of primary sources concerning Norwegian serial killer Arnfinn Nesset.

Contents

Introduction ix

Section I—Profiteers and Plunderers
Chapter I—Johann Otto Hoch—Bluebeard Extraordinaire. 3
Chapter II—Vasili Komaroff—Vampire of Moscow 23
Chapter III—Raymond Fernandez and Martha Beck: Lonely
        Hearts Killers 41

Section II—Victims Of Society?
Chapter IV—Fritz Haarmann—Lustmord in Weimar. 69
Chapter V—Carl Panzram—"The World's Worst Murderer" 91

Section III—The Vengeful Killer
Chapter VI—Bela Kiss—Vengeance in Oil 117
Chapter VII—Robert Hansen—Hunting Women in Alaska 133
Chapter VIII—Lucian Staniak—The Red Spider 153

Section IV—Sado-Sexual Crimes
Chapter IX—Henry Lucas and Ottis Toole—The Tag Team
        from Hell 169
Chapter X—Leonard Lake and Charles Ng—Sex Slave
        Masters. 195
Chapter XI—Andrei Chikatilo—Teacher, Grandfather,
        Sadistic Killer 213
Chapter XII—Dean Arthur Corll—Texas Candy Killer 235

Section V—Stereotypes: Intelligence, Race

Chapter XIII—Marcel Petiot—Doctor of Holocaust
    Atrocities 255
Chapter XIV—Cleveland Torso Killer—Mad Butcher of
    Kingsbury Run 277
Chapter XV—Carlton Gary—The Stocking Strangler 295

Section VI—Serial Killers for the 21st Century—Power Over Life and Death

Chapter XVI—Arnfinn Nesset—Scandinavia's Most Prolific
    Murderer 315
Bibliography 337

Introduction

On "The Osgood File," March 20, 2000, Charles Osgood spoke of serial killer Michael Ross, who was on death row for killing eight women and girls. Ross's attorney argued that he should not be put to death because he was an Ivy League graduate who could tell the world much about the mind and workings of a serial killer. Ross was executed in 2005.

Perhaps that was true, but even without Ross, we have learned much about the hundreds of serial killers who have come to the world's attention. Since the 1990s, the public interest in and fascination with serial killers has heightened greatly.

In a 1993 *New York Times* review of books on Ukrainian serial killer Andrei Chikatilo, Julian Symons wrote of the "contemporary fascination with physical violence, the fascination that has helped to make books and films like *The Silence of the Lambs* immensely successful."

According to Mark Seltzer in his *Serial Representation*, 1998, "serial murder and its representations ... have by now largely replaced the Western as the most popular genre fiction of the body and of bodily violence in our culture."

Statistics report the rise of serial killers in America. In the first half of the twentieth century, 1.2 serial killers were identified every year. At the close of the century, more than twenty-five were being recorded annually.

Serial killers have become an important factor in America's unsolved murders. They may very well account for many of America's five thousand unsolved killings each year. In addition, serial killers may be responsible for a large number of unknown murders each year, since many of their victims are drifters and prostitutes, so many have nobody to report them as missing.

Harvey Rosenfeld

Our fascination with the gruesome, with depravity can be traced to our study of Elizabethan tragedy at St. John's University. Our mentor was the late Prof. Leonora Brodwin, author of *Elizabethan Love Tragedy*. Our interest was heightened with the inauguration in 1974 of the bimonthly periodical, *Martyrdom and Resistance*, published by the International Society for Yad Vashem. We served as founding editor and edited the periodical for more than three decades. We learned of man's most wicked acts of the Holocaust and genocide.

In 1982 we focused on the battle of depravity versus humanity in our book, *Raoul Wallenberg: Angel of Rescue*, the story of the legendary hero of the Holocaust.

In discussing serial killers, one must make a distinction between serial killers and mass murderers. It is essential to look at the factors responsible for the development of serial killers and what spurs them on to their somewhat sociopathic "careers."

Everyone agrees that Adolf Hitler, Saddam Hussein, and Timothy McVeigh are mass murderers, not serial killers; however, there is no unanimity in distinguishing between the two. According to Symons, the distinction is more euphonic than substantive: "In the past, Mr. Chikatilo would have been called a mass murderer. Now the description has been softened to serial killer. The change is significant. A serial sounds agreeable, something to watch on television, and killing is what we do to vermin."

In 1990, Eric Hickey defined serial killing without consideration of motive, including all offenders who through premeditation killed three or more victims over a period of days, weeks, months, or years.

Later that decade, Colin Wilson and Damon Wilson and Harold Schechter and David Everitt offered differing views. In *Killers Among Us*, the Wilsons distinguish between the sexual versus the materialistic: "We are once again confronting the problem of the dividing line between the serial killer—whose motive is rape—and the mass murderer, who kills for gain." The Wilsons were very thorough in their presentations of serial killers, but their distinction was too limiting. The "rape motive only" definition excludes the likes of Petiot, Beck and Fernandez, and Hoch, all of whom are most often included in the serial killer rosters.

In *The A to Z Encyclopedia*, Schechter and Everitt present a more acceptable distinction between the mass murderer and serial killer, accenting the mind-set and actions of the individual. The mass murderer "suddenly goes completely berserk, slaughtering a large number of random victims." On the other hand, the serial killer is a planner, "the hunter of humans."

Schechter and Everitt's definition can be further refined: A mass murderer—political or not—does not have to be, as they state, "suddenly ... completely berserk." Neither does there need to be a reason for the victims to be murdered suddenly (e.g., contract killings). The serial killer does plan, most often at different locations.

In 1998, Steven A. Egger (*The Killers Among Us: An Examination of Serial Murder and Its Investigation*) widened the definition to those committing a second murder. He did challenge, however, views that include material gain as motive. In his definition, "There is generally no prior relationship between victim and attacker; generally, the murderer seeks power or dominance over his victims, and victims may have symbolic value for the murderer and/or are perceived to be prestigeless and in most instances are unable to defend themselves or alert others to their plight."

In defining "serial killer," we need to know how many murders it takes for someone to "qualify." According to the criterion of the FBI-created National Center for the Analysis of Violent Crimes, there must be at least four victims for someone to be considered either a mass murderer or a serial killer. The criterion was determined at a 2005 symposium of the National Center for the Analysis of Violent Crimes.

In *Thrill Killers* (1986), Clifford L. Linedecker argues there is no fixed number required. What he stresses, and what can be added to the definition of serial killers, is the continuation of their operations: They continue their crimes until imprisonment or death, or, if they are never caught, the cessation of their murder sprees may simply mean they abandoned their criminal careers.

One of the earliest students of serial killers was William Bolitho in 1926, who was intrigued by the phenomenon of Germany's Fritz Haarmann. Bolitho included four other serial killers and categorized them as murderers for "profit." He concluded that each is unique with his "black literature," yet he also concluded that in many ways the serial killer is much like the ordinary individual:

"These are men, certainly not deranged automatons that we will observe; the worst men, not madmen; even on the slightest acquaintance, nastily like ourselves. They do not despise in their technique of life any of the anodynes that we 'of the virtue' use against poverty, loneliness, hunger, the contempt of our fellows, or predatory competition ... they very commonly construct for themselves life-romance, a personal myth in which they are the maltreated hero, which secret is the key of their life. In such comforting day dreams, many an honest man has drugged himself against despair."

Bolitho goes beyond these murderers for profit to place serial killers in three categories that combine motivation and upbringing: the biological killer, whose crimes are triggered by a physical defect or malady or injury; the psychologically demented killer, whose problems are related to a traumatic childhood; and the sociological or "made-by-society" killer, who feels society has cheated him and owes him something.

More contemporary serial killer scholars have analyzed serial killers in terms of their fields of operations, their relationships to their victims, and the reasons for their crimes. In Michael Newton's *Hunting Humans* (1990), the author writes of the locale of these crimes: "territorial," staking out of a specific region; "nomadic," roaming widely in search of prey; and "stationary," setting traps in the killers' own homes or places of employment.

Brian Lane and Wilfred Gregg, the editors of *The Encyclopedia of Serial Killers*, approach the study of serial killers as an analysis of those who have "separate and distinct characteristics," among them "the single incident killer" who has one victim at a time; minimal prior connections or relationship between killer and victim; "spatial mobility," which does not restrict the killer geographically; "overkill," in which there is "total enjoyment of the use of violence, heightened by excess;" and the absence of rationality for the crimes. However, they are far from convincing on this last point because if no rationality existed, serial killers would all be judged insane and not punished. Moreover, after making the point, the editors proceed to discuss motives, identifying three serial killer personalities: "missionaries," who seek to aid society by ridding it of "undesirable elements;" "hedonists," who derive pleasure, thrills, lust, or financial gain from their murders; and "power seekers," who view their murders as a means of exercising control over other people's lives. The hedonist also derives great satisfaction by outwitting those who pursue him or set out to trap him.

Lane and Gregg cite Ronald M. Holmes and James De Burger, whose *Serial Murder* (1987) called gain killers "comfort-oriented killers." According to Lane and Gregg, these murderers "exhibit the comparatively rare motive among serial killers of personal, usually financial, acquisition. For this type of murder the act of killing is an incidental, often irksome necessity in the pursuit of some other goal."

During the 1990s, Newton and Colin Wilson ("The Age of Murder") focus their explanations of serial killings by examining the sado-sexual overtones, Satanism, and black magic. Serial killers possess average or even above-average intelligence. They do not make an active or positive use of their intelligence. Instead, they act, in part, because they resent a society that does not permit them to productively use their intelligence.

Synonymous with existentialism of the twentieth century, John

Paul Sartre has received added attention from serial killer scholars in the past fifteen years. His essay "Herostratus," first translated into English in 1941, examined the inner life of a serial killer. Leyton begins his 2000 study of serial killers by describing Sartre's serial killer as having the qualities that contemporary scholars note: "self-absorption ... anger and desire for revenge for real or imagined slights, the pleasure in the suffering of others, the need to demonstrate their 'superiority' by taunting the authorities, the urge for lasting celebrity, and the peculiar mixture of reality and fantasy in their lives."

Mark Seltzer in *Serial Killers* deals with Sartre's *Critique of Dialectical Reason*. Seltzer views Sartre as considering seriality as a mode of human interaction, a "radical failure of individuality." Seltzer further quotes Sartre: "All the while I am modeling myself and my behavior on the being of other people outside me, all the rest of them are doing exactly the same thing; in fact there is no Other, only an infinite regression."

According to Thomas C. Anderson, Sartre sees those who commit senseless acts as individuals who fear loss of personal freedom. Therefore, they refuse to cooperate or work together with others, over a long period of time. "That is why the threat of violence is necessary," writes Anderson. "That is also why the group tends to dissolve into seriality, no matter how harsh the steps taken to prevent it."

Serial killers, according to Sartre, think illogically. In speaking of the "insanity" of serial killers or their "senseless" acts, Colin Wilson in "The Age of Murder" relates the actions to Sartre, who terms this phenomenon as "magical" thinking. Explains Wilson: "completely illogical thinking that cannot possibly accomplish its objectives—like an ostrich burying its head in the sand." Wilson argues for the importance of magical thinking as "a vital clue to the psychology of crime." Thus, Wilson systematically argues that serial killers can be explained with a link to Sartre.

"They are free individuals who have decided to kill by following a certain thought process. It is because the thought process is magical—because it contains a fallacy that they end as serial killers. Magical thinking ... is the child's attempt to avoid the effort of self-control, based on the spoilt child's assumption that he deserves freedom."

Perhaps no writer has dealt as thoroughly with serial killers as has Colin Wilson; however, as incisive as "The Age of Murder" and his other writings are, his theories do not always hold true; nor do the theories of the other writers cited here, nor of many other psychologists and criminologists who have labored to fix a theory for the crimes of serial killers. Some have advanced the theory of "motiveless" aggression; others have described serial killers as those who act out of insanity or paranoia.

In short, no one theory can explain all serial narratives. What is helpful, however, is a series of observations: (1) The serial killer must be intelligent, clever, and/or crafty, otherwise he or she would not succeed as long as he or she does in the serial killer "career;" (2) The motive of financial gain has spurred on serial killers, but in recent decades, this motive seems to have become less important; (3) Today, the most common forces driving serial killers are sex and power; and (4) The drive for power and life-and-death control over another human being has resounded in the past few years, as in the cases of New Jersey nurse Charles Cullen, who, in December 2003, reportedly admitted killing thirty during his sixteen-year career, and British family physician Dr. Harold Shipman, who hanged himself in jail in January 2004, having been blamed for killing some two hundred fifteen elderly patients over several decades.

What influences shape the development of a serial career? Again, there is no one set answer. More than one contributing factor may exist, including "non-personal" factors like ethnic, cultural, and economic situations, and "personal" factors like brain or physical damage, an abusive parent who is on drugs or alcohol or excessively possessive, or a socially frowned-upon parent like a prostitute.

In *Serial Murder*, Elliott Leyton offers "modern scientific perspectives." In this exhaustive study, Leyton closes with a section on future research. One of the "unresolved questions" is whether serial killers were victimized by "savage child abuse."

Leyton notes that early researchers found no solid link between abused children and serial killers. However, more current research has stressed the link and backed it up with statistics. This research insists, writes Leyton, that "child abuse is the significant and recurring factor in the personal history of these killers."

Yet Leyton is not convinced and asks for more proof. More important, he asks: why do not all abused children develop into serial killers? Some lead a life of alcoholism, drug addiction, or "religious or political fundamentalism." *Depravity* notes many who were victimized as children. While not answering Leyton's question, this book emphasizes that serial killers were craftier and more cunning than the drug addicts or alcoholics whose beginnings were marred by child abuse.

Another fruitful avenue for future research suggested by Leyton: "the still unknown role of biological/chemical hormonal imbalances in the construction of the murderous personality." The stories of Raymond Beck and Fritz Haarmann, among others of the sixteen, confirm the value of such investigation.

Depravity introduces a group of serial killers spanning the twentieth century and spanning the globe. In varying degrees, all were intelligent or crafty in their ability to outsmart others or elude pursuers. Their development or motivation offers multidimensional looks. Among others, we find:

A Russian, Komaroff, who killed for profit;

A German, Haarmann, emotionally damaged in childhood, who personified lust-morde;

A Pole, Staniak, with artistic skills, who was driven to a serial killer career to avenge the death of a family member;

A Hungarian, Kiss, who merged vengeance with a thirst for plunder;

A Norwegian, Nesset, who moved from a deprived childhood to wield power and death as manager of a nursing home;

Two Americans, Beck and Fernandez, who joined as a team, bringing a childhood of sexual depravation, in her case, to advance his lust for money;

An American, Lucas, who launched a horrific life of murder after being raised by a possessive mother;

And another American, Carlton Gary, whose career as a serial killer brought to the fore questions about why there have been relatively few African American serial killers.

SECTION I—
PROFITEERS AND PLUNDERERS

JOHANN OTTO HOCH

Bluebeard Extraordinaire

"Women are all right in their place, but marry only one at a time."

The advice was offered to a newspaper reporter by Johann Otto Hoch before the swindler, bigamist, and murderer was hanged in 1906. During a near-two-decade period, from the end of the 1880s to the first years of the twentieth century, Hoch married at least fifty-five women, and the number of those he murdered range from twenty-five to fifty. The police designated him "America's greatest mass murderer."

Hoch also earned notoriety as a bluebeard killer, which Michael Newton in *Hunting Humans* describes as a "generic term for any man who murders a series of wives or fiancées." The term "bluebeard" is derived from a fifteenth-century slayer of children, the French nobleman Gilles de Rais. His facial hair was blue-black; so the designation.

The American bluebeard is known in American serial killer literature as Johann Otto Hoch, but he often adopted as a pseudonym the name of his most recent victim. He had a medley of names: Johann Hoch, Otto Hoch, Jacob Joch, Jacob Schmidt, Jacob Erdorf, Jacon Huff, Henry Bartels, Dewitt C. Cudney, Albert Buschberg, Dr. L. G. Hart, Martin Dotz, C. A. Meyer, Jacob Duss, H. Frick, John C. O. Schulze, Heinrich Valzand, Henry F. Hartman, James C. A. Calford.

The bluebeard was born Johann Schmidt in Horweiler, Germany, in 1862. The family setting seemed quite positive. Both his father and two brothers were clergymen. And the family expected he would follow the same path.

However, he was first apprenticed as a metalworker, and then chose to study medicine, pharmacy, and chemistry in Vienna. He gained experience in chemists' shops in Germany, which would serve his later needs—drugs and poisons.

Who was the "lucky" first Mrs. Hoch? All that is known of Anna Hoch is that he married her in Vienna in 1881 and buried her in 1883. Cause of death: unknown. That same year, he married wife number two—at that point people were still counting—the wealthy Christine Ramb, who bore him four children. In 1887, Hoch walked out on the marriage and wed once more—wife's name unknown—in a town near Vienna. That marriage lasted less than a year.

Hoch was now ready to immigrate to America with funds available from the dowry collected before marrying Christine Ramb. But bluebeard wasted no time en route to America. He romanced an immigrant servant girl on board, married her after the ship docked, and collected her niggardly savings as he buried her after a two-month marriage.

He settled in Chicago, where he continued to swindle, marry, and murder. Few specifics have been detailed, but police would later learn that he posed as a religious worker, Jacob Erdorf. He swindled the Herzfeldt sisters, first his wife, Martha, of eighteen hundred dollars. He told Martha that her savings were in a bank that would surely fail, so he offered to take her savings and deposit them in a "safe" bank. Soon after the transfer, he buried Martha.

He next turned attention to sister, Rose, and sweet-talked her into marriage. "Now, my dear," he told her, "I am alone in the world. You stick to me, and I will make you happy. I will do everything for you I possibly can. Your sister told me you were a good businesswoman. When things get straightened out, I will open a hotel, and we will work hand-in-hand.

"It would be a pleasure to be a father to your ten children. Then they will be our children. I want a wife who has had a bad husband, so she will appreciate a good one. Therefore, you will appreciate me when you get me ..." Married now to Rose, he convinced her to withdraw eight hundred dollars from the bank and entrust the funds to him. He never came back from the bank but used the funds for a return visit to Germany.

Back in Horweiler, he took to speculating in barley futures, but he was an absolute failure as a speculator. When a note for three thousand marks fell due, he boarded a ship for Wheeling, West Virginia, in 1895.

He assumed the name of Jacob Huff and played the role of a charming, happy-go-lucky fellow with a well-cared-for handlebar moustache. He first worked in a saloon as an itinerant bartender, and soon he opened his own saloon. By this time, Huff was an accomplished swindler and bigamist. Before he was hanged, the *Chicago Sun* and the *New York Evening Journal* reported the six rules the bluebeard had crafted for succeeding with women:

"Nine out of every ten women can be flattered."

"Never let a woman know her own shortcoming."

"Always appear to a woman to be the anxious one."

"Women like to be told pleasant things about themselves."

"When you make love, be ardent and earnest."

"The average man can fool the average woman if he will only let her have her own way at the start."

However, a Wheeling pastor was not fooled. Pastor Herman Haass of St. Matthew's German Lutheran Church was the first person who was wary of Huff. Huff's clients were the local German immigrant population, who savored beer, zither playing, and nonstop old-country singing of Heidelberg drinking songs. It was at this saloon that Huff met a woman. She was a widow with a large house and a twenty-five-hundred-dollar life insurance policy.

The reverend started sizing up the saloon keeper when Huff began befriending the well-to-do widows of his church. "Huff's romantic technique," writes Schutzer in the 1964 *American Heritage*. "He proposed marriage to just about every wealthy widow in the neighborhood. 'He wants to settle down,' the minister later remembered one of his Hausfrau parishioners telling him. 'He said he needs a woman to care for his home,' she continued. 'And he said he would be willing to provide for me.'"

Haass advised his parishioners to proceed cautiously. However, Caroline Huff, the widow with the large house, would not wait, fearing she would lose out to another widow. Reluctantly, the reverend performed the ceremony. Immediately, Jacob Huff moved into the widow's house.

Caroline Huff had always been a healthy woman, so all were amazed when she was stricken ill within three months. The situation worsened. Summoned to her bedside, Haass watched Huff dose his wife with a white powder, which the cleric assumed at first was potion or medicine. After leaving the room, Haass rethought the situation and noted that Caroline reluctantly took the medicine.

The minister agonized. What should he do? Should he go to the police? If he were wrong, and she were really sick and the powder were medicine, his reputation as minister would be damaged, and worse, it would have been sinful—perhaps an unpardonable sin—to suspect an innocent man.

So Haass waited until deciding to go to the professionals. He called Dr. Gregory Ackerman, a local physician, and took him to visit the sick woman. When they arrived, they noticed Mr. Huff sitting alongside the bed.

Quickly, Dr. Ackerman grabbed the minister. "We must leave," he said. "Dr. Ford is treating her."

Dr. Ackerman's medical ethics are questionable in light of a 1905 interview he gave to the *New York American*. "Mrs. Huff had been dying," he said. "Her hands were swollen and her stomach was distended. She vomited continually. Either she had peritonitis, or she had been poisoned. However, Dr. Ford was the regular attending physician, so I had no right to interfere."

The day after the visit by minister and physician, Caroline Hoch died in agony. When the minister went to the Huff house, he found the body unattended. The minister searched for the husband; after a long search, he found Mr. Huff calmly waiting for a haircut. The widower immediately wept, but the reverend could not be fooled.

After Mrs. Huff was buried the next day in a cemetery on the outskirts of Wheeling, the minister commenced an investigation. He learned that Huff's saloon had been shut down and the owner was heavily in debt. What about the powder? No prescriptions had been filled in Wheeling's pharmacies. Neither had Dr. Ford written a prescription, for he believed that Mrs. Huff was suffering from the kidney disease nephritis. No treatment existed.

"Detective" Haass then went to Mrs. Huff's bedroom to retrieve the powder for analysis. No trace remained. Perhaps the husband had the same thought and was covering up his trail.

Haass suspended the investigation because of his own illness. After recovery, some two weeks after Caroline Huff's death, the minister sat down to dinner with his family. The meal was interrupted by noise in the bedroom. A prowler? No, Jacob Huff.

"What are you doing here?" the minister demanded.

"I want to talk with you," said a timid Huff.

"But why did you sneak into the bedroom?" responded the annoyed minister. Without answering, Huff ran out of the room, out of the house, never to be seen again in Wheeling.

The minister's own medicine was over the fireplace in the bedroom. "He was trying to poison me," concluded the cleric. Immediately, he emptied the bottles. He later regretted that action. If the bottles had been tested, that might have clinched the case against Huff.

Certainly, Huff knew that he was under suspicion. The Wheeling police told Haass that they had found Huff's clothes, hat, a German silver watch with Huff's photo, and suicide note. All this was found on the banks of the Ohio River.

Clever criminal that he was, Huff's footprints led down to the river. "We must conclude," said the police, "Huff committed suicide because he was depressed about his wife's death."

The police dredged the river for two days at the place where Huff had left his clothes. They found nothing. A report from the Red Men's Cemetery revealed that Mrs. Huff's grave had been tampered with. No purpose could have been served with the tampering, reasoned the police. The matter was dropped. The reason for the tampering, unfortunately, only became clear years later.

The pragmatic Huff had already taken care of business. He sold the house, withdrew the wife's savings, and cashed the twenty-five-hundred-dollar life insurance policy.

Pastor Haass continued his interest in the case, always on the alert for news and leads. Approximately one week after Huff's supposed suicide, a salesman of religious articles called on Haass about someone fitting Huff's description on the other side of the Ohio River in Janesville. Naturally, Huff was with a woman, arm in arm. The minister notified the Janesville police, but they showed no interest.

Haass was persevering. He was a voracious reader of the press, both German and English. In particular, he enjoyed perusing life cycles—birth, marriage, and obituary notices. Was he looking for news of suddenly dead widows and disappearing husbands?

Haass's readings bore fruit. One story, in 1897, told of Otto Hoch, who married in Dayton and deserted his wife few days later—with her savings, naturally. Haass reached for his scissors after reading about a mysterious death in Cincinnati of Mrs. Clara Bartels. The three-month marriage mate was Otto Hoch. He then read of a Jacob Otto Hoch who married in Milwaukee.

That was it. He quickly sent a missive with a warning to the Milwaukee police. Again, the police refused to act.

Haass continued to read and clip through 1898. Mrs. Janet Spencer of Chicago was married to C. A. Calford and ripped off of seven hundred dollars after a two-month marriage; Mrs. Minnie Rankin married Frank Warnke, who disappeared one month after the marriage ceremony; DeWitt C. Cudney fled with five hundred dollars, leaving Charlotte Andrews one hour after the nuptials.

But it was the name of Martin Dotz that would finally serve the mission of the pastor. As was his custom, Haass sat down with his paper after breakfast. He read about Martin Dotz, arrested for bigamy and for swindling.

The swindling charge did Dotz in. The alleged victim was F. J. Magerstadt, a Chicago used-furniture dealer. At first, the name of Dotz meant little to the minister. But then he read the physical description of the bigamist crook: weight, height, beard-whisker, the drooping eyelid, and huge teeth.

Setting aside his unfinished breakfast, Haass rushed off a letter to the chief of police detectives in Chicago, Captain Luke Colleran. Haass was convinced that the alleged criminal was Huff, murderer of Caroline Huff. He also attached a copy of the photograph on Huff's abandoned pocket watch.

Enter inspector extraordinaire George Shippy. The inspector confronted Hoff, now Hoch, with the photo. "Yes, it's my picture. So what? I never set foot in Wheeling," retorted the bluebeard.

At this point, nothing could be proven concerning bigamy or murder charges. But the swindling charge stuck, and Hoch was sent to Cook County jail for a year.

Meanwhile, Shippy persevered. Hoch was his number-one pursuit. The investigation began with Magerstadt. Aside from being a furniture dealer, he was a Chicago realtor who rented apartments to Hoch after his marriages. In fact, he had rented Hoch more than a half-dozen flats, a new flat for each marriage.

The merchant-realtor told the inspector that the new brides came to his store to choose furniture. Women would fill his ears with tales of the courtship, including zither serenades. One of the women told

Magerstadt, "With my money and his brains, he'll make a fortune for both of us."

Magerstadt continued his narrative for the inspector. "One day, I asked him, 'Why is it that you marry under so many different names?' 'Very simple. Women would not marry me or any other man if they knew I had been a widower so many times.'"

Magerstadt was fascinated, so he decided to attend one of the numerous funerals of a Hoch wife. The rite was for Mrs. Julia Steinbecker, married for but two months. Suddenly, the family of the deceased joined the coroner in insisting that the burial not begin. Julia swore on her deathbed, claimed the family, that her husband had poisoned her with white powder.

However, Hoch had not left things for chance. He produced a death certificate signed by the attending physician that Julia had died of natural causes. Shippy was not convinced and followed all leads.

Next, the inspector headed for Wheeling to gather evidence from the cemetery. Shippy contacted Chicago Police Chief Colleran, who reached out to West Virginia State Attorney William C. Meyer. Permission was granted to exhume the body of Caroline Hoch and perform an autopsy.

But Hoch had seemingly outwitted the inspector. He had been to the cemetery three years ago. When the grave was opened, the workers gasped. "Her body has been cut open," they screamed. There was no midsection or vital organs. In short, it was impossible to test for poison.

After Hoch left Cook County jail in 1900, Shippy was waiting with a demand that he go to Wheeling on a murder charge. But without evidence—without the organs—there was no case. Hoch was released from custody.

Anxious to resume activity after a year in prison, the bluebeard—now Albert Buchsberg, a wealthy Chicago druggist—desired Mrs. Mary Schultz, recently widowed. He married her and pocketed the two-thousand-dollar policy on her late husband's life. He then prevailed on Mary and her daughter to move to Chicago with him. Mother and daughter—and an additional fifteen thousand dollars in savings—were never heard from again.

With Shippy and Haass unremitting, why didn't Hoch quit? Didn't he realize that at one point he would be caught?

According to Shippy, "It seems doubtful Hoch possessed an arrogance so monumental that he believed he could murder without end and never run afoul of the law. More likely, murder had become a habit. Wife-killing was his trade. He could make a living at nothing else."

Shippy monitored Hoch's activities. He read of courtships in San Francisco, western New York, St. Louis, St. Paul, and Milwaukee. Still, Shippy had no smoking gun. Meanwhile, Hoch was honing his trade. He enrolled in a hypnotism course in Jackson, Michigan, and earned a diploma as a graduate hypnotist. He hoped to entrance widows to take out large insurance policies.

Hoch continued swindling and murdering through the fall of 1904 and had returned to Chicago. He posted a matrimonial advertisement in the German-language paper *Abendpost*: "German, with his own income, wishes acquaintance of widow without children. Object, matrimony."

He lured Marie Welker and wasted no time. On the wedding day, he borrowed four hundred seventy-five dollars from his bride to furnish their new flat. "My money is all tied up in real estate and investments," he lovingly told the bride. She fell ill the day of the wedding and was diagnosed as having nephritis by Dr. Reese. But Hoch had arrived first with white powder.

Hearing of her sister's grave condition, Mrs. Emilie Fischer—also a widow—came to visit and offered one thousand dollars for medical expenses. Hoch turned down the offer. But the dying woman sensed that Emilie was readying a marriage to Hoch. "I'll soon be dead," said an angry Marie, "and then you can have him." The sisters bitterly argued for hours.

It was too late to go home, so Emilie planned to bed in the kitchen.

"I apologize for Marie's words," Hoch told her. "She is very sick, you know."

With one wife ready for the grave, Hoch advanced another romance. Hugging Emilie, he pleaded, "I cannot be alone in the world. Marry me when she goes. I will be a widower. The dead are for the dead. The living are for the living."

Early the next morning, Hoch left his still-cursing wife and returned with the physician. "She's dead," pronounced Dr. Reese.

Hoch "restrained" himself. He waited four days before marrying Emilie. "If Marie had not insulted you with her accusations," Hoch told his would-be sister-in-law and new wife, "I would have mourned at least six months for her." Not long after the new bond, Hoch thought about the thousand dollars he turned down. "Emilie." He turned to his new wife. "I have an eighty-one-year-old ailing father in Germany. He plans to leave me fifteen thousand dollars. Then we can open a hotel. Don't you think I should visit Germany and protect our interests?"

Within a week, the new bride advanced seven hundred fifty dollars. Hoch left and never returned. But Emilie became suspicious. After all, her sister had seemed in good health. She contacted the Chicago police and met inspector Shippy.

In January 1905, the court ordered the body of Marie Welker Hoch exhumed. Inexplicably, Hoch had not covered his tracks this time. The autopsy showed a substantial amount of arsenic: 7.6 grains in the stomach and 1.35 in the liver.

Shippy had the evidence; now he had to find Hoch. Throughout America, ads were placed looking for Hoch. Understandably, Chicago police were bombarded with calls from ex-wives, and relatives of Hoch's victims. Perhaps sniffing trouble, bluebeard left for New York as Henry Bartels and resided in Manhattan, at 47th Street near 10th Avenue. He found the room through an advertisement in the German-language paper *Das Morgen Journal*.

As was his practice, he wasted no time. Arriving at night, he waited until the next morning and proposed in the kitchen. Actually, he did peel potatoes for the landlady, Mrs. Catherine Kimmerle, twenty minutes after putting down his suitcases.

The lady, of German descent, was stunned but very polite. "Why don't I introduce you to my friends," she said. "Many are widows anxious to get married."

The next morning, Mrs. Kimmerle took a trolley ride down to Chambers Street. Staring her in the face across the aisle was a photo in the *New York American* with the caption "Bluebeard Murderer"—her boarder and would-be husband.

Immediately, she called the police, who hurried to the boardinghouse and Bluebeard's room. "How d'ye do, Mr. Hoch?" was the greeting of detective John O'Neill. Hoch was relaxing, unruffled by the police intrusion, and did not resist arrest.

"First-rate," responded the lodger, "but you have made a large mistake. My name is not Hoch, but Bartels, and I sell wines from the Rhine. Our home office is Frankfurt am Main."

They searched his room and found some seven hundred dollars, a wedding ring, some dozen suits with labels from different cities, and a loaded revolver. The most valued find was a hollow fountain pen containing fifty-eight grams of arsenic.

The four detectives were not convinced of his expressed innocence. "Well," said O'Neill, "You look enough like my old friend Hoch to be mistaken for him, and I guess you'd better come over to the station house and convince the captain that you are not Hoch. They want a man that looks very much like you in Chicago."

The police station was one block from the boardinghouse. Hoch was questioned intensely and seemingly endlessly, when the captain asked about the arsenic. "I am a very depressed widower," said the suspect, "and am planning suicide."

Hoch was released, but that quickly came to an end when his widely circulated portrait caught the attention of one of the living swindled in Chicago, Mrs. Anna Hendricks Schmidt. She took the next bus to New York and identified Hoch.

"I am Hoch," admitted the bluebeard, "and I am a much-abused man."

As extradition procedures were readied in Chicago, police gathered information from victims and heirs. At the start, the police announced that they had evidence that Hoch once had five furnished flats with a wife in each—at the same time.

Physicians were queried by the press. How did Hoch baffle them? Why the diagnosis of nephritis when victims were poisoned with arsenic? There were at least eight irritants, said physicians, capable of concealing their own presence behind symptoms of nephritis itself. This frustrated post-mortem examinations and chemical analyses.

After one week, the police had identified some fifteen ex-wives who had been swindled out of more than fifteen thousand dollars.

As February 1905 began, Hoch was becoming annoyed at his detainment and the "extradition business." Reporters were unimpressed with the physical quality of the prisoner. Reported the *New York Times*, "Hoch does not look like a Don Juan. He is short and chubby with big hands and feet. He has a tinge of gray and his forehead is high. His eyes are shifty."

"I'm Hoch, all right," he told detectives on the way to the courthouse, "but I haven't murdered anybody or committed any crimes. This story about my marrying all these women is nonsense. Do you think I'm a Mormon? I've only had two wives—and these not at the same time."

On February 1, the Grand Jury in Chicago returned two true bills against Johann Hoch, both in bigamy cases. On February 4, Illinois Governor Deneen requested extradition of Hoch.

Bluebeard arrived in Chicago February 9. None of his alleged wives were at the police station to greet him. "Where are those fourteen wives you talked so much about?" Hoch queried Detective Loftus upon arriving at the station. He now admitted to only one illegal marriage—to Mrs. Marie Gorek Hoch. Before the evening's end, one ex came by—Mrs. Emilie Fischer. "You old hog," she shouted at Hoch. "You got my seven hundred fifty dollars, did you not?"

The next day, Hoch issued a statement about his "romantic" activities: "I want to correct one impression of me given to the public. All are led to believe that I am a regular Romeo. I am not. I did not love any of my wives. I have no use for women.

"It was purely a business proposition with me. When I found they had money, then I went after that. When I got it, I left them. They had no charms for me. I advertised for women over forty-five. I found they were easier to separate from their money.

"Flattery was my chief stock in trade. You can woo a woman quicker that way than any other.

"Believe me, all those women married me, not because they loved me, but because they thought I was wealthy ... they gave me their money because they thought they would receive it back with more."

The trial opened in April 1905, Hoch being charged with the murder of Mrs. Marie Welker Hoch. The most devastating testimony came from the only identifiable survivor who was married to him: Mrs. Emilie Fischer Hoch, sister of Marie.

Emilie testified that she saw Hoch giving her sister light-colored powder in water two days before her death. She also related the following incident after her own marriage to Hoch:

One day, the Hochs were met at the door by Mrs. Bauerborck. "Don't go in there," Mrs. Bauerborck warned. "Mrs. Sohn is here, and she says that Hoch murdered your sister."

Emilie continued, "I looked at Hoch and said, 'What are you changing colors for? If you haven't done anything wrong, you should not be afraid.' He said nothing, but sat down on the bed ... I never saw him again until I faced him in the police station."

Against Emilie's testimony, the defense could not present a strong case for the accused. Added to Emilie's words were other witnesses who testified about his swindling.

With the evidence and testimony against his client, defense attorney Plotke tried to move the jury by charming them with beautiful poetry. Plotke pleaded to the jury for a direct acquittal and said, "I ask you to take to the jury room a few lines of poetry and consider them. With these verses in your minds, you should give this man the liberty which he should have."

Plotke read the first two verses from John Henry Cardinal Newman's "The Pillar of the Cloud." He then passed out copies of the poem to the jurors:

> Lead kindly light, amid the encircling gloom,
> Lead me thou on!
> The night is dark, and I am far from home,
> Lead me thou on!
> Keep thou my feet: I do not ask to see
> The distant scene; one step enough for me.
> I was not ever thus, nor pray'd that thou
> Should leadst me on.
> I loved to choose and see my path, but now
> Lead thou me on.
> I loved the garish day, and, spite of fears,
> Pride ruled my will: remember not past years.
> So long, Thy power hath blest me, sure it still
> Will lead me on,
> O'er moor and fen, o'er crag, and torrent, till
> The night is gone.
> And with the morn, those angel faces smile
> Which I have loved long since, and lost awhile.

Perhaps this was Plotke's poetic message of penitence. Certainly, the jury grasped the beauty of the verses, but still found Hoch guilty and recommended the death sentence. Three votes were needed: on the first he was unanimously guilty, but two of twelve jurors voted for life imprisonment.

Upon hearing the word "death," Hoch stared at the jurors and turned pale. He denied having killed Marie Welker Hoch and asked for the death penalty rather than life imprisonment.

Plotke announced that he would appeal, but Hoch was resigned to death and had little interest in the appeal. "I wish they would hang me tonight, now that they have found me guilty," he said. "I am not afraid to die, and the sooner it is over the better. My life was 'gassed' away by the jury. They did not give consideration to the testimony."

Hoch took on a stoical air as he whistled a lively tune on the way back to his cell. But all the bravado collapsed the next day when Hoch was reportedly seen weeping all day in his cell. Fellow prisoners were not moved. "Brace up and die like a man," they jeered.

Hoch was sentenced to be hanged June 23. Judge Kersten asked why the sentence should not be carried out. "Judge," said Hoch. "I am willing to die tonight if you think I am guilty. I am innocent of the crime…"

And he had a message for all responsible for the sentence—police, prosecutors, jurors, and witnesses: "May God have mercy on your souls. I am convinced that my wife was murdered, but I am not her murderer."

The June hanging was postponed. Governor Deneen granted a stay after five hundred dollars had been raised for an appeal. The "benefactor" was an attorney, a friend of counsel Plotke, who said that he was "moved by humanitarian reasons."

Hoch cheated the gallows in August when State Supreme Court Justice Magruder ruled that that there was enough evidence for a review. The news was relayed to a cigar-smoking Hoch. "I am not guilty of this horrible murder, and now the highest court in the state will prove me innocent. I have never felt that I would go to the gallows. I may be guilty of other crimes, but never of that murder."

The delays in execution not only spared Hoch momentarily, but he also received several proposals of marriage. Fortunately for these women, all appeals and reviews failed.

Preparations were made for Hoch's hanging on February 23, 1906. When Hoch was informed he was on death watch, he responded calmly,

"I feel fine, but I guess I have to die tomorrow. This is the fourth time I have been near death—and the last.

"Me take my own life? Why, do you know what that would mean? It would be an absolute confession of guilt. Why should I not be brave and drop from the scaffold if I am innocent?"

The scheduled hanging time was set at 1:30 in the afternoon. Lawyers, without Hoch's knowledge or approval, were busy at the U.S. Circuit Court, asking for a delay. They filed an application for a writ of habeas corpus. Judge K. M. Landis denied the writ because proper application had not been made from the State Supreme Court to the U.S. Supreme Court.

As the Reverend J. R. Burkland recited the prayer for the dead, jailer Whitman told the minister that time was up and asked Hoch if he had anything to say.

Hoch's last words: "Father, forgive them. They know not what they do. I must die, an innocent man. Good-bye."

Burial was not without complications. An undertaker had agreed to inter at his own expense, while clergymen present at the hanging sought to choose the burial place. Every cemetery sought to avoid notoriety, so those who were hanged were denied burial. At last, the body found rest at Potter's Field, a field adjoining the county poor farm, at Dunning.

Deserved satisfaction had finally come for the persevering duo: the Reverend Herman Haass and Inspector George Shippy. The indefatigable Chicago crime officer had followed all leads and sightings of Hoch, and now justice had been attained.

For Haass, it had been a long journey. His initial suspicions of Hoch—then Huff—had been justified. Now pastor of St. Matthew's German Lutheran Church in Utica, New York, he could not save Caroline Huff in 1895, and many swindles and murders followed. But the case was finally closed.

The Hearst newspapers had headlined the pastor as "Hoch's Nemesis." He was asked about his feelings about Hoch finally being brought to justice and responded, "No punishment that can be meted out to this man Hoch will be too severe. I have followed him for ten years, and I know him to be the biggest scoundrel of the century. Certain it is, whatever may be proven, he is a murderer and a multimurderer …"

For many, Johann Hoch was the scoundrel of his era: bluebeard, swindler, serial killer of those he knew—even married. His goal was financial gain. The story of Vasili Komaroff of Moscow illustrates how different serial killers are, even if their motives are similar. Komaroff also killed for financial gain, but he was no bluebeard. Those he killed were complete strangers. And while Hoch came from a middle-class background with a formal education, Komaroff fought in the Russian Revolution and was engulfed in the depressed economic conditions of Moscow.

VASILI KOMAROFF
Vampire of Moscow

Excitement gripped Moscow on the sizzling summer day of June 6, 1923. The oppressive poverty of the post-Revolution years seemed forgotten as Muscovites were fixed on the news of the opening of the murder trial of the Wolf of Moscow, also referred to as the Human Wolf. The extraordinary interest had forced the relocation of the trial from a courtroom in Moscow to the more spacious Polytechnic Museum.

The celebrated Moscow correspondent of the *New York Times*, Walter Duranty, covered the event. He wrote, "Never was there such interest in Moscow in any non-political event."

Vasili Komaroff, aka Ivan Komaroff or Petroff Komaroff, fifty-two, stood trial for killing thirty-three people from 1921–1923. Beyond the number of victims, the murders recalled the "murder den" legends of Central Europe.

Investigators had been totally baffled in a two-year manhunt. The victims, males, were always bound up in sacks—always in the same manner. One inspector described the bodies "trussed like chickens for roasting." Twenty-one of the victims were discovered in various parts of Moscow on waste ground, most in the Shabolovki quarter, in districts south of the Moskva River.

After Komaroff's confession, five additional victims were found. Six victims were lost in the Moskva River. The detectives also reported other interesting findings. The bodies most often were discovered on

Thursdays and Saturdays. Further detective work showed that the burial sacks contained hay or oats.

The Shabolovki district featured a horse market on Wednesdays and Fridays. The clues led to a dealer named Vasili Komaroff. While Komaroff rarely was seen doing business at the market, he was often seen leaving with prospective buyers.

Coincidence? The Muscovite inspectors were patient. They spoke to other traders in Shabolovki. On May 20, 1923, the detectives came to his home. "We are searching for illegal liquor," the raiding party told Komaroff, who was stunned to find a search in his stable.

The case was solved. Under a pile of hay, the detectives found the body of the latest victim in a sack. Komaroff escaped through a window, but was caught several days later, on May 26.

According to his confession, Komaroff was motivated by robbery. He brought the victims to his home on 24 Shablofka Street with the promise of a bargain. He served them tea, and while they drank, he approached them with a hammer, hit them on the front side of the forehead, strangled them using a pillow, and then tied the victims' necks, removed the clothing, and bound the bodies to the dimension of the sack. The procedure took a half hour, and, with experience, was trimmed to fifteen minutes.

The average gain from each victim was eighty cents. Komaroff described the murders as "an awfully easy job." He didn't like to be overcome in these "discussions." The Wolf told the media before his trial, "I killed a man who tried to beat me in a horse trade. He was the only one who ever resisted. I just knocked them on their heads with a hammer or strangled them."

The Wolf's wife, Sophia, was also charged with murder. Although not put on trial, the prosecutor said, "Sophia Komaroff knew of the crimes and certainly had a role in hiding the bodies."

"Make quick work of this trial," Komaroff told an Associated Press correspondent. "I am fifty-two, have had a good life, and don't want to live any longer. If the court so decides, then shoot me quickly."

Depravity

Indeed, the prisoner had shown no will to live. While in captivity, he thrice unsuccessfully attempted suicide.

The eagerly awaited trial lasted one day. Komaroff was alert and relaxed throughout the proceedings. The only apparent sign of nervousness was the quick fingering of his small beard.

During the interrogation, he reviewed his wolfish deeds. "I do not remember the names of my victims," he said. But he had an accurate recall of other information. The first murder was in February 1921. By the year's end, seventeen had been murdered. In 1922, an additional ten were murdered. In 1923, Komaroff added six more to the total. Nearly half of the corpses were dumped in a dilapidated lodging on Conway Lane and near an adjoining house on 26 Shablofka. Later in the killing spree, Komaroff acquired a horse, and conveyed the corpses to an embankment of the Moskva River and in the canals.

The judge asked Komaroff, "Why did you commit such atrocious crimes?" Komaroff answered without emotion: "I needed money for food and drink. My wife liked to eat delicacies. The horse was the way to get these things. When she found out about the murders, she started to cry. But soon she said, 'Let's get accustomed to this.'" Walter Duranty evaluated the answer in his *Times* report: Komaroff gave "the eternal Russian excuse for any knavery in which they are caught."

The Criminal World of Moscow, published in 1924, recorded the response of Komaroff: "Petroff Komaroff displayed complete indifference to what he had done as he was calm in detailing the crimes he committed. If sixty more people had come to his home, he would have killed them too. He used the Russian expression, 'Then once and kvass [Russian fermented drink].'"

The decision was announced at 2:00 AM June 7. The Komaroffs were sentenced to be shot within seventy-two hours. Not given to court etiquette, the crowded court broke out in applause upon hearing the verdict.

The court had deliberated most of the day and through the night. A large crowd stood outside the Polytechnic Museum awaiting the verdict.

The building was heavily guarded by a strong force of gendarmes with fixed bayonets on their rifles.

Komaroff greeted the verdict stoically. As he left the court, he announced, "Well, it's my turn to be put in the sack now." Reported Duranty, "Komaroff's callousness is that of the typical Asiatic."

Although the court spectators favored the decision, the crowd outside was not supportive of the court. Interestingly, the execution was only made possible because the Russian penal code permitted the death sentence to be carried out upon those who were a menace to society.

Duranty interviewed a well-dressed citizen. "What is the good of killing him?" she wondered. "Why not send him to work? He is strong enough."

An elderly woman was not an advocate of capital punishment. "The execution would not deter murder," she insisted. "If they cut Komaroff slowly in bits, others might be frightened, but shooting—bah. That's nothing. They ought to give him to the doctors for experiments."

The Wolf's bravado vanished quickly after leaving the courtroom. He explored every avenue to save his life. He demanded a new trial. "The facts were not presented accurately," he stressed. The request was flatly rejected.

His next appeal was a combination of a plea for clemency buttressed by his reading of Russian criminal law. "I have been wrongly convicted," he maintained. "Besides, criminal law provides for imprisonment, not death." Komaroff did not succeed. Having been rejected, he put in a special plea for clemency for his wife, Sophia. However, the Central Executive Committee gave a "nyet" to the plea.

Death came to the Komaroffs on June 21 by a Moscow firing squad.

Before Komaroff rose to notoriety, no one had a bad word to say of him. His neighbors knew him as an amiable family man. He greeted all neighbors with a smile and "dobri den." He was often described as "a mild-eyed peasant." The police report described him as "a genial, smiling man with nothing strange about him save that the pupils of his eyes were unusually small in comparison with the white." He was a member of the Red Guard during the Revolution and a former Moscow Cabinet officer.

Yet, as reporters continued to probe the personal life of the Wolf, they realized that he was not so pleasant—apart from the murders. Obviously, he was a sadist. At eighty cents a victim, he made less than twenty-seven dollars for all his killings. Once, he tried to hang his eight-year-old son, but the mother saved the youngster by cutting him down.

As soon as the manhunt caught Komaroff, investigators sought to learn all the facts, the modus operandi of the killings, as well as put together a profile of modern Russia's first serial killer. The assignment was completed by the Moscow Criminal Investigations Department (MCID).

The central museum of the Ministry of Internal Affairs on Seleznyovskaya Street followed the trial with an exhibit featuring the heavy shoe hammer, the weapon of the crimes. Komaroff was long known in Russia as the "greatest disemboweler of the twentieth century."

The Russian criminal records had no previous record of such a premeditated killer. Komaroff's story reminded criminologists of the career of Lobas, a "human hunter" in the taigas of Siberia.

One of the investigators, Dr. Krasnushkin, said, "Komaroff's attitude was seen in his deep cynicism, bottomless moral obtuseness who possesses no power over his soul.

"This moral obtuseness was shown in his craving for pleasure. Yet, at times he showed feelings of love for his children. During some of the questioning, he cried and couldn't be calmed for a while. He definitely had a strong attachment to his wife. Surprisingly, he possessed religious feelings. For example, he would say, 'I was praying in my soul to my angel all the time.' The criminal personality astonishingly harmonizes with the theoretical propositions of the psychologist Ferry."

Komaroff was born in the Vitebsk region into a family with twelve children. The family was indigent, and the children didn't receive proper care. His father was a hard worker, an alcoholic who ended his life like a true alcoholic. While drunk, he beat his wife. One day while drunk, the father stumbled into a canal and fell facedown into the water, choked, and died.

When Komaroff was born, his father was fifty-five years old. The alcoholic influence was dominant in the family. The mother was also an alcoholic, and five of his six brothers were heavy drinkers. In fact, one of the brothers, while drunk, killed his superior in a factory and was sentenced to a long prison term in Sakhalin.

As for Vasili Komaroff himself, from the age of fifteen, he was a hard drinker. Because the family needed money, Komaroff was not sent to school. Instead, he remained at home, and at age twelve went to do chores for the landlord. He had his first sexual encounter at age fifteen with a domestic servant.

That started a series of changing landlords and jobs. The reasons were in part poor working conditions and in part an affinity to vagabondage. He served in the Russian army for four years, seeing action in the Russo-Japanese War. At age twenty-eight, Komaroff was married. Accompanied by his wife, he was assigned to a mission in the Far East. They traveled to many towns and spent all their money. The marriage was a failure. They both drank and fought often.

Vasili Komaroff's first crime was committed in 1911 when he was forty. He stole apples from a warehouse he was in charge of and was sentenced to a year in prison. Gaining his freedom, he went home only to find out that his wife had died of cholera.

Komaroff took his second wife in 1914 in Riga, a Polish widow with two children. She was terribly oppressed and terrorized by Vasili Komaroff. "My head was never cured of beating," she said. "I was always running out of the home with the children."

During the war, the Komaroffs fled Riga and settled in the Volga region. Komaroff got a position as a loader in a warehouse. The rate of his drinking intensified. In 1917, he joined the Russian Civil War as a volunteer in the Red Guard. The illiterate Komaroff learned to read and write. He rose to the rank of platoon leader-commander and

Depravity

took part in a number of military actions. As platoon commander, he was in charge of executing soldiers of the enemy White Russians. His commander told him, "You are devoted to the idea of internationalism. And besides, you are a Party member. Get someone to help you so that we can rid ourselves of our class enemies."

Komaroff needed no help, he told the Moscow investigators. "Why did I need help? I could handle the business myself. The enemies were tied up, so they could not run, and could not hit back. My philosophy has always been: do the job and then kvass! I had a large drink of alcohol after every killing."

As a prelude to his killing spree, Komaroff set out after the victims' money. "I also carefully checked the victims' pockets to find money or tobacco. Believe me, once I found a silver watch on one officer. The other idiots who searched the officer found nothing. But I squandered the watch in drink."

Added Komaroff, "Since my army days, after drinking alcohol, especially when I was drunk, I want to kill somebody!"

His good fortune was halted when he was taken prisoner by the army of General Anton Denikin. "I changed my name to Petroff," he said, "and I was concerned that should I be freed I would be killed since I killed many of my White brothers. But my first worry was Denikin's soldiers. But no, they have the bourgeois agenda. The commander was a very young-looking man with a mustache who listened to music on the gramophone."

"Let this Red live," said Lieutenant Semyonoff. "He was probably taken against his will to fight."

Komaroff went along with this line. "Yes, Mr. Lieutenant. I don't fight for ideas. I was forced." However, he confided to the Moscow interrogators, "Not true at all. I went to the front in November 1917. I wanted to beat all of the rich people, the bourgeois. I hated all those educated people who finished high school and could play the piano."

Komaroff was spared. He was assigned to chop wood and heat

the stove for Semyonoff. The lieutenant treated his prisoner well, even offering him choice cigarettes.

"Again, a change in my life happened," Komaroff continued his war tale. "Our Red Guard unexpectedly attacked the White army and took many prisoners, including Semyonoff. Barefooted, the lieutenant was taken behind the house, placed against the wall to be shot."

The lieutenant was in disbelief. Komaroff, the man he had spared, was poised to kill him. "He stared at me defiantly and said, 'Rascal, rabble.'"

Komaroff responded: "You dark soul. You understand nothing. When you decide on someone's life, you feel that you are a tsar and god. But consider this. You can listen to the gramophone and understand music, study in different high schools. However, I with my power will put an end to your life. This is my will and there is no escape!"

Komaroff told the Moscow detectives that he was proud that he killed the lieutenant. "For my courage," he said, "I was rewarded with a deed of merit and a gun. The deed is at my home on the wall, and I proudly show it to all who come to my house."

When the war ended, Komaroff settled in Moscow and took work as a wagoner in the Evacuation Center of Tsentroevak. This was one of the units of the Popular Committee of Internal Affairs, headed by Comrade Dzherzinski. Unfortunately, the criminal career began a new phase. He stole materials from the Evacuation Center.

Having pieced together fragments from the life of Vasili Komaroff, the Moscow investigators offered their conclusion: "After tracing the developments in the life of Petroff Komaroff, we can say that his childhood was destroyed by alcohol. He left childhood psychologically traumatized. That carried over into his teenage years, worsened by weak family bonds, and by relationships with strangers. His involvement in war with its legalized killings worsened the situation. All these factors combined to sow the seed of a massive killer that came to life in 1921."

Komaroff recalled the first of his thirty-three killings; February 1921.

He began the day stealing a new harness from a fellow worker.

Depravity

Before the victim realized the theft, Komaroff threw five sacks of peat in the sledge and headed for the government agency, Auto Industrial Commerce, located at 15 Karetney. Looking to earn some money, he took an old woman to the Brest-Litovsk station.

Komaroff drove to the horse section at Smolensk Market. The timing was good. A well-known gypsy, Grisha, sold a gelding to an individual—it was an ancient creature, with bad teeth, and a right eye missing. Thought Komaroff, "The gypsy should have given some drink to the gelding or done something else to the horse because it was so unnatural-looking. This horse was better suited for the abattoir."

Perhaps the muddleheaded purchaser was the perfect victim for Komaroff. The man was duped by inferior quality. Komaroff noticed that the man was affixing an old rope-harness to the sad-looking horse.

Komaroff merrily winked to the fellow. "A broken harness is like a man without his …" said Komaroff. "Here, take my harness. It looks like a king's harness, and it's new. And it's free."

The man was agreeable. "Let's have a drink to the future good work from your horse," proposed Komaroff. "A bar is like death. You cannot overcome it."

Komaroff's new companion showed his agreement by shaking his head. "He still has a lot of money," thought Komaroff, taking the man to the bar, where they had many drinks.

They returned to the Evacuation Center. "I feel sick," Komaroff told his chief, Rosa Radek, sister of the popular Bolshevik Karl Radek.

"All right," she said, "but come back to work on Monday. We have a closed Party meeting."

After the gelding was put in the stall, Komaroff and his comrade went to the tobacco shop, where Komaroff bought tobacco. While another customer turned his back, Komaroff stole a new pair of leather gloves. They then left for a long night of partying at a bar.

The man was taciturn, but he seemed to be a good listener, so Komaroff told the fellow about his life, especially his war experiences.

When Komaroff came to the story of his being honored by gun and proclamation for killing the White lieutenant, Komaroff said, "The deed is hanging on my wall. The gun—well, I squandered it on alcohol. I feel bad about that since a gun is very useful in life."

Komaroff noticed the man was anxious to go home for the evening. "Are you hurrying back to your woman?" asked Komaroff. "The gypsy cheated you, but I gave you a free harness. I am generally a good person. Look, I am bringing home sweets for my children."

The man walked away in the night, down Kaluga Street, dark and silent, with only occasional lights shining in the windows. Suddenly, Komaroff aroused himself. "Why am I letting him go? The man still has a lot of money. The harness I gave him is new, and I could get some money for the gelding.

"I can hit him with a rock in the head, and then once and kvass. Nobody will look for this man. Who has need of this proletarian?"

Unfortunately, Komaroff missed his chance. A noisy group appeared from the alley, singing songs. They headed in the same direction as that man—to the center of Moscow, with lights, streetwalkers, and many members of the militia.

Komaroff returned to 26 Shablofka. He got up the next morning an unhappy individual. "I should have hit the man yesterday," he lamented. "With the money, I could have drunk wine for three, maybe four days and bought sweets for the kids."

But Komaroff comforted himself. "What the hell. Is he the only one in the world? The devil will bless me with luck and send someone else."

As soon as he got up that day, he opened the wall closet, looking for the spirits hidden by his wife. As soon as he started drinking the strong-smelling liquid, he felt much better, more relaxed. He thought that this would be the ideal day for a crime. He wife and children went to friends in Podolsk. "This is the best. Today, I am going to do it."

But he needed some money for drink, so he visited his neighbor Vasili Marcarovich Andreef. "Vasili Marcarovich, give me some money for a bottle of alcohol. I swear I'll pay you back soon." Before the

Depravity

Revolution, Vasili was a landlord with many buildings. He hated his neighbor Komaroff, whom he considered a burglar, one who destroyed his previous life. While he hated Komaroff, he was afraid of the proletarian, so he gave Komaroff the money.

Meanwhile, Komaroff's destined victim in the nearby village of Pavlovka was in a heated conversation with his father. "Egor," said the father, "you have been delaying long enough at home. Go and harness your horse and go to Moscow to buy a horse. Moscow is about two hours from here. It is important to be at the market when it opens."

Egor was thirty, a strong, tall man with light hair and blue eyes. The old man, Vasilev, was a peasant. Egor had a wife and three children.

The family had the largest farm in Pavlovka, with two workers. With the triumph of the Bolsheviks, the family did not fare well. The house was robbed several times; chicken and grain were plundered. But the tide had turned. They were blessed with plentiful harvests.

They were also helped out by the father's younger brother, Zachar, who had an influential, well-paid position with the Tea Department on Miasnitscaya Street. The father intended to accompany the son to the market, but Zachar sent a letter telling his brother that he would visit him that day. He wanted to speak about family matters and about the latest economic developments.

"Egor," advised the father, "buy a strong, healthy horse." This was really unnecessary advice because Egor had been an expert on horses while serving in the cavalry. One look at a horse, and Egor could tell you about its strengths and weaknesses.

"Yes, father," Egor said cheerfully.

His wife served breakfast. "Now," said the wife with a loving look at Egor, "the road will be much easier." He hugged his wife and children, and the father blessed him.

"Bring us some sweets, Father," said the children. "Some cookies."

With spring approaching, they needed one more horse. Egor harnessed Romashka, the family's sole horse that survived the Revolution. He headed for the city. The sun was shining on this beautiful February day.

The "big market" was the Smolensk Market. It occupied a large area with thousands of people, from honest and naive peasants to an assortment of criminals and prostitutes. Egor couldn't miss seeing that mass of humanity. The entrance was from Mojaisk Road. He read the poster hanging on a nearby building:

The Big Smolensk Market

A huge selection—MANUFACTURED ITEMS, MEAT PRODUCTS, FISH, SHOES, LEATHER, FURNITURE, MUSICAL INSTRUMENTS, AND SO FORTH

Open Every Day, including holidays

Tramways B 4, 5, 7

Egor wondered what "and so forth" meant. He discovered that it meant a huge collection, including gold and stolen diamonds—and horses. Finally, he found the horses' row. The horse selection did not appear promising. The horse trade was still suffering from the influence of World War I, when half the horse population was taken to war. Those that stayed behind suffered from the Civil War or times of hunger.

And the season was not auspicious. Sowing time was near, and the peasants did not sell their horses except under severe financial crises. Once again, the gypsy came with an ancient gelding. A few other sellers brought old horses, good only for the abattoir.

"Are there better horses elsewhere?" asked Egor.

The gypsy realized that Egor knew his horses and would not go for the gelding, so he directed Egor to the Sucharev market. "However," he added, "you will not find much, and what you do will be three times more expensive than at this market."

"Well, we wasted the day." Egor looked sadly at Romashka. "Let's go home."

Vasili Komaroff took all this in. Egor noticed the skinny man, with an alcoholic face, expressionless blue eyes, wearing dressy box-calf shoes.

"What type of horse do you have?" asked Komaroff. "That's a beautiful horse you have."

Egor relished the praise. The initial disfavor he found in Komaroff's appearance changed. "Romashka's father was beautiful pure racehorse. From him she got long and fast legs," responded Egor.

"What about work?" asked Komaroff.

"Works a lot, but I came to buy one more."

"Yes, in today's times, it is hard to find a horse. If someone is selling, it must be a very old or sick horse."

The conversation halted as Komaroff and Egor smoked their cigarettes. Suddenly, Komaroff continued, "What can I tell you? That's life. But I want to sell you a very good stallion. I'm in the carrier trade in the state department. Therefore, the state has given me a horse. It is of a pure breed, three years old, a devil on the road."

An excited Egor said, "What could be better! How much do you want?"

Answered Komaroff, "We will come to an agreement. The most important thing is that the horse will be in good hands."

"Then let's get going. Where will we drive?"

"I live on Shablofka," said Komaroff. "The mare is there."

Egor smelled deceit. "Hey, hold on. You hide something, man. In the beginning, you spoke about a three-year-old stallion. Now you speak about a mare!"

Komaroff fought this off. "A stallion is a stallion! My neighbor, Andreev Vasili Makarich, wants to sell a mare. It's a pity you don't know him. Before the Revolution, he owned four apartment buildings on Shablofka. Now he lives on 25. He is a very good friend of mine. He is very rich. If you change your mind about my stallion, we'll go see his mare. Stay here and I'll go buy a bottle of vodka. We will drink: after once and a kvass."

"I don't drink alcohol," said Egor.

In one minute, killer and victim were headed to Shablofka. The trip was short from Smolensk Market to Shablofka. Komaroff drank and did all the talking, reliving his past, trying to gain sympathy from Egor as he reviewed a sad childhood.

The good feeling about Komaroff wore off for Egor. Perhaps it was the alcohol. Egor felt very uncomfortable, as if a press were rolling over his body. Finally, they arrived at the Komaroff home on 26 Shablofka. Komaroff told Egor, "Stop. It's here." Komaroff got off to open the gates.

"Put your horse here under the roof," said Komaroff. "This house was given to me by the Soviet regime since I am a veteran and Party member. This trader Kirikoff lived here before. Now it is mine because I served in the war for the proletariat."

All was silent in the courtyard and in the street.

An anxious Egor asked, "Where is the stallion?"

"There in the shed," pointed Komaroff. "But before the sale, let's drink this bottle of alcohol. And I will get you the documents on the stallion. You will see the entire genealogical tree."

The Komaroff house was dark and humid. Two dark, old icons hung in one corner room. The bed was dirty. The pillows were torn. As they opened the door, a big fat rat jumped off the table.

"Sit here, man," said Komaroff, who directed Egor to a table with an old cover. "You have no idea how much I want to drink alcohol."

Komaroff poured the alcohol from an already opened bottle into two glasses.

"No," refused Egor. "Now, how about the papers?"

"Oh, yes," responded the killer host. Komaroff acted as if he were searching for the pedigree passport. He opened a drawer filled with blank papers, magazines, newspapers, and miscellanea. He took out a large folder with papers and placed it in front of Egor. "I'll find the papers," Komaroff said. "They must be here, but I don't see without glasses."

Facing the window, Egor seemed confused as he looked at the papers. Komaroff returned with his hammer, hidden under a pillow; approached Egor from behind; and hit the victim in the front side of the forehead. He then tied a loop around the neck, and removed the

Depravity

clothing from the still-warm body. Komaroff learned during the Civil War that the victim's clothing could bring money.

The body was then fitted into a sack. Komaroff had begun has career as serial killer.

Egor's family waited in vain. The wife, Anastasia, and children cried for days. They did not learn about the fate of husband and father until two years later, when the Wolf of Moscow was arrested. Egor's father died in grief without identifying the killer. The once-prosperous family was destroyed financially in a short time.

The murder of Egor was the first of thirty-three murders, nearly all in the manner that Komaroff killed Egor.

Beyond the family life and military experiences of Komaroff, it is important to factor in the woeful economic conditions of post-Revolution Moscow. For a description of Moscow life in the twenties, one can turn to Walter Benjamin's *Moscow Diary*, which covers his two-month stay from December 6, 1926, to the end of January 1927.

For the entry of December 15, 1926, Benjamin relates a visit to a friend's mother's apartment.

"We decide to drop in and say hello. Like all the rooms that I had seen so far … it contains only a few pieces of furniture. Their bleak, petit bourgeois appearance is all the more depressing because the room is so sparsely furnished. Completeness is an essential feature of the decor of the petit bourgeois interior: the walls must be covered with pictures, the sofa with cushions, the cushions with coverlets, the consoles with knickknacks, the windows with stained glass. Of all this, only a few items here and there have indiscriminately survived. If people manage to bear rooms, which look like infirmaries after inspection, it is because their way of life have so alienated them from domestic appearance. The place in which they live is the office, the club, the streets …"

Vasili Komaroff was post-Revolution Russia's first serial killer. Eighty years later, he still attracts attention in the ghoulish universe of serial killers.

Rustlings in the Wind, an online publication of prose and poetry, in 2001 posted a portrait of Vasili Komaroff, with a description as an "elusive killer who terrorized" Moscow for two years. Subscribers were asked to respond with a brief poem or reflection.

Pam Stollings observed, "He doesn't look like a killer."

Jeneral offered this poem:

> *Friendly eyes know death*
> *Friendly death knows why*
> *But 'e ain't talkin'*
> *Friendly eyes are sorry*
> *Sorry wonders why*
> *A moment too late*
>
> *Friendly eyes shine warmer*
> *Chilling why's hammer*
> *Down upon his head*

Leonardo offered these thoughts:

> *I walked alone and feeling wolfen tired*
> *but never tired enough*
> *I held secrets*
> *that no hands could ever hold …*

Both Hoch and Komaroff murdered for financial gain, although their approaches obviously differed. Hoch murdered women; Komaroff sought victims who were horse traders. From Hoch and Komaroff, we move to Raymond Fernandez and Martha Beck. The motive was money; the victims were women seeking romance and marriage; the setting was the forties and Lonely Hearts Clubs.

RAYMOND MARTINEZ FERNANDEZ AND MARTHA BECK

Lonely Hearts Killers

The phenomenon of woman as serial killer is intriguing. In *The A to Z of Serial Killers*, Schechter and Everitt pose this question: "Is there such a thing as a woman serial killer?" No decisive answer is offered. On one side, the crime histories identify women who have been mass murderers. "The problem arises," according to the authors, "when you try to find a female criminal who matches the model of the modern-day serial killer epitomized by Jack the Ripper, the lone psychopathic lust murderer."

However, Robert Hale and Anthony Bolin have no problem identifying "The Female Serial Killer," the title of an article in the anthology *What Is Serial Murder?* They stress the notoriety—albeit not modern—of "Countess Dracula" of Hungary, who murdered eighty women before bathing in their blood. Those crimes were committed between 1580–1610. Hale and Bolin have counted—in their 1990s article—183 other women who have committed "multicide."

The former FBI agent Robert K. Ressler is credited with coining the label "serial killer." While noting the clear majority of males as serial killers, Ressler was wary of a definite rise in the number of female serial killers: "The fact that women are getting involved at all is alarming. Women have always provided a balance to male violence, and I'd hate to see them tip that balance." Ressler expressed his fear in the late eighties; since then, Stephen T. Holmes, Eric Hickey, and Ronald M.

Holmes have authored an article on "Female Serial Murderesses" for *The Contemporary Journal of Criminal Justice*. In addition, Michael D. Kelleher and C. L. Kelleher in 1998 authored *Murder Most Rare: The Female Serial Killer*.

Can one argue with Rudyard Kipling, who wrote in *The Female of the Species*, "The female of the species is more deadly than the male"?

Hickey found that females made up 17 percent of all serial killers. He did find, in 1991, that females were more likely to be motivated by material or social gain. This runs counter to the research of Deborah Cameron and Elizabeth Fraser (*The Lust To Kill: A Feminist Investigation of Sexual Murder*). They argued that sexual murderers were always male; the murder of women for sexual pleasure was the natural expression of male identity.

Holmes, Hickey, and Holmes fit female serial killers into five categories: the "Visionary Serial Killer," whose actions are from without, such as with spirits; the "Comfort Serial Killer," whose motivation is materialistic; the "Hedonistic Serial Killer," whose goal is pleasure; "Power Seekers," who seek to control others; and the "Disciple Killer," who is ruled by her partner.

The Kellehers divided the female serial killer into categories: "Team Killers"; the "Black Widow," who murders spouses, other family members, or partners for monetary reasons; the "Angel of Death," whose victims are served or cared by her, with the motivation being diverse; "Sexual Predator," with clear sexual reasons; "Revenge," with the added motive of jealousy; "Question of Sanity," whose motives reflect insanity; "Unexplained," for their motives cannot be fully explained; and "Unsolved," for it is not provable that the murderer was a woman.

How does one categorize Martha Beck and Raymond Fernandez, both executed on March 8, 1951, in Sing Sing? Obviously, they are team killers. Martha killed for materialistic reasons. Certainly, Martha was ruled by her partner. On the other hand, while Martha Beck was executed for murder, some students of the case are convinced that she was not the murderer but took the rap for her love, Raymond Fernandez.

Depravity

Unlike other team killers, notably Lucas and Toole, only Fernandez had embarked on a criminal path, although murders allegedly committed before the pairing were not marked by violence. If Beck had not met and teamed with Fernandez, she probably would have been spared from her notoriety.

Together, the Beck-Fernandez team offers many facets for study in the world of the serial killer. While they were not committed with the scope of Johann Hoch's, Raymond Fernandez's murders were clearly in the bluebeard tradition. And the early years of Beck and Fernandez showed devastating influences in the home and in the school. Both, in different parts of their lives, evidenced mental and physical disabilities that greatly impacted their lives. In their criminal careers, they displayed—like other serial killers—a craftiness or intelligence in the commission of their crimes.

The trial of the two in New York City spotlighted the problems of justice in serial killer cases as never before. Questions of justice had arisen before (e.g., the Panzram case). However, the Beck-Fernandez trial took place in a media-circus atmosphere for more than forty days, with conflicting testimonies of psychologists and psychiatrists.

And the Lonely Hearts killers forced American culture to examine the dangerous nature of these clubs, which now has been transformed into Internet dating with attendant dangers.

Both Martha Beck and Raymond Fernandez had troubled childhoods. Born in 1920 in Milton, Florida, the youngest of five children, Martha was raised by her mother and stepfather after her parents' divorce. Her mother was forty-four when Martha was born, and perhaps that accounted for remarks that she was not a planned child. Moreover, Martha spoke of being looked on as "unwanted," "different," and "queer."

What contributed most to an unhappy childhood was her obesity. That was worsened by a pituitary-ovarian gland disorder that made her body blotched and swollen. She was menstruating at age nine and had prominent breasts. She was physically an adult female without having experienced the joys of childhood. This disorder would later prevent her experiencing pleasure from "normal" sexual intercourse.

Martha's mother treated the daughter cruelly. Martha had no fond memories of school. Fellow students laughed at her. Most teachers were not caring or concerned about her personal life.

But the greatest agony of childhood was being raped by her brother when she was thirteen. He threatened to kill her if she told anyone. One rape was near the river; a second, in her room. She did tell her mother. The mother whipped Martha, and from that time on labeled Martha as "bad" and "sinful." Martha was impregnated, and an abortion was performed. Afterward, Martha was confined to her room and would not leave the house alone.

When all her other daughters left the household for work or marriage, the mother placed all her vigilance on Martha. In Wenzell Brown's *Introduction to Murder*, the devastation all this had on Martha is stated: "The mother's domination served to stunt Martha's emotional growth. On the emotional level, Martha remained a small child throughout her life. Psychologists … diverged widely in their analysis of her character … Martha at times [could] make mature and wise decisions, but whenever she had to face an emotional problem that dealt with her own security, it was as though she were crazed by fear, hate, panic, and, above all, the need to act, even though blindly and in a fashion that would lead to her own destruction."

With age, the problems diminished somewhat. The other girls had grown physically, so she no longer stood out—as much. Yet the rape by her brother left great scars. She craved sexual satisfaction, but that experience implanted horror. The mother continually followed Martha, and on one occasion even broke up a movie date and struck the boy.

School gave her an outlet for fulfillment and approval. She graduated third in her Milton High School class. Martha was accepted to the Pensacola School of Nursing. "I chose this profession," she wrote in an application letter, "for in this field of endeavor I sincerely believe that I can do my best in aiding humanity. I chose this profession without thought of self and want to prepare myself for this profession, not for material gains but for the purpose of aiding humanity and rendering service to others."

She graduated first in nursing school, but job offers were not forthcoming. Clearly, her physical appearance, with swollen, fat arms and swinging breasts, turned off prospective employers. She therefore settled for a job with a local mortician, washing, embalming, and preparing female corpses for burial.

To "compensate" for sexual fulfillment, she turned to the world of fantasy, with true confession magazines and romance novels. But the emptiness of her life and the grisly mortician hours forced her to look elsewhere.

Napa, California, was an ideal choice, with its large Naval and Army hospitals. Employment opportunities were available—she was now a nurse at the Park Victory Memorial Hospital—and so were personal opportunities. Unfortunately, she spent after hours at city bars and bus depots. One of her many sexual encounters left her pregnant. The father was a soldier who reluctantly agreed to marriage, but then attempted suicide in a nearby bay. The message to Martha was death rather than marriage to her.

The situation never improved. Martha decided that she would be better off in Florida, even with an ill-willed, ill-tempered mother. But she needed a story to explain her pregnancy.

As was proven during her short life, Martha was crafty. She bought a wedding ring and fabricated a story for use in Pensacola: she met Joe in California; had a breathtaking, frenzied romance; and met his family in Norfolk. He was now on active Naval duty in the Pacific.

As the birth of her child drew near, some wondered, "Where is Joe Carmen?" Others wondered if this was a fantasy from the romance-reading Martha. Leave it to Martha. In 1944, she orchestrated the sending of a telegram to her with the sad news: her husband was killed in action. Neighbors consoled her, and then Willa Dean was born.

Martha took a position as nurse at a local hospital. Then she returned to the bus depots; met a driver, William Beck; and again became pregnant. Reluctantly, the driver married her. The unhappy marriage ended in divorce in 1945.

Frustrated with her love life, she put all her energy into work, joined the Pensacola Crippled Children's Home, and was later promoted to superintendent. With two young children and an unfulfilled personal life, she now found a new fantasy. One evening, she went to the local cinema and was enraptured by the French actor Charles Boyer. She bought an autographed photo of Boyer and placed it on her dresser. Any Boyer movie found Martha at the theater, and she would see the same film several times.

Adding to her problems was that Martha Beck, twenty-five, now looked forty-five, and her supervisory role gave her an appearance of coldness and sternness.

Enter Pensacola neighbor and former classmate, Ned, and the lonely hearts club. A practical joker, Ned once sent Martha's name to a dieting group. And it was he who forwarded her name to a lonely hearts club. One day in 1947, an envelope arrived in the mail from Mother Dinene and the Friendly Club for Lonely Hearts. Testimonies thanked Mother Dinene for helping them find happiness. The advertisement proclaimed that her list had men who "are gay, witty, charming, and have good positions or are independently wealthy. Why not meet such men?"

Martha Beck was convinced. Wasn't she entitled to happiness? She enclosed the required five-dollar bill and filled in details, and, naturally, omitted weight, divorce, and two children. She wrote that she was "witty, vivacious, and oozed personality."

One of the detectives would later ask her, "Weren't you afraid about the type of men you might meet?"

"Not exactly frightened," she responded. "I did think some old man or some funny-looking guy might come nosing around—someone whose looks I'd be ashamed of. But I reckoned I could handle anyone like that all right."

But what was her ideal prospect? Charles Boyer would have been lovely but totally absurd. However, Raymond Fernandez was a con, a seedy one. "I guess I hadn't thought about it much," she said. "But I didn't think I'd ever meet anyone like Ray." And Raymond Fernandez never thought he would meet Martha Beck.

Like Martha Beck, Raymond Fernandez had an unhappy childhood. He was born in Hawaii in 1914 to parents of Spanish descent. The family moved to Bridgeport, Connecticut, when Raymond was three. His father was tyrannical in dealing with the family. Raymond was a frail and sickly child, but his father imposed hard work on him in the house and outside so as to bring in more funds. If it was work or school, the father made the boy work.

The father's cruel side also showed when he made the boy work at night even though Raymond was afraid of the dark. Still, the boy finished grade school and high school and impressed teachers with his intelligence. In fact, his IQ of 135 was borderline genius.

The father's stinginess resulted in Raymond's first criminal act. The father refused to "waste" money for Thanksgiving on a turkey or chicken. "If you want a chicken, you go get chicken," said the father. Raymond took the advice literally. Raymond and two friends stole chickens—twenty-three of them—from a nearby farm. Because Raymond's father did not cooperate with the police, Raymond was the only one of the three boys sentenced to sixty days in the county jail.

Raymond was resentful that only he was punished. Writes Brown, "He was aflame with the injustice that imprisoned him while his companions in the escapade had gone scot-free. He was deeply resentful of his father and determined to break loose from his domination as soon as possible. And he felt shame and humiliation over his imprisonment, which he felt would mark him forever as a jailbird."

With the onset of the depression, the family returned to Spain; the father prospered there, and father and son improved their relations. Raymond married Encarnacion Robles in Orgiva. At the age of twenty-one, Raymond had a son, the first of four children. But home worsened quickly, aggravated by his father's intrusiveness.

Raymond hoped to return to America and sailed there to establish himself before leaving Spain for good. However, his son was critically ill, forcing him to leave America, and when the Spanish Civil War broke out, business opportunities stopped. After the war, relations with his father and wife went downhill. His employment status was uncertain, as he took jobs as stevedore, gardener, paperhanger, and plasterer.

He found work as a dockworker in Gibraltar when World War II erupted. Raymond offered his services to Great Britain as a spy. He would have people believe that he passed on valuable information. However, the Defense Security Office in Gibraltar released a statement: "Raymond Martinez Fernandez was entirely loyal to the Allied cause and carried out his duties, which were sometimes difficult and dangerous."

Once more, Raymond set out for America, via a freighter headed for Curacao in the Dutch West Indies. It would prove to be a disastrous journey; life would never be the same. He was struck directly on the head by an open hatch cover. The injury was a heavy indentation on the skull, high on the forehead. A long scar remained on the brain tissue.

He was hospitalized for three months in Curacao, but never received medical or psychiatric care after release. While imprisoned a short time afterward, prison reports spoke of the condition and described the frontal lobes as controlling "the executive functions of the mind in which are bound up the self-control potentialities of the individual and the complex group of reactions which are comprised roughly under the name of conscience."

Another report added that Fernandez "may have suffered an alteration of personality to such an extent that his moral judgment was impaired. Thus, while legally sane, with the powers of reason unimpaired, he may have become a moral monster."

And the personality change was quite evident. He was no longer amiable and courteous. He frequented the brothels in Aruba and quickly exhausted his funds. Penniless, he headed for Mobile, Alabama. On leaving ship, for "some dumb reason," he stole clothing, sheets, pillowcases, and towels—all with government stamps. "I don't know. I can't think. I can't say why I did it. I just saw other men putting a towel or two in their bags, so I thought I'd do the same. Only I just couldn't seem to stop." His first crime, on Thanksgiving, now seemed minor: this time, he was sentenced to one year in the Federal Penitentiary in Tallahassee, Florida.

It was an inauspicious stay. A Haitian cellmate taught Fernandez voodoo and black magic. He was initiated into the world of the occult and was thrilled when he heard talk of mass hypnotism, charms, curses, and control of women. All one needed was possession of a woman's hair or nail clippings.

To test his powers, be wrote the sentencing judge and complained that his one-year sentence was too long. Actually, court officials had just then told the judge that they had advised Fernandez not to retain counsel. The judge reduced the sentence to six months. "You see, my hypnotism worked," ecstatic Fernandez told his cellmates.

Upon release, he preached spiritualism and boasted of his powers. "I can make any woman fall in love with me." Now living in Brooklyn with relatives, he started writing to women through lonely hearts clubs. At first, this pursuit was purely sexual egotism. He placed a sprinkling of "magic powder" on the letter. He then asked the women to send him locks of hair or fingernail clippings, and then fashioned a miniature figure or doll representing the woman. Then he placed the doll under a hypnotic spell.

During the first two years after his release, Fernandez corresponded with hundreds of women and conducted affairs with as many as fifteen at a time. At one point, he realized that his activities could be profitable, so he turned his charms and "powers" to swindling these women, especially widows, out of their resources.

To enhance his powers, Fernandez put on a toupee to cover his scar, and in 1947 met Jane Lucilla Wilson Thompson through a lonely hearts club.

Recently separated from her husband, Mrs. Thompson was an

ideal Fernandez target. After a correspondence courtship, they met and roomed in her Manhattan apartment. She was a dietician and had a nice apartment and some money. With her funds, they purchased cruise ship tickets for a Spain vacation.

Although separated, Raymond Fernandez was still legally married to Encarnacion Robles. Was that a problem? Not for Fernandez. Although no record exists of a ceremony, he and Jane traveled as a married couple. Arriving in La Linea, Fernandez introduced Encarnacion to Jane as Señora Robles.

For several days, the trio traveled and dined together. Suddenly, without full explanation, during the first week of November 1947, an argument erupted between Jane and Raymond. The next day, a maid found Jane dead in her hotel room. While unproven, Jane Thompson might have been the first victim of Fernandez. It is known that Fernandez purchased digitalis from the hotel pharmacy, and a half-empty bottle of digitalis was found in Jane's medicine chest.

Fernandez quickly left Spain and headed back to Jane Thompson's apartment, also shared by the victim's mother, Mrs. Pearl Wilson. He had previously encouraged—successfully—Jane Thompson to sign her name on two blank sheets of paper. With this trick, he took over the apartment and all possessions. In fact, before all ended, Mrs. Wilson had been swindled of almost all her property.

Now Raymond Fernandez returned to letter-writing and informed prospective lovers that he was back in New York. In the new listing from Mother Dinene's Friendly Club, one name captured his attention. He liked her profession—nurse; he liked her age—twenty-six, much younger than other writers. He was enticed most by her name: Martha Seabrook Beck. "Seabrook, what a name," thought Fernandez. William Seabrook was the author of *Magic Island*, a fascinating narrative of the occult.

Fernandez gave his letter to Martha Beck more attention than he did other letters. And he sprinkled it with his "magic powder."

The letter arrived in Pensacola a few days before Christmas 1947.

Depravity

What a holiday present for Martha! She was thrilled as she read and reread the letter. Fernandez said that he was attracted to her by some "psychic power." The letter exchange intensified. He had to come to Florida immediately, according to the last exchange.

Now Martha Beck had to face reality. She had not mentioned her weight, her children, or her divorce. How could she catch a charming Spaniard? Without waiting for an answer, Fernandez said that he would be in Pensacola before New Year's Day.

The arrival was a magical moment for Martha. Not only was he charming, but he also looked like her idol Charley Boyer. In fact, one court official later proclaimed that he looked like the movie star, but "a seedy Charles Boyer."

Certainly—and he later said so—Fernandez was shocked at the sight of the fat nurse. Ever the businessman, he knew she had money, and he had dealt with other gross opportunities.

They dined at her apartment, and then Martha had her sexual gratification from a master schooled in all erotica. She vowed that she would not let him go. But Fernandez learned that she was not as rich as he had hoped; he had no marriage plans, especially concerning her. After the second day, he told Martha that he must leave for New York but would return soon. Fernandez felt blessed that he had escaped a not-so-tender trap.

But Martha had other ideas. She took his romantic sentiments literally and even told friends of an impending marriage. A shower was planned. He had been "misunderstood," Fernandez wrote Martha. "Without you I cannot live," Martha wrote in a suicide letter.

Fernandez was worried. An investigation linking his name might lead to other love inquiries, so he agreed to let her visit him in New York.

Martha wasted no time, taking a two-week leave of absence from the Crippled Children's Home. While in New York, she served Fernandez in any and every matter: cooking, cleaning, et cetera. Something in Martha met his need. Writes Brown, "The feeling of vagueness, insecurity, and wavering uncertainty that had been with him ever since he had his accident was diminished in her presence. She fulfilled a need within him, although he was unaware of exactly what the need was."

Still, two weeks later, Fernandez had had enough. The lonely hearts business could not move on until she did. He tried to convince her that they could not stay together—he was already married. "I will be your mistress," Martha pleaded. An unhappy Martha took the train back to Florida.

She was stunned as she came to work. She was greeted by a delegation from the Children's Home. She had been fired; no explanation was given—although the Fernandez affair was probably the reason.

Only one course of action remained. Unannounced, she arrived in New York with her children. Fernandez was quite displeased to find Martha and two children on his doorstep.

"All right," he thought to himself. "She serves my needs. But I can't have the children here. And, more important, she must help me in my plans." Martha cried and begged to no avail. The children or Raymond. She chose Raymond. No agency would take the children. Finally, Martha's mother agreed, with the provision that she pay some thirty dollars weekly for their care.

Previously a very caring mother, Martha Beck never contributed a cent to her children's care, nor did she attempt to see them. Only while in Sing Sing on death row did she again think of them.

Martha did not disappoint. She helped convince Mrs. Wilson to leave the apartment. Fernandez explained to Martha all the details of his "line of business." Even if bigamy was involved, Martha was ready to help. Her first "job" was Esther Henne, whom Raymond married and swindled. In fact, Martha pawned Esther Henne's rings. However, Esther Henne was as determined as Fernandez. She turned the matter over to her attorneys and got back most of her money. Fernandez was not used to losing.

The next target was Myrtle Young of Green Forest, Arkansas. Another bigamous marriage followed. However, Martha intruded on the "bridal couple" in Chicago, determined that the marriage not be consummated, and demanded to share Myrtle's bed. Fighting broke out. The bride was given a heavy dose of barbiturates and died several days later from "cerebral hemorrhage and liver inflammation." Neither Martha nor Fernandez admitted administering the barbiturates. But one of them obviously was the murderer.

Martha and Raymond returned to Queens, New York. Christmas 1948 approached and funds were scarce. Then a sixty-year-old widow from Albany, New York, beckoned—Janet Fay, who had a long-running involvement in lonely hearts clubs. Unfortunately, she was easy prey, with suitors looking for her money in the bank. A year before meeting Charles Martin, aka Raymond Fernandez, she was bilked, so friends and family warned her to stop writing letters.

On December 30, 1948, Martha and Raymond arrived in Albany, with Martha posing as Raymond's sister. Janet quickly accepted Raymond's wedding proposal and planned to move to Long Island. Awaiting marriage, Janet closed out her bank accounts. The three left for Valley Stream on January 4, 1949.

That night, Janet Fay was murdered. The full details are only known to Beck and Fernandez—and they have changed stories. The following is a summary of their statements until Martha changed her narrative shortly before execution.

While Raymond slept on the couch, Martha and Janet shared the bedroom. The prospective bride bombarded Martha with questions about Raymond's past. Already annoyed that Raymond had fondled Janet, Martha became irascible. Janet then shouted at her roommate, "I won't allow you to live with us. You're the most brazen bitch I've ever seen."

Awakened by the shouting, Fernandez told Martha, "Martha, keep this woman quiet. I don't care what you do. Just keep her quiet."

Martha testified that she blacked out and couldn't remember additional details. The next thing she knew, Mrs. Fay was lying on the floor, blood pouring from her forehead. The murder instrument was a ball-peen hammer used by Fernandez to tack up pictures.

Making use of her experience as a nurse, Martha stopped the bleeding. They swathed her head with towels and dumped the body into a closet. The next day, they put the body into a large trunk and stored it in the basement of Raymond's sister's house. More than a week later, they retrieved the body and buried it in the cellar of a rented house in South Ozone Park, and then covered up the grave with cement. A few days after "burial," they gave up their lease.

They then cashed Janet Fay's checks. Before the murder, Fernandez contrived this scheme: he wrote the word "surprise" on blank sheets of paper, and convinced the eager bride to sign her name since they would surprise friends and relatives with a wedding announcement. They now took those sheets, and with Clorox deleted "surprise," leaving the signature.

One such letter reached Mrs. Mary Spencer, Janet Fay's stepdaughter:

Dear Mary,

I am all excited and having the time of my life. I never felt as happy before. I will soon be Mrs. Martin and will go to Florida.

Mary, I'm about to ask you a great favor. I would like you to call on the American Express Agency and have them ship my trunk and boxes that I have there to me. The address is on the various stickers I am enclosing in the letter ... I will close now with my best wishes for you both and love and kisses for the children. I really do miss you all, but I am sure that my prayers are granted to me by sending me this wonderful man.

God bless you all,

Janet J. Fay

However, there was one major goof. Mrs. Fay did not have a typewriter, nor could she type. Mrs. Spencer went to the police, and her stepmother now was a missing person. Authorities were now searching for Janet Fay.

While the "accepted" story was that Martha Beck became jealous and blacked out, she hammered Janet Fay to death. Dr. Richard H. Hoffman, the psychiatrist for the defense at the trial, secured a confession from Martha Beck before the executions, which appeared in abridged form in the 1951 fall edition of *True Crime Detective*:

"Ray must have heard the argument between Janet and I, for when she slapped me, he prevented us from having a free-for-all. He told me to go back to bed, that he wanted to talk to Janet. I left the room crying and threw myself on the bed and to drown out my crying buried my face in the pillow. Some minutes later, Ray called to me and the sound of his voice frightened me as he sounded frightened. I ran into the room and was horrified at the sight. Ray was standing around Mrs. Fay with both hands around her neck and she was moaning faintly …"

Dr. Hoffman showed the confession to Fernandez. In an interview with Wenzell Brown, he related the reaction of Fernandez. "It's all true, every bit of it, but if I go to the chair, Martha goes too."

Hoffman told Brown, "Martha Beck acted under duress and could not be held responsible for her acts. Fernandez told her, 'If you don't do what I tell you, I'll kill you too.' He continually made threats against her. She acted to save her own life."

Certainly, Martha Beck was no longer the same individual after the Fay murder. As Brown writes, "Through murder, she had become for the first time in her life an integral part of something larger than herself. She and Raymond were no longer separate entities. The ties of birth, love, and marriage could all be broken, but the common bondage of a shared murder would bind her to a paramour as long as both should live. For the first time, Martha possessed a security of sorts. No longer was she alone."

And that would be reinforced in the next lonely hearts adventure in Michigan.

In Fernandez's line of "business," one could not sit still. He chose Daphne Downing of Grand Rapids, Michigan, as his next target. Living with two-year-old daughter, Rainelle, Daphne Downing was forty-one, a widow whose husband had been a successful businessman. He simply adored children, Raymond, or Charles Martin, wrote Daphne, and he would be coming with his sister, Martha.

They arrived in Byron Center, a Grand Rapids suburb, in January 1949—less than a month after Janet Fay was dispatched.

Not unexpectedly, Charles Martin hit it off with the widow. And, also expectedly, Martha was enraged with his intimacies with the widow. January turned into February, as a New York wedding was planned and the widow's properties were transferred to cash.

Then one day, the crisis came. One day, Daphne caught Fernandez leaving the bathroom without his toupee. She was horrified at his baldness and the scar on his forehead. Daphne accused Fernandez of fraud and wanted out. Not having resolved this crisis, another arose. Daphne's menstrual period had not arrived, so she feared pregnancy.

While Daphne did not care for Martha, she turned to the nurse for help. Martha gave her sleeping pills, which she thought would hasten death. The pills worked to the extent that Daphne began to menstruate.

Rainelle began to cry, fearing the goings-on. Martha began choking the child into unconsciousness to silence her, leaving the child with bruises on the neck. "If she wakes up and sees Rainelle, she'll go the police," said a worried and angry Fernandez.

"Do something, Ray!" Beck pleaded. He went into the next room, took a pistol belonging to the late husband, wrapped the gun in a woolen baby blanket to muffle the sound, and shot the widow twice in the head. The widow was wrapped in sheets, carried into the basement, and dumped into a large hole.

The child had witnessed the murder. For two days, she cried and refused to eat. To pacify the child, they bought a puppy. Unfortunately, the puppy licked, clawed, and scratched the child's face. And the screaming intensified.

Meanwhile, Beck and Fernandez cashed all checks and stripped the house of all valuables. But Rainelle remained—and that was a problem.

Remembering past experiences, Martha knew that no shelter would take the child.

"Then stuff a pillow over her face," demanded Fernandez. "Smother her. We'll have the whole neighborhood aroused if you don't get her quiet."

Pleaded Martha, "I can't do it, Ray. I can't!" But she consented. She had abandoned her children to be with Fernandez. Now this trained nurse, who headed a home for crippled children, would do the unthinkable: kill a helpless two-year-old. She would do anything to remain with Fernandez.

Martha carried the child while Fernandez filled a tub with water. Martha held Rainelle under the water until she drowned. Fernandez dug another grave for Rainelle, next to the mother's.

Some neighbors dropped by to purchase some household goods. Fernandez explained that mother and child had been taken to Daphne's mother-in-law. For whatever reason, Fernandez and Beck tarried for hours and decided to take in a movie in Grand Rapids.

When they returned, the police were waiting for them. The neighbors had been suspicious. One man told police, "I didn't like this man, Martin. He was supposed to be a wealthy man in New York, but he didn't look or act the part. Not to me, he didn't."

They were arrested on February 8, 1949. The police searched the house and found the newly cemented patches in the cellar. "You got me dead to rights," Fernandez told police. "I ought as well come clean and tell everything. I'm no average killer." Without legal representation, Beck and Fernandez signed a seventy-three-page confession.

True, the police were investigating the Fay case, but Beck and Fernandez were not considered the suspects. Yet they confessed to the Fay murder. They seemed relieved that Michigan, without the death penalty, would never turn them over to New York, which did have the penalty. Seemingly, they were assured by Kent County D.A. Roger O. McMahon that they would not be extradited to New York.

Why did Michigan reverse its policy? Undoubtedly, newspaper

headlines nationwide, and in particular New York, demanded justice (i.e., execution). The papers had a field day demeaning and demonizing Martha: "Big Martha," "a two-hundred-pound figure of wrath, "a weird woman," "a degenerate." Obviously resentful of all the publicity, Martha protested, "What am I being tried for—murder or because I'm fat?"

According to Brown, great pressure was exerted on Michigan: "Individuals and groups put pressure on officials to surrender the pair to New York in order that they might be executed. Feelings ran so high that no one, certainly no public figure, dare speak out openly for moderation and thoughtful consideration of the facts that lay behind the Lonely Hearts Murders."

New York Governor Thomas E. Dewey prevailed. Martha Beck broke down. "I don't want to go back to New York. Never. I'm afraid of the electric chair."

Stoical Fernandez took things calmly. "They ought to kill me," he told the press. "I've done a terrible thing, but I'm not afraid of the chair. I guess that's the way I ought to die."

Obviously, Beck and Fernandez were both accused of the Fay murder, but their situations and defenses needed to be different. Yet the court gave them the same attorney: Herbert Rosenberg. That was a violation of ethics and legality. What Rosenberg achieved was changing the venue from Long Island, scene of the murder, to Bronx County. The case, opening in July 1949, was heard before Judge Ferdinand Pecora.

The public thirst to read of and view this trial could not be satisfied. Writes Brown, "A seething mass of struggling, shoving semi-hysterical women swarmed into the big air courtroom … and overflowed into the corridors." All of them were anxious to catch a glimpse of the Lonely Hearts Murderers and to hear the lurid details, which the newspapers had indicated would be made public during the trial. During the recesses, most of them pretended to be shocked at what they had deliberately come to hear, while some openly admitted they thought Fernandez "handsome," "so virile," or "just like Charles Boyer."

And throughout the proceedings, Fernandez had a good volume of fan mail with marriage proposals—if he survived the proceedings. To a lesser degree, Martha Beck attracted admirers.

Jury selection had been difficult. Rosenberg was determined—unsuccessfully—to get a jury that would not convict simply because of attitudes toward sexual perversity.

District Attorney Edward Robinson Jr. lined up an army of witnesses, including the medical examiner and Fay's Albany friends. The defense sought to plead insanity for Martha Beck; as for Fernandez, he was only an accessory after the Fay murder. The state psychiatrist, Dr. Perry M. Lichtenstein, said both of the accused were sane. Martha Beck knew "she was directing the hammer to the skull of Mrs. Fay and she knew when she had done that, she was causing damage to Mrs. Fay's skull."

The defense lost a major point when Judge Pecora rejected the contention that the Michigan confession was made under duress and as part of a deal of a trial in Michigan.

From beginning to end, the trial was conducted in a carnival atmosphere. The best "shows" featured Fernandez and Beck on the stand. On July 11, Fernandez said that he was retracting his confession, made only for love. Said the gentleman Spaniard, "All my statements were made for the purpose of helping Martha. I love her. It couldn't be anything else." But Robinson was persistent and brought up other misdeeds: the Downings, Jane Thompson, and Myrtle Young.

As for Fay's murder, Martha's confession was read before the gasping gallery: "I can still hear it! The blood was dripping, dripping, dripping, and the sound of it just sounded like it could be heard all over the house!"

The lurid details never ceased during more than a week of testimony. Fernandez matter-of-factly related an experience with the swindled Mrs. Esther Henne. The three-way game of strip poker came down to a last hand. The winner won Fernandez in bed. The *New York Times* recorded spectator interest. Testimony was so revolting that "unauthorized persons were not permitted to loiter outside the courtroom. Many of the would-be spectators, predominantly women, did without lunch in order not to lose their places."

But no anticipation matched Martha Beck's taking the stand on July 25. There was absolute silence. No one wanted to miss a word, as she narrated her life story: a tyrannical mother, incestuous relationships, failed romantic relationships and marriage, six suicide attempts, abandonment of her children.

As for her relationship with Fernandez, she said emotionally, "We loved each other and I consider it absolutely sacred … you referred to the love-making as abnormal, but for the love I had for Fernandez, nothing is abnormal … I loved him enough to do anything he asked me to."

At times, the three-day interrogation became raunchy. Squeamish spectators left when Martha detailed aspects of the sexual relationship. On the other hand, The *New York Times* reported that when Martha narrated sex acts connected with voodoo, two dozen policemen were sent to the courthouse to prevent spectators from shoving their way into the courtroom. "The lonely hearts murder trial was disrupted yesterday afternoon," said the paper, "by a near riot of would-be spectators outside the courtroom."

At the end of forty-four days, the jury heard summaries. The prosecution's case was clear-cut: two sane individuals had committed an abominable murder. The defense offered a tedious six-and-a-half-hour defense, much of which attacked the D.A. and state psychiatrist.

An exhausted jury filed out in the early evening of August 18 to decide the fates of Beck and Hernandez. They came back to ask for a reading of Beck's confession and to get a definition of "premeditation." On the first ballot, Martha Beck had one vote for acquittal on grounds of insanity and Fernandez had one vote for manslaughter because there was no proof of premeditation. The juror relented, and early the next day a verdict of first-degree murder was brought in for Fernandez and Beck.

On August 22, Judge Pecora sentenced the pair to die in the electric chair on August 31, 1950. They were immediately sent to Sing

Depravity

Sing to await execution. The State Court of Appeals reviewed the case on July 11, 1950. The vote was 5-2 in favor of the trial court. The three reasons given by the minority are noteworthy: the court's failure to permit proper examination of jurors on their opposition to capital punishment; the permitting of one counsel for both defendants; and the failure to give proper instructions to the jury. A compelling dissent, but of no power to change the death sentence.

The condemned were on death row for some nineteen months. The public was still hungry for news, and they got it—sort of. A rumor in the fall of 1950 linked Martha sexually to one of the guards. An exasperated Martha wrote to Sing Sing Warden Denno:

To print or say that I am having an affair with a guard is one of the most asinine and ridiculous statements ever made! Approximately 25 million persons heard Winchell's broadcasts tonight—including members of my own family. And I admit it, it will be a shock and embarrassment to them.

And Fernandez fumed that the "triangle subjects him to mental torture beyond endurance."

Dr. Hoffman hurried to Albany to plead with Governor Dewey to stop the execution. He waited outside the governor's office in vain. It was against precedent for a psychiatrist to discuss a case with the governor.

Execution was set for March 8, 1951. They had their last meals. Two hours before execution, Fernandez sent a message to Martha: "I would like to shout my love for you to the world."

Martha was ecstatic and hugged the matron who brought her the message. "Now that I know that Raymond loves me, I can go to my death beaming with joy."

She issued a final statement:

"What does it matter who is to blame? My story is a love story, but only those tortured with love can understand what I mean. I was pictured as a fat, unfeeling woman, True, I am fat, that I cannot deny, but if that is a crime, how many of my sex are guilty? ... The prison and the death house have only strengthened my feeling for Raymond, and in the history of the world, how many crimes have been attributed to love?"

Fernandez also issued a final statement: "I am going to die. That is all right. As you know, that's something I've been prepared for since 1949. So tonight I'll die like a man."

Fernandez died first; Martha died some twelve minutes later. The press circus continued. Nobody said it like the *Daily News* as it captured in headlines the end, especially Martha's grimace: "Heart Killers Die in Chair; Martha Goes With Smile, Wink."

In his treatment of the Lonely Hearts Killers, Brown also noted the cold, cruel press coverage of the executions. "Newspapers gleefully reported the struggle to fit her huge bulk into the chair, and the prolonged writhing as the electric shocks struggled to have an impact through her flabby flesh. Such was the public distaste for the Lonely Hearts Killers that more people laughed at that last ordeal than felt pity for its victim."

Martha Beck was the eighth woman in New York State to die in the electric chair. Two years later, another pair of lovers was electrocuted in Sing Sing: Julius and Ethel Rosenberg.

Beyond discussions of the motivations and lives of Fernandez and Beck, there were examinations of the insanity defense. An August 8, 1954, article by Dr. Frederic Wertham, a psychiatrist in the criminal field, dealt with the Lonely Hearts murderers: "The idea that all murderers must be abnormal and therefore exculpated came up in the Lonely Hearts murders … I was asked by the defense to examine Martha Beck and Raymond Fernandez with a view to laying the foundation for an insanity defense.

"I examined them and unearthed a great deal about their lives. Especially in the case of Martha Beck, I tried my best to find medical evidence that I could recognize as symptoms of disease and not as signs of personality. I could not find any. The motive of naked greed overshadowed everything else. I refused to testify for the pair; to condone their cold-blooded deeds on the grounds of illness would not have only been unscientific but unjust to those who are genuinely ill."

Many students of the American scene turned their criticism on the existence of lonely hearts clubs. Reportedly, when Martha Beck was arrested in Grand Rapids, she turned angrily to Sheriff Clarence E. Randle. "You're a policeman. Why don't you put an end to these matrimonial bureaus? The sooner you do, the better it will be for everybody in saving lives and money. They are nothing but a racket."

Lonely Hearts Clubs have been "transformed" into Internet dating. In 2001, Financial Times Information released a report from the national police agency on the first half of the year. Crimes stemming from those who met through online personal sites soared three times beyond the number of similar crimes in all of 2000. Most of the crimes involved child prostitution but also included killings and rapes. All told, there were 283 victims of lonely hearts crimes.

SECTION II—

VICTIMS OF SOCIETY?

FRITZ HAARMANN
Lustmord in Weimar

In the 1920s, when public interest in serial killers was not at today's level, William Bolitho authored *Murder For Profit*. The five he studied were William Burke of Scotland, J. B. Troppmann of France, George Joseph Smith of England, Henry Désiré Landru of France, and Fritz Haarmann of Germany. Burke and Troppmann were of the 1800s. Bolitho considered Haarmann the "chief murderer" of the group, "the worst man, the last of the human race."

Bolitho elaborated: "For in him, the ogre of Hanover ... there are characteristics of all the rest, and his is the sum of all their guilt. Haarmann was possessed of all their guilt. Haarmann was possessed by the ghoul of Burke and the wild beast of Troppmann. He bettered the satanic economics of Smith; and was damned in deeper erotics than Landru."

In a more contemporary study, in 1995, Maria Tatar, professor of German Studies at Harvard University, placed Haarmann in sharp focus. Her work was titled *Lustmord: Sexual Murder in Weimar Germany*. In studying society's fascination with sexual violence, Tatar found that Haarmann personified a small group of serial killers, of "sexual psychopaths" ... "a conspicuous presence, yet also a closely guarded secret, in Weimar's artistic, cinematic, and literary production."

Fritz Haarmann was born in Hanover in 1879, the youngest of six children. His father was a locomotive-stoker who left work when

Fritz was five to retire on his wife's dowry, which was a small fortune, including several houses. From his earliest years, Fritz hated his father.

Olle Haarmann had a nasty temper and was a grumbler, mean-spirited, and malcontent. He was frequently seen at night at Hanover bars. Father and son continually argued. When the father taunted his son and threatened to institutionalize him, the son vowed to go to authorities with the accusation that the father killed a train driver.

The mother, Johanna Clouds, forty-one, was seven years younger than her husband. She became bed-ridden after Fritz' birth and remained a withered, prematurely aged parent. He always remained close to his mother and spoke of her with tenderness and much emotion. With the type of household Fritz was raised in, it would not surprise that his childhood would not be like that of other youngsters.

Of the siblings, Alfred, the oldest, was a respectable, hardworking factory foreman with proper family values. The second brother, Wilhelm, was sent to a reformatory for a sexual offense against a neighbor's twelve-year-old daughter. The three sisters were all prostitutes and all divorced after brief marriages. One died in World War I; a second sister never fared well with Fritz. So the youngest sister, Emma, was Fritz's only family link.

In fact, when his mother died in 1905, the family structure was further weakened as the family fought over her inheritance.

As soon as he passed infancy, he chose to play with dolls and loved sewing. At times he dressed in his sisters' clothing. While he got great pleasure from helping his sisters with homework, he was shy and scared of playing with boys.

As an adolescent, he also gained pleasure in acts that discomforted and frightened others. He regularly tied up his sisters and tapped on windows in the post-midnight hours, hoping to inspire fear of ghosts and werewolves.

While stocky, he was a handsome fellow who enjoyed popularity among schoolmates. Having failed his locksmith apprenticeship, Fritz at age sixteen was enrolled in a training school for commissioned officers at Neubreisach. He excelled as a gymnast and was a disciplined soldier, but was a poor student. One day while marching he had a fainting spell and epileptic fit. The school records attribute the incident to a concussion contracted while doing bar exercise or the result of sunstroke during exercise.

"I don't like it here any more," he pronounced after recovery and left the academy.

His career of perversity mounted after leaving school. At first, his father sought to employ him at a cigar factory he opened in 1888. But sexual offenses against children were a daily occurrence. He was sent to the Provincial Asylum at Hildesheim. He was examined by the town doctor, Dr. Schmalfuss, who deemed him incurable and deranged.

He so bitterly resented the institutional life and it so traumatized him that the threat of sending him back to an asylum managed to subdue him temporarily. At his later trial, he told the court: "Cut off my head, but do not send me back to the madhouse."

He only remained at the asylum for six months. As the institution celebrated Christmas with a tree-lighting ceremony, Fritz bolted to his freedom and fled to Switzerland. He found employment, first with a boatmaker, then with a Zurich apothecary.

In 1889, at age twenty, he returned to Hanover. The return home was not well received by the father, who engaged in many physical battles with Fritz. The father purchased a fried-fish business for his son, but Fritz ruined the business with plundering. However, Fritz seemed to achieve a period of normalcy. He seduced and married the attractive Erna Loewert. Both sets of parents hoped that the union would create a settling-down phase for Fritz. However, he deserted his pregnant wife and left for military service.

He enlisted as substitute and was dispatched to the highly skilled 10th Jager Battalion in Colmar, Alsace.

He was the ideal soldier, much like William Burke and Henri Désiré Landru, soldiers turned serial killers. One captain engaged him as batman.

Fritz was known as an excellent soldier full of obedience and esprit de corps. He carried even the most menial of details and assignments. The army stint was "the happiest years of my life," according to Haarmann.

However, in 1901, he collapsed during an army exercise. The illness was diagnosed as neurasthenia. He was released with the designation of "recht gut," equivalent to honorable discharge. The following diagnosis was made: "The patient has a mental deficiency, which becomes apparent only during systematic examination … It appears probable that he contracted dementia praecox in 1895, which led to considerable mental deficiency, appearing as congenital idiocy; subsequently, there was some improvement."

Still, he was eligible for a pension, which he received until his final arrest in 1924. Interestingly, the other convictions didn't interfere with his pension.

Back home in Hanover, the family feuding reached new levels. The father had Fritz examined. In the medical report of May 1903, Haarmann was evaluated as lacking morals, unintelligent, crude, vengeful, selfish, and "easily amused." To the dismay of the father, however, the doctor concluded that he was not in the medical sense "mentally ill, so that there are no grounds for sending him to a lunatic asylum."

It was in 1905, following his contracting gonorrhea, that Haarmann turned to homosexuality. Haarmann told of his association with a count's valet. Haarmann met the fellow at a fair and accompanied the valet home: "He made fresh coffee. He kissed me. I was shy. By now it's turned midnight. He said, 'It's late. Stay with me.' I did. He did things I never imagined. I was frightened. I messed the bed. But later I met hundreds of others like him."

Thus, at age twenty-four, Fritz Haarmann was free to engage in any activity without fear of institutionalization. Haarmann sat in prison for one-third of the next twenty years, on charges of petty theft, burglary, fraud, and indecency.

Haarmann was very clever in his thievery. In one stint, he purchased a disinfection system and rented a room. He found his clients by reading the obits in the papers. He visited the bereaved as an official of the town's disinfection department and advised them to have the rooms and possessions of the deceased disinfected. While disinfecting, he plundered the family's possessions.

Whenever Haarmann entered prison, he came out more crafty, and the crimes increased. "Typical of the twentieth-century penal system," according to Prof. Theodore Lessing, "whenever Haarmann was released from jail, both his craftiness and his crimes increased."

In his study of Haarmann, Bolitho wonders at a society that functions in such a contradictory manner. It institutionalizes him, then doles out an army pension, refuses to institutionalize him, and sends him in and out of prison:

"The proper interpretation of the medical reports which decorate the period of his life is that the State was unwilling to content itself with the simple removal of an irritating parasite to the safe keepings of an asylum, but must also scratch. It indulges itself with a revengeful assertion of his responsibility, in order not only to segregate but to punish."

When the Great War broke out, Fritz Haarmann, called the "born soldier" by Jager officers, was in prison. Post-war Germany was in chaos. The city of Hanover, with some four hundred fifty thousand citizens, was filled with swindlers, thieves, prostitutes, perverts, and countless fugitives from the law.

The only way to survive was to get food near the rail station. Outside the rail station, writes Bolitho, "was the card system, stupid, proud, honest, by which all honest, proud, or stupid men were doomed to slow starvation, to death. The only way to obtain meat, bread, milk enough to keep body and soul alive was Haarmann's way—opposite the railway station, in the Scheiber market."

Hanover was only four train hours from Berlin, eight hours from Cologne, and a good place for smuggling, a thieves-market. He joined a smuggling ring. Following the collapse of Germany, Hanover flourished as a hub of international transit and the black market. Haarmann started a business as butcher or meat-hawker. He outdid his father's success as cigar manufacturer. He undersold all competitors, and was loved by housewives who appreciated his huge stock of meat. He was also a police spy, giving him the revered title of Detective Haarmann in the Scheiber Market.

In fact, he was thought of as a model citizen: a self-employed butcher, a friend to homeless boys, who would be offered a meal and lodging. Haarmann was thought of in the community as a benefactor of the unfortunate, especially to the homeless. He distributed clothes daily. Those who received them knew he was homosexual but did not care.

The police welcomed the services of Haarmann. He was ideal for informing against those who were plotting attacks against property and government. And Haarmann knew where these undesirables were. The Hanover authorities could not deal with the crisis following the war. People were starving. Only twelve Hanover constables and detectives were available to handle four thousand registered prostitutes and five hundred male prostitutes. The police estimated that the number of prostitutes in Hanover was about forty thousand.

Understaffed and underpaid, the Hanover police could not cope with lawlessness. They needed informers like Haarmann. The best reward was immunity from crime. Haarmann was highly welcomed by the Hanover police.

The crime spree began in September 1919. The first victim was Freidel Roth. His father was in military service; the mother could not handle the undisciplined teen. He left home with his father's civilian clothes and sold them. He wrote his mother that he would return when she was "nice again." He was spotted at the Scheiber Market.

One of Freidel's friends, Paul Montag, later told police that Freidel had met a "fine gentleman," a detective who had taken him for a ride in the park. Freidel confided to Paul, "I have been to his room; there we smoke and amuse ourselves."

After several days, the parents went to Haarmann's lodging at

Depravity

Cellarstrasse. The parents demanded the police search the house. They did not find the missing lad, but they surprised Haarmann in bed with another youngster. Haarmann was sentenced to nine months in prison for seduction. Years later while awaiting trial, Haarmann confessed: "At the time when the policeman arrested me, the head of the boy Freidel was hidden under a newspaper behind the oven. Later on, I threw it into the canal."

After release from prison, Haarmann moved to Nikelaastrasse. The landlady refused to tolerate the continual stream of new visitors, so he moved farther down the block. Where did these youngsters come from?

Daily, the rail station brought a new detachment of these youngsters of the war generation," observed Bolitho. "They stepped out, covered in coaldust, from goods-wagons where they had ridden hundreds of miles without a ticket; they crawled from under the axles of expresses sometimes, and very often they arrived on foot, limping and pale from the villages within a hundred miles round. They had left home because their fathers were dead in the war and there was no food at home, or sometimes because their fathers had returned safe from the war, and there were two masters in the house."

Settled in his new home, Haarmann met a youth who would change his life. Now, it was Fritz Haarmann and Hans Grans. Haarmann was forty; Grans was sixteen. The youth was very effeminate and appealed to Haarmann's homosexual needs.

Lessing describes this odd couple: "Picture a tough wily crab in the bottom of the ocean, lodged in the dark cavern of a slimy giant polyp, and you will have an idea of the strange symbiosis of compulsive crime and parasitic intelligence, of madness of mind and spiritual parasitism, which irrevocably bound together Hans Grans, young, gentle, and girlish, and the effeminate, rough, bloated Haarmann, Grans' senior by twenty-four years."

The couple at first did not engage in murderous activities—at least none were proven. They had a well-organized operation of thievery. They prospered. Haarmann supplemented his thievery with social security payments because he was deemed an invalid. As police informer, he was able to extract huge sums.

The killings were renewed in early 1922 when they settled at 8 Neuestrasse. The modus operandi was the same as in the Freidel Roth case. Haarmann, often with Grans, would go to the rail station in the evening and choose a youngster. Under the guise of a friendly police official, he would take the lad home, kill him, hack up the body for further use, or throw the corpse into the river. They then would sell the clothing or other possessions on the thieves' market.

Their hovel was near the town synagogue. Perhaps sensing the future, Lessing observed how fortunate it was that Haarmann was not Jewish: "Imagine what ritual pogroms would have been carried out by the people had Haarmann been a Jew."

Rumors surfaced that human flesh was being sold on the open market. While suspicions fell on Haarmann because he was seen with young boys, they never were followed up. As a butcher, Haarmann could easily answer questions about a bloody knife, a bloody apron, or buckets of bloody water.

After February 1923, details are available of twenty-seven disappearances in which Haarmann was involved, either through his own confessions or unchallenged opinion. The first of the twenty-seven occurred on February 12. Fritz Franke, seventeen, came from Berlin after stealing goods from his father's house. The runaway was accompanied by another youth and met at the Hanover station by Haarmann, who said that he was a police officer inspecting the waiting rooms. The other youth, less attractive, was dismissed. Franke went home with Haarmann. Grans claimed the effects of the deceased.

The murder was also noteworthy because two women, friends of Grans, visited the Haarmann residence while the two were away. Looking in the closet, they discovered a quantity of strange-looking meat. They brought a sample to the police, who maintained that it was pork. How could anyone suspect Haarmann? According to Bolitho,

Depravity

Haarmann might have also come into service for the police against suspected Communists.

No incident against Haarmann or Grans was followed up. In fact, in one situation one paper carried a story asking for information about a missing lad. Haarmann came to the door of the anxious family and announced that he was a criminologist. As he said at the trial, he left "laughing hysterically."

The following is a gruesome sampling of the Haarmann crime log:

William Schulze, seventeen, came looking for work. His clothes were discovered in the possession of Haarmann's landlady.

Raymond Hoch, fifteen, sought a career at sea. His clothing was sold by Haarmann.

Hans Sennenfeld, twenty, had his clothes sold by Grans to an individual, who turned them into scouring rags.

Ernest Ehrenberg, thirteen, a son of Haarmann's neighbor. His knapsack was found in Haarmann's room.

Heinrich Struss, eighteen, whose possessions were found in Haarmann's room, including a key ring that locked Haarmann's box, wardrobe, and violin box.

William Erdner, sixteen, arrested for vagabondage by a detective, who was later identified as Haarmann.

Adolf Hannappel, seventeen, killed by Haarmann because Grans coveted Hannappel's trousers.

Ernest Spiecker, seventeen, met in the dance hall; when arrested, Grans was wearing the boy's shirt.

Willi Senger, twenty, whose overcoat was found in Haarmann's room.

Robert Witzel, eighteen, was found in the Leine River. The skull was identified by his teeth.

Almost all of the victims were disillusioned youth: runaways, without jobs, unhappy at home. Parents, either angry or estranged, did not immediately report the disappearances. With the clothing and the meat of the victims distributed around Hanover, tracings were very difficult.

The Witzel case rang an alarm in Hanover. On May 17, 1924, the human skull turned up in the Leine. As May ended, another skull turned up further down the river.

Seventeen-year-old Erich de Vries disappeared on June 14, 1924. Haarmann offered him some cigarettes and lured him to his room.

On July 24, youngsters frolicking on the riverbank found a sack of human bones and a skull. Previous findings had been dismissed by the police doctor as a medical school prank, remains from the anatomical institute in Gottingen, tossed into the river by grave robbers fleeing the scene of looting, or the bones were washed down from Alfeld, suffering from a typhus outbreak.

The newest finding could not be dismissed. The talk of Hanover went as follows: "There are killings in the Old Town. Young children have been done away with in cellars. Boys have been drowned in the river … a werewolf is among us."

The newspapers ran stories about six hundred disappearances in 1924, mostly boys between ages fourteen and eighteen. Police decided to dredge the river and found five hundred bones of twenty-two different bodies. Every thief and sexual pervert the police could locate was brought in for questioning.

The police followed the lead offered by Witzel's best friend, Fritz Kahlmeyer, who visited the local circus the night of Witzel's abduction. Kahlmeyer said they had gone to the circus with a police official who matched Haarmann's description. While not abducting Kahlmeyer, Haarmann procured the youth for "society gentlemen." The police searched Haarmann's apartment and found Witzel's possessions, but Haarmann insisted that this was his market trade only.

However, one day a couple chanced to enter the police station,

Depravity

where the Witzel family was waiting to query the police. "Where did you get that jacket? It's my son's!" Mr. Witzel screamed at the man. The name Witzel was on an identification card in the trousers.

The man said that the pants had come from Haarmann. The police grilled the Vampire of Hanover, who confessed to thirty or forty murders. And under incessant questioning, he fingered Grans as instigator and accomplice. At the time relations between them had somewhat cooled. The questioning stretched out over seven days. Haarmann finally snapped and called for the superintendent and examining magistrate. He would make full confession.

After the "unburdening of the conscience," Haarmann led police and court officials on a murder circuit of the city. Corpses were shown: parts hidden in bushes, bones dredged from a lake, skeletons in different parts of the city. The publicity encouraged additional witnesses to step forward, with evidence of clothing or meat obtained through Haarmann or Grans.

In its report, the police called Haarmann's appearance "far from evil." They noted his feminine mannerisms: wiggling of his behind, licking of his lips, and his feminine pastimes, such as baking and cooking. Yet he still smoked strong cigars.

True, Haarmann confessed, but the procedure was thoroughly brutal. One report said that his testicles had been crushed. One detective told a parent of one of the victims, "I certainly gave Haarmann something to think about with the rubber hose."

At the end of August 1924, Haarmann was sent to Gottingen for psychiatric examination. The question of his sanity has never been fully resolved. But, as will be seen, three psychiatrists at the trial deemed him sane.

The trial opened the first week of December 1924, with Fritz Haarmann as Germany's most prolific serial killer. With sixty volumes of files available, the case was unparalleled in German history.

Massive crowds blocked the streets leading to the Berlin courtroom, as citizens wanted to glimpse Haarmann and Grans. Fearful that relatives would carry weapons to murder the accused, the police carefully searched all witnesses. Some one hundred ninety witnesses were prepared to testify.

More than twenty press representatives came, including the French and American media and four artists.

The court set up an exhibit of the clothes of the victims arranged in small heaps and ticketed with their names. Some carried a note: "identified by parents."

Haarmann asked and was permitted to tell his story and conduct his own defense. His narrative was explicit, chilling, and gruesome:

> I never intended to hurt those youngsters, but I knew that if I got going, something would happen and that made me cry ... I would throw myself on top of those boys. They were worn out by the antics and debauchery. I bit through the Adam's apple, must have throttled them at the same time.
>
> I'd put the body on the floor and cover the face with a cloth so it wouldn't be looking at me.
>
> I'd make two cuts in the abdomen and put the intestines in a bucket, then soak up the blood, then I'd make three cuts from the ribs toward the shoulders, take hold of the ribs and push until the bones around the shoulder broke....Now I could get the heart, lungs, and kidneys, and chop them up, and put them in my bucket. Then I'd take the legs off, then the arms. I'd take the flesh off the bones and put it in my waxcloth bag.... It would take me five or six trips to take everything out and throw it down the toilet or river. I'd cut the penis off after I had emptied and cleaned the chest and stomach cavities. I would cut it into lots of little pieces. I always hated doing this, but I couldn't help it—my passion was so much stronger than the horror of the cutting and chopping.
>
> I'd take the heads off last. I used the little kitchen knife to cut around the scalp and cut it up into little strips and squares. I'd put the skull, face down, on a straw mat and cover it with rags so that you wouldn't hear the banging so much. I'd hit it with a

blunt edge of the axe until the joints on the skull split apart. The brains went in the bucket and the chopped-up bones in the river opposite the castle … Clothes were given away or sold. The more I did this, the more efficient I became.

Many Germans were unhappy in reading the press. The Federation of German Women's clubs, with more than a million members, called on the press to cease publishing the horrific details.

"We speak for all responsible women and mothers," said the appeal. "Incredible harm accrues to our youth from the publication of the terrible details involved in the trial."

Not all was gruesome in the two-week proceedings. The nonchalant Haarmann was flippant, comic, and satirical.

When queried whether a certain youth was among the victims, he countered, "No, I did not kill that chap, but let his name stand on the list—I do not mind."

When the lights were switched on, he quipped, "Just like a pretty Christmas tree."

However, when shown the picture of Heremann Wolf as a possible victim, he roared. "No, he is ill-dressed, ugly. I could never consider such a grotesque victim."

To the news that it might be a two-week trial, he pleaded, "Oh, finish it up. I want to be executed as soon as possible." So he told the jury, "Keep it short, I want to spend Christmas in heaven with Mother."

And he admonished the press, "You are not to lie; we know you are all liars."

He rebuked one witness, whose son was allegedly murdered by the accused. "What kind of father are you to let your son be dressed in rags!" Three German psychiatrists—a university professor, a local prison official, and a nerve specialist—testified that Haarmann was sane.

Ernest Schultze of the University of Gottingen spoke of the

accused's "inordinate vanity." Responding to Haarmann's demand for a public beheading, the witnesses observed:

"Haarmann rejoices in a possible beheading as though it were his own wedding. He wants a big monument erected over his grave with an inscription testifying to his breaking the world's record for wholesale murders. During one of my interviews with him, he told me, 'I am now a famous man; the whole world talks about me.'"

As for his partner in crime, Grans, the younger murderer, was more serious on the stand. He sought to preserve his life, trying to place of the blame on Haarmann, who encouraged him.

At the trial, Haarmann spoke of his close relationship with Grans. "I had to have someone I meant everything to. Hans often laughed at me. Then I got mad and threw him out. But I ran after and fetched him back. I couldn't help it; I was crazy about the boy."

Yet there was sniping between the two at the trial. In fact, Haarmann placed the blame on his friend. "Grans just didn't bring the boys to me for me to kill them. He just didn't use all sorts of tricks to get me going … He took advantage of my madness and for days on end he'd try to persuade me to kill boys whose trousers he wanted. He killed too!" Lessing described Haarmann's actions as a "suppressed desire for sexual revenge."

Defense attorney Dr. Teich summed up with his question: "What is truth?" Nothing could have saved Grans, according to Lessing: "Had the good Lord himself appeared in the courtroom and stood protectively in front of the young man, of whom nothing, but nothing at all could be proven, no god could have saved him in this unpleasant atmosphere of hatred and resentment and anti-justice." Any sympathy for Grans was lost when he told the court: "I expect to be acquitted and to have my honor restored by an impartial court."

On December 19, 1924, Haarmann was found guilty of twenty-four murders and sentenced to death. Upon hearing the verdict, Haarmann reacted calmly: "I accept the sentence fully, and entirely, though I am innocent of some of the murders attributed to me." His counsel objected to the hasty acceptance without appeal.

"I have thought carefully what I am doing," Haarmann insisted. "I want to be executed in the marketplace. On the tombstone must be put this inscription: 'Here Lies Mass-Murderer Haarmann.'" Haarmann was decapitated, but in Hanover prison.

The welcoming of death was described by Lessing as "one final orgasm." Added Lessing, "This person, normally devoid of feeling, experienced a self-extinguishing overexcitement that far exceeded anything he experienced in his ordinary day-to-day life."

Grans was sentenced to death for his incitement in the murder of Adolf Hannappel, seventeen, who was dismissed from a milkman's farm for overeating. During the trial, Haarmann testified that Grans instigated the killing against Haarmann's will because Grans wanted the victim's trousers. Throughout the trial, Grans denied any knowledge of Haarmann's murders, a fact contradicted by Haarmann. Grans was visibly shaken by the death sentence.

T. R. Ybarra, covering the trial for the *New York Times*, reported: "Thus, closed the worst murder case in German annals of crime. It has filled German newspaper columns for a fortnight—not counting the huge amount written about it before it came to trial—and has been followed throughout the country with extraordinary interest mixed with intense horror and disgust."

The trial ended, but Haarmann had not finished his jousting with the law. Several days after the verdict, a messenger found a letter on the street, addressed to Albert Grans, whose son had been condemned to death. The letter soon reached the Hanover court.

The four-page letter was a confession from Haarmann, written as the prisoner was taken back to his cell. "Hans Grans has been sentenced unjustly," Haarmann wrote, "and that's the fault of the police, and also because I wanted revenge … Put yourself in Grans' position; he will question the existence of the Lord and justice just because of me … May Hans Grans forgive me for my revenge and inhumanity."

What was the reason for this letter? Was he troubled by his conscience? Was this a stall? Possibly, as suggested by Lessing, Haarmann had been pressured by the police, and he wanted to get back at the legal system. Fritz Haarmann felt a "judicial murder was committed." So, like his other victims, Haarmann killed the one he loved by seeking to manipulate the German legal system.

Prof. Lessing was enraged by the case. His book was completed and ready for publication in February 1925. His greatest anger was directed at society, which bore responsibility for all Haarmann's victims. Instead of rejoicing at the death of Haarmann, Hanover should observe "communal guilt." The remains of the victims should be placed in a communal coffin; "decorate it with flowers and lower it into the earth at our town's expense ... And all of us, the whole town, will follow it: senators, clergymen, senior council members, chief of police ... to accept and acknowledge our collective guilt."

After Haarmann's decapitation, an additional note of the Vampire of Hanover was found, a declaration of revenge against the police:

"You won't kill me; I'll be back—yes, I shall be amongst you for all eternity. And now your yourselves have also killed. You should know it. Hans Grans was innocent! Well? How's your conscience now?"

Nevertheless, Grans's sentence was carried out.

Haarmann forecast that he would not be forgotten. He proved he was right. Debates continued about his execution, mind, and motives. And he became a legend in the history of Weimar culture.

Because of all the influences Haarmann was subjected to, Bolitho insists Haarmann is not responsible for his crimes:

> "The unnatural marriage of his parents, the corruption of a town, which he did not invent, the asylum that allowed a homicide to escape, the science and the revenge that would not send him back again, the army that taught him the theory of manslaughter, the prison that gave him bad dreams, the enthronement of his life over the economic system in consequence of the war, the

police that gave him license and power: for none of these things is Haarmann responsible, even in the ambiguous arithmetic of law. Take them from the crime, and what remains of Haarmann?"

Lessing, an observer at the trial, was completing his book *The Story of the Werewolf* at the time of the trial. He felt society and its institutions created Haarmann the killer. "Prison produces homosexuality," he wrote. "Nature did not create the evil monsters. They were created by the cage … Our madhouses provide madness, our prisons create criminals."

Lessing also theorizes that Haarmann, like many others "consumed by passion … indulge in sex murder." He cites the lines of a man abused in prison in Oscar Wilde's "Ballad of Reading Gaol":

> Yet each man kills the thing he loves,
> By each let this be heard,
> Some do it with a bitter look,
> Some with a flattering word,
> The coward does it with a kiss,
> The brave man with a sword!

In his introduction to the 1993 Nemesis edition of *Monsters of Weimar*, Colin Wilson stresses that Haarmann was the first illustration of the sadistic-homosexual killer, followed in more modern times by Dennis Nilsen and Jeffrey Dahmer.

Not surprisingly, the Communist daily *Die Rote Fahne* (*The Red Flag*) linked the death sentence to the morally corrupt Social Democratic government, which gave a pass to violence through its capitalistic activities: "The beast Haarmann, a blood sucker who works on his own in a primitive way, lives in the shadow of the bloody weapons used by the capitalist state." Haarmann's crimes were minor, said the paper, compared to the World War I generals Hindenberg and Lodendorff.

Others blamed Haarmann's deviant behavior on the homosexual and immoral behavior promoted by Jews. A 1924 pamphlet accused the Jewish press of "unleashing a contagious plague."

In 1929, a Nazi newspaper reviewed the Haarmann case and concluded, "Jews are forever trying to propagandize sexual relations between siblings, men and animals, and men and men." Their propaganda is "nothing but vulgar perverted crimes. The punishment should be banishment or hanging."

Alexander Gilbert in his essay for The Crime Library comments on three influences: biological, the traumatic childhood, and sociological factors. Like other killers, Haarmann experienced head injuries in youth. He also endured epileptic fits in early childhood.

Haarmann's childhood was not psychologically sound. He was pampered; he engaged in feministic activities; he was sadistic with his peers.

Society contributed to the making of the Vampire of Hanover. He was traumatized by stays in prison and at the mental asylum. With every release from prison, Haarmann sharpened his crime techniques and increased his hatred of the judicial system.

In the words of Gilbert, "Haarmann's psychological examiners … believed that he saw his execution as one final intense orgasm and the excitement of this possibility exceeded anything he had experienced in his day-to-day life. He rejected the inhibitions that society attempts to place upon us and manipulated love and crime into a sexual game… Haarmann murdered for profit, both sexual and financial—and, yet, while often racked with remorse, he never at any time in his life felt the burden of fear upon him. Fritz Haarmann lived his entire life for his own destruction."

Fritz Haarmann has not been forgotten in Germany. Fritz Lang's film *M* opened in 1931 with the following rhyme chanted by a child:

> Just you wait 'til it's your time,
> The black man will come after you,
> With his chopper, oh so fine,
> He'll make mincemeat out of you.

It is clear, according to Tatar, who studied sexual murder in Weimar

Germany, that "the black man" is Haarmann. "Much as collective cultural memory has excluded Fritz Haarmann from the historical record," writes Tatar, "and preserved the historical record, it was impossible to eradicate his real-life existence entirely."

Tatar relates a bizarre, scandalous attempt in the 1970s to "celebrate" Haarmann's black deeds in his Hanover hometown. Architect Alfred Hrdlicka suggested a monument to the serial killer. Not surprisingly, the plan was never approved.

Hrdlicka explains his position in *Grafik*:

"Haarmann the mass murderer … was not only a lightning flash revealing the state-sanctioned mass murders that were to come; his antisocial occupations and drives were, above all, what made him a prototype of his time."

Perhaps Hrdlicka has overdone his stress on Haarmann, argues Tatar, but the episode focuses on the importance of lustmorde in Weimar Germany. A serious student of German history should not overlook Hrdlicka's "refusal to erase Haarmann from the historical record and his determination to investigate his deeds as symptomatic of something larger than the murderer himself."

Beyond the lustmorde vis a vis Weimar Germany, the Haarmann case is notable for the negative spotlight on the state, which must take much of the blame for the serial killer. According to Bolitho, "The state had used all its best tools upon him: church, prison, army, school, family, asylum—it can hardly disclaim responsibility for the result."

And the analysis of Bolitho, more than eighty years ago, is valued for his conclusions about mass murderers in general. Society should not view them as crazed, "deranged automata," but rather the "worst men."

Criminals such as Haarmann, argues Bolitho, construct for themselves a life fought against what they perceive as the evils of society. They delude themselves into a "life-romance, a personal myth in which they are the maltreated hero, which secret is the key of their life; in such comforting daydreams many an honest man has drugged himself against despair."

CARL PANZRAM
"The World's Worst Murderer"

In his 2000 book offering a "modern scientific perspective" on serial murder, Elliot Leyton places the Panzram case into the "proletarian rebellion." Leyton labeled Panzram as "one of a small proportion of murderers who come from anything resembling a truly oppressed segment of society."

According to Leyton, the early twentieth century saw the emergence of "a new homicidal theme … Proletarian revolt became a minor expression, in which those … who glimpsed their utter exclusion, who felt their torture at the hands of the bourgeois institutions constructed for their 'rehabilitation,' wreaked a similar havoc."

Panzram was one of those who were stung and bitter at his exclusion. His years of oppression were documented in his prison journal.

His message to the world was clear: "I have done as what I was taught to do. I am no different from any other. You have taught me how to live my life, and I have lived as you taught me. I have no desire to reform me. My only desire is to reform people who try to reform me. And I believe the only way to reform people is to kill 'em."

Yes, to understand Panzram—and other serial killers—is to understand his anger at society. Beyond that, the story of Panzram also shows the intelligent side of the serial killer and the disastrous parenting and schooling experience that would be translated into the tragedy of a lifetime.

It is nearly eighty years since Carl Panzram was hanged at Leavenworth. With twenty-one murders, according to his admissions—the actual numbers might be higher—he was among the more notorious of American serial killers in the early twentieth century. One newspaper headline called him, in 1930, the "World's Worst Murderer."

However, the story of Carl Panzram and his criminal career are made up of many fascinating facets: a debate on the causes of his depravity—innate demonism, wretched family life, or horrid correctional and penal institutions; a unique friendship with a sympathetic prison guard that produced an extraordinary twenty-thousand-word confession smuggled out of the cell; the involvement of celebrated essayist H. L. Mencken and psychiatrist Dr. Karl Menninger; sharing of a solitary block with the famed "Bird Man of Alcatraz;" and an appeal of the condemned to President Herbert Hoover not to interfere with the scheduled hanging.

The out-of-prison career of Panzram was variegated in terms of positions and habitats. He was a muleskinner, carnival worker, soldier, railroad guard, strikebreaker, seaman, watchman, caretaker, and labor foreman. He served in Connecticut, Kansas, Massachusetts, Pennsylvania, Scotland, Panama, and the Belgian Congo.

Carl Panzram was born in 1891 on a small farm in Minnesota, the youngest child of Prussian immigrants. He had five siblings: four brothers and one sister. When Carl was seven, his father walked out of the marriage, left the farm, and never came back.

He was abused from his earliest days. As he stated in his *Confessions*, "Right or wrong, I used to get plenty of abuse. Everybody thought it was all right to deceive me and kick me around whenever they felt like it pretty regular. That is the way my life was lived until I was about eleven years old."

That marked the commencement of a criminal career, as he broke into a neighbor's home, stealing food, but notably a "great big pistol." He headed for the train tracks and adventures as a cowboy. However, he was caught, brought back to be pummeled to near unconsciousness by his brothers, and sent to jail, and the next year to the Minnesota State Training School at Red Wing.

It was at the correctional school that young Carl learned about "man's inhumanity to man." He was continually abused and beaten by authorities. "Then I began to think that I was being unjustly imposed upon," he said. "Then I began to hate those who abused me. Then I began to think that I would have my revenge just as soon and as often as I could injure someone else. Anyone at all would do. If I couldn't injure those who injured me, then I would injure someone else."

The beatings were with wooden planks, leather straps, whips, and paddles. For a start, the revenge was petty. He would "urinate in their soup, coffee, or tea and masturbate into their ice cream or dessert and then stand beside them and watch them eat it." His biggest thrill was burning down the paint shop, with damages of over one hundred thousand dollars.

He was discharged. Now fourteen, he returned home, kicked out of school after attempting to kill his teacher, and went back to the farm. It was time to set out on his own. On the freight train, heading west, he endured a life-defining experience. Four men approached him and offered clothes and shelter. "But first they wanted me to do a little something for them," Panzram wrote. He was gang raped. "I cried, begged, and pleaded for mercy, pity, and sympathy, but nothing I could say or do could sway them from their purpose." This experience brought a life motif: "If I was strong enough and clever enough to impose my will on others, I was right ... Another lesson I learned at that time was that there were a lot of very nice things in this world. Among them were whiskey and sodomy."

Caught in a petty larceny in Butte, Montana, Panzram was sentenced to one year at the Montana State Reform School. He escaped before completing his term.

While in a Helena, Montana, tavern, he heard a speech from an Army recruiter and enlisted in the army. The sixteen-year-old lied about his age. It wasn't long before he was caught stealing army overcoats, a civilian suit, and gold buttons. He was given three years in the U.S. Military Prison at Fort Leavenworth, Kansas.

Among tortures, he was chained to a fifty-pound ball and had to carry the weight even while sleeping. His assignment: breaking rocks in a quarry, ten hours a day, daily.

When discharged in 1910, he was the spirit of meanness personified. "Well, I was a pretty rotten egg before I went there, but when I left there, all the good that may have been in me had been kicked and beaten out of me."

His goal for the future was to stir as much mayhem as possible: "All I had in my mind at that time was a strong determination to raise plenty of hell with anyone and everybody in every way I could and everyplace I could."

Panzram's post-prison trek took him through Colorado, Texas, and California before enlisting in the Foreign Legion of Northern Mexico. That stint lasted a month before his desertion. "All the churches I ever saw had all been robbed before." He changed his name to Jeff Davis, then Jack Allen. He rode around burglarizing and sodomizing; he was in prisons and escaped. His next wanderings were in Oregon, Idaho, and Montana.

His first full sentence was at the state prison at Deer Lodge, Montana. "At that place and time," he wrote in *Confessions*, "I got to be an experienced wolf. I knew more about sodomy than old boy Oscar Wilde ever thought of knowing. I would start the morning with sodomy, work as hard as I could all day and sometimes half the night."

After release in 1915, he was back to his activities as burglar: money, food, clothes, and guns. Only a few months later, he was caught stealing clothes and other items that were worth less than twenty dollars. The DA asked him to plead guilty for a light sentence; however, the sentence was seven years at the Oregon State Penitentiary in Salem.

Warden Minto made prison cruelty more unendurable. The tortures are described in detail in Gaddis and Long's *Killer*. They included "The Jacket," "A Dose of Salts," "The Bat or the Paddle," "The Restraint

Machine," and "The Humming Bird." The Spanish Inquisition was tame compared to these, observed Panzram. "Torquemada, chief inquisitor of the Spanish Inquisition, was known as the world's greatest torturer. The methods and all of the instruments that he used to inflict torture on other human beings were all very ingenious, but they were crude compared to those in use today."

The more Panzram violated prison regulations, the greater the severity of the punishment. He started several fires and razed three buildings. Solitary punishment always followed. He helped another inmate escape, who killed Warden Minto in a nearby town. The public became enraged. Prison conditions worsened, and so did voices for reforming the penitentiary system.

Through all this, Panzram continued his attempts at escape. He was initially frustrated in cutting through the bars of his cells. When he did escape, he was recognized by a policeman, subdued in battle and brought back to Salem unconscious. But he made it out again, for good, in the spring of 1918. He ran into the woods and grabbed a freight train heading eastward.

He was now John O'Leary, on the run in the midst of World War I. His stops were short and frequent: Army enlistment in Meyersdale, Pennsylvania; Baltimore, for a hotel robbery; New York, to acquire a Seaman's Identification Card; to Panama, Peru, and Chile; back to Panama, for the stealing of a schooner, killing the owner, captain, and crew—a total of six, with the help of a sailor; to Texas and Scotland, where he robbed a ship and passengers, for which he served a short prison term.

The next round in the journey took Panzram from London to Paris to Germany, and back to New York, for a robbery of a jewelry store. His next activity was a forty thousand dollar robbery of a mansion, former home of President William Howard Taft. Having signed on with the yacht *Manchuria*, he enlisted other sailors to rob other yachts stationed around South Street.

Some of the victims were brought to City Island, where the Panzram yacht was tied. He promised them work; instead, he robbed them, killed them, and dropped them into the channel.

Aware that the neighbors were becoming suspicious, Panzram headed for New Jersey, then Connecticut, and added rounds of burglary. However, he was arrested for burglary and gun possession—six months in jail.

Upon release, Panzram was in the middle of a labor battle involving the Flying Squadron of the Seaman's Union. He became involved in a gun battle with the police, was arrested, jumped bail, and boarded a ship in Norfolk, destined for Europe. He landed in the Belgian Congo and made his way to Angola, where he took a job driving riggers for Sinclair Oil Company.

In Luanda, he killed and raped an eleven-year-old boy. He bashed the victim's head with a rock. As Panzram detailed in his *Confessions*, "His brains were coming out of his ears when I left him and he will never be any deader."

After the murder, Panzram returned to Lobito Bay. His next venture was a jungle hunt for crocodiles, for sale to European speculators in the Congo. He was joined in the hunt by six natives, who demanded a share of the profits.

Panzram had other ideas. He shot and killed all six, some preteens. After killing them, admitted Panzram, " I threw them all overboard and the crocodiles soon finished what I had left of them."

He could not stay in the Congo since people had seem him hire the victims. Escape was necessary, so he took a route for the Gold Coast, then to the Canary Islands, and on to Lisbon. But the government was informed of his crimes; he found another ship that brought him to America in 1922.

Having arrived in New York, Panzram sought another yacht to replace the *Akista*, which had been wrecked two years earlier. He searched in Providence and then in Salem. He did not find a boat but found another victim, a twelve-year-old boy, George Henry McMahon. "I stayed with the boy about three hours," he said. "During that time, I committed sodomy on the boy six times, and then I killed him by beating his brains out with a rock … I had stuffed down his throat several sheets of paper out of a magazine … I left him there with his brains coming out of his ears." The murder would remain unsolved for years.

Panzram returned to New York and moved to Yonkers in the summer of 1923. He stole clothes, jewelry, guns, and money. One of his adventures was on a yacht, from which he stole a .38 caliber handgun. The owner of the gun and yacht was the police commissioner of New Rochelle. He tried Providence again, and this time stole a yawl.

He repainted the boat and looked for a buyer. Instead, the buyer turned out to be a fellow thief. He was shot with the gun Panzram stole from the police commissioner's yacht. Panzram and a teen he had picked up reached Newburgh, New York. The teen jumped ship and then tipped off police, who collared Panzram and seized the yacht in Nyack. Panzram was arrested on charges of sodomy, robbery, and burglary. He unsuccessfully tried to break out of the city prison in Yonkers.

Panzram jumped bail and drifted to Connecticut, looking for another boat. He arrived in New London, found a youth that he sodomized and strangled with his arms. Without getting a boat, he returned to New York, hopped a train at Grand Central, and got off in Larchmont. He broke into the depot, looking to steal suitcases, scheduled to leave the following August day. He was spotted by an officer, who battled Panzram, disarmed him, and arrested him.

Panzram said that he had just escaped from Oregon and a seventeen-year term.

Police thought he had contrived the story for the purpose of a detention site. Panzram was sentenced to five years in Sing Sing and finish his sentence in Oregon, where the police learned he was "wanted badly."

Apart from a few days in jail—before jumping bail—Panzram had been free for five years and had been through thirty counties. He did not stay long in Sing Sing. New York's prison authorities took a very careful look at Panzram's history and decided Panzram was better suited for the prison in northern New York, the Clinton prison for incorrigibles, at Dannemora.

Killer offers this 1920s description of Dannemora:

"America's worst prison in the corruption-ridden twenties. A pain-and-punishment mill of almost legendary repute, Clinton Prison had virtually lost its name years before in favor of Dannemora—a mournful sound to prisoners. Even as early in 1905, it had been known as the Siberia of America … troublemakers, escapees from Sing Sing, drug addicts—anyone hard to handle—would be shipped to this prison. Dannemora carried a symbolism that was replaced nationally by Alcatraz in 1934 and, for a brief interval in infamy, by Tucker Prison Farm in Arkansas after Alcatraz was abandoned in 1961."

Having taken note of the prison, he vowed not to complete the five years. Nothing succeeded: his plan to burn down the workshops, his attempt to kill a guard, an escape attempt by climbing a prison wall. Finally, he was thrown into solitary. "I suffered more agony, for many months," said Panzram, "always in pain, never a civil answer from anyone, always a snarl or a curse or a lying, hypocritical promise which was never kept. Crawling around like a snake with a broken back, seething with hatred and a lust for revenge, five years of that kind of life, the last two years and four months confined in isolation with nothing to do except brood … the more they misused me, the more I was filled with the spirit of hatred and revenge. I was so full of hate that there was no room in me for such feelings of love, pity, kindness or honor or decency. I hated everybody I saw."

He dreamed of revenge; the most satisfying was to drop a large quantity of arsenic into a stream that fed into a reservoir, thereby killing the entire population—human and animal—of the village of Dannemora.

Panzram could not realize these plans for revenge. With the sentence over, Panzram quickly resumed his notoriety. In the span of about a month, he committed a murder in Baltimore, and some

Depravity

dozen burglaries in the Baltimore-Washington area. In August 1928, the arrested Panzram was brought back to the nation's capital. Panzram was sent to the Washington District Jail.

One of the most remarkable stories of guard-prisoner relationship unfolded at that jail. Henry Lesser, twenty-five, first began his service that year. His father was a Jewish immigrant from Russia who eked out a living as a salesman in Fall River, Massachusetts. Young Lesser devoted his efforts to bettering the lot of humanity, whether as a union organizer of clerks, as a hospital attendant, or now as a guard.

"What was your crime?" Lesser asked innocently.

"What I do is reform people," Panzram coldly responded.

The answer stunned and fascinated the guard. The prison administration learned quickly about Panzram's past. Superintendent W. L. Peak told his staff to beware of the prisoner and be prepared for extraordinary disciplinary measures if necessary.

The opportunity came early when Panzram tried to escape by chipping away at the concrete surrounding the metal bars of his window. Panzram was handcuffed around a wooden pole and a rope was tied to his handcuffs. He was then hoisted up so that his toes were touching the ground and his arms were lifted beyond his shoulders. He was kept this way for twelve hours. He cursed his parents for bringing him into the world. "I will kill everyone if I have the chance," he screamed.

He later confessed to a number of the murders, including the youth in New London. "If there ain't enough," he boasted, "I'll give you plenty more. I've been all over the world but hell, and I guess I'll see that now." Whatever the reason, Lesser pitied Panzram: he offered him extra food and gave him money to buy cigarettes. When the prisoner realized the sincerity of the gift, he was even moved to tears and thanked Lesser. "No screw has ever done this before," he said.

"When are you going to ask me about my life?" Panzram queried Lesser.

"Whenever you want to talk, I'll listen," said Lesser.

What followed set the wheels of revelation in progress.

"I'm going to see," said Panzram, "that you get the story of my life. All of it. Just keep me fixed with pencil and paper."

Lesser started smuggling the writing materials to Panzram. "I want to write it before I kick off," said Panzram, "so I can explain my side of it. Even though nobody ever hears or reads it except one man."

Even before *Confessions* was written, Lesser learned much in conversation with Panzram, who was an avid reader of Kant, the pessimistic philosopher Schopenhauer, and the nihilistic Nietzsche.

For the new few weeks, Panzram detailed his life: twenty thousand words reflecting hate, depravity, and murder. As Lesser began reading of Panzram's early life, Lesser sensed something unique. As recorded in *Killer*, "Henry Lesser began to feel the nudge of something unusual … He felt the grip of a life and the horror of a personality flexing the heavy muscles of retaliation and revenge."

Certainly, Lesser was not prepared for what followed, especially some of Panzram's keen analyses of the world outside:

> I am 36 years old and have been a criminal all my life. I have 11 convictions against me. I have served 20 years of life in jails, reform schools and prisons. I know why I am a criminal … I know the facts. If any man ever was a habitual criminal, I am one in my lifetime. I have broken every law that was ever made by man and God. If either had made any more, I should very cheerfully have broken them.
>
> All they think is necessary to do is to catch me, try me, convict me, and send me to prison for a few years, make life miserable for 'em while in prison and then turn me loose again. That is the system that is in practice today in this country. The consequences are that anyone and everyone can see crime and lots of it. Those who are sincere in their desire to put down crime are to be pitied for all of their efforts which accomplish so little in the desired direction. They are the ones who are deceived by their own ignorance and by the trickery and greed of others who profit the most by crime.

Depravity

And Lesser was struck too by Panzram's thoughts on controlling crime:

> Before you can ever put down crime, you must change the system a whole hell of a lot. Also, you must change your educational system. You must absolutely divorce the schools and prisons from all politics. As things are now, you are making criminals much faster than you are reforming those who are already in existence....
>
> The main cause of why we are what we are is because of our improper teaching, lack of knowledge and our environments.
>
> If you put a lot of powers in the hands of your public servants and they misuse their power, then you are at fault also. I have only a little knowledge, but I have as much knowledge as the average person, and I know that I was taught wrong. I could have been taught properly, and if I had been, I feel sure that I would have led a far different life than I have done...

Throughout the document there is neither guilt nor regret. Apart from his cogent comments on education, crime, and justice, the document is overwhelming in the preciseness of his crimes: dates, times, places, and the details provided from 1900–1928.

Arrest warrants arrived at the DC prison from Philadelphia, for a choking and strangling homicide, and from Salem, Massachusetts, for the killing of George Henry McMahon. Yet his trial in the Washington DC Court was for burglary and housebreaking charges in Baltimore.

Panzram served as his own attorney and expectedly was his usual combative self. Staring at a witness, he growled, "Take a good look at me," as he put his finger across his throat. "I've promised it to you and you'll get it."

At the summing up, he turned and confronted the jury: "You people got me here charged with housebreaking and larceny. I'm guilty. I broke in and I stole. What I didn't steal, I smashed. If the owner had come in, I would have knocked his brains out.

"There's something else you ought to know. While you were trying me here, I was trying all of you, too. I've found you guilty. Some of you, I've executed. If I live, I'll execute some more of you. I hate the whole human race.

"You think I'm playing crazy, don't you? I'm not. I know right from wrong. No delusions. I don't hear anything you don't hear. My conscience doesn't bother me. I have no conscience. I believe the whole human race should be exterminated. I'll do my best to do it every chance I get."

Judge Walter McCoy told Panzram and the silenced courtroom the sentence: twenty-six years in the Federal Prison in Leavenworth. A delighted, grinning Panzram responded, looking squarely at McCoy, "Visit me!"

Panzram arrived at the Big Top, Leavenworth, on February 1, 1929. For Panzram, the formidable prison differed little from any other prison. "I have been in two reform schools, nine big prisons and hundreds of jails. None of them were any different from the others. All were run under the same system by the same sort and the results were exactly the same in all of them."

Panzram's arrival had been preceded by warnings from other prison officials about the dangerous nature of the prisoner. He wrote the warden, demanding an assignment that would isolate him from other prisoners: "I am doing a long time and I am an old crank and I want to be by myself. I am a cripple … I don't like standing on my broken ankles."

Deputy Warden Fred Zerbst called in Panzram to tell him that he was assigned to the laundry room. He would wash inmates' clothes and have little contact with others. After Zerbst read him the rules, Panzram responded matter-of-factly, "I'll kill the first man that bothers me."

Meanwhile, Lesser and Panzram corresponded; so did Lesser and H. L. Mencken, editor of *The American Mercury* and celebrated worldwide as a giant among American critics. Having read Panzram's *Confessions*, Mencken responded, "This is one of the most amazing documents I have ever read … I can't recall reading anything more shocking." The critic recommended a book be written.

Panzram's supervisor was Robert Warnke, detested by prisoners for reporting prisoner violation of rules, which brought revocation of privileges, solitary, and sometimes torture.

Not unexpectedly, prison food was horrid; to get better fare, prisoners needed more funds to purchase in the prison commissary. To purchase more food and cigarettes, Panzram began, in violation of rules, to launder extra handkerchiefs. Warnke learned of the infraction. Punishment was in solitary, the Hole, and a reduction of future privileges.

However, Panzram saw a positive note in the punishment. Those punished in this manner were regularly transferred to other assignments. However, in spite of Panzram's early warnings, the prisoner went back to the laundry under Warnke's supervision.

Panzram had made his decision and intimated this in a June 1929 letter to Lesser: "I am still on my same job and like it less each day. I am getting all set for a change. It won't be long now."

Five days later, Panzram struck. Working in the laundry room, Panzram was met by Warnke, who was checking out supplies. Near Panzram was a four-foot-long iron bar used to support the wooden transport cranes. Immediately upon seeing Warnke, Panzram picked up the ten-pound bar and smashed it on Warnke's head. The skull was crushed instantly. "Here's another one for you, you son of a bitch," Panzram roared. Panzram continued to pound the skull of the dead man.

Other inmates watched in horror as Panzram chased them, looking for more victims. All tried to get out of the room, but it was locked. Finally a door opened, as a prison alarm was sounded. Guards with submachine guns and high-powered rifles stormed the laundry room. Panzram was totally out of control, covered with blood from head to toe.

"I just killed Warnke," he informed the guards, as he readied himself for isolation. "Let me in," he told guards.

"First, drop that bar," they ordered.

He hurled away the murder implement. "Oh," Panzram said, looking at the bar. "This is my lucky day."

Panzram was placed in the isolation tier, which only held three prisoners, two of whom had killed prison guards. His neighbor was Robert Stroud, the Birdman of Alcatraz. Having escaped the gallows for murdering a guard in 1916, Stroud was in his thirteenth year in solitary confinement. Among other "achievements," Stroud was a world authority on canary diseases.

Although prisoners in isolation could not meet, they could communicate by talking loudly with the tier guard. Although they rarely communicated, Stroud was very interested in Panzram and his possible march to the gallows.

In August 1929, Panzram wrote Lesser a long letter ending with, "I expect to go up for trial next month, and I would have to wait until I see if I get my wish then …" Lesser was taken aback by the thought that Panzram wished his own death.

Guards also overheard Panzram was talking with enthusiasm about his own death. Prison officials worried that Panzram was planning an insanity plea. Officials carefully examined his letters to Lesser. Panzram would have no part of their thinking, he wrote Lesser. "There are some folks," he told Lesser, "who actually believe I am just a little bit nutty. But I don't worry about that because they don't know me like I know myself.

"I know myself far better than anyone else knows me and I am firmly convinced that I am not crazy … I don't care what they do to me just so they don't try to prove I am crazy. I don't want no part of that."

Panzram moved a step closer to the gallows in December, with his indictment for first-degree murder by a grand jury in Kansas City. Lesser still hoped for a defense crafted by an insanity plea that would lead to reform or rehabilitation and eventual freedom for Panzram. He would have none of Lesser's urgings.

"I believe it is absolutely impossible for me to ever gain my freedom in a legal way because I have too much against me and too many people wish my death.

"I could not reform if I wanted to. It has taken me all my life so far, thirty-eight years of it, for me to reach my present state of mind. In that time I have acquired some habits. It took me a lifetime to form these habits and I believe it would take more than another lifetime to break myself of these same habits even if I wanted to.

"I prefer death before spending more years in prison. My belief is that life without liberty is not worth having. If the law won't kill me, I shall kill myself."

Perhaps the calendar was crowded; the trial would not be before April 1930. Ironically, although in isolation, Panzram was well treated, better treated than ever. In fact, he wrote Lesser, "No one lays a hand on me. No one abuses me in any way ... I have been trying to figure it out, and I have come to the conclusion that, if in the beginning, I had been treated as I am now, then there wouldn't have been quite so many people ... that have been robbed, raped, and killed."

Judge Richard J. Hopkins appointed well-known attorney Captain Ralph T. O'Neil as Panzram's counsel. Panzram stunned the judge by refusing to accept counsel. "My conception of justice is that I'm found guilty of murder in the first degree and then sentenced to death, and that sentence carried out."

The judge refused to dismiss O'Neil.

"How do you plead?" the judge asked Panzram at the trial.

"I plead not guilty! Now you go ahead and prove me guilty, understand?"

The defense attorney moved that the court appoint a Sanity Commission. That same day, a three-member commission examined Panzram. They found Panzram was of unsound mind, but he "knew what he was doing." Moreover, the trial could proceed because Panzram understood the nature of the charges against him and was capable of assisting in his own defense.

The press reported Panzram's remarks to the commission: "There isn't a man in this room I wouldn't kill … I don't believe there is any good in any man. I'd like to have the opportunity to go away, gain power and brains, and then I'd like to kill all the rest of the world."

For the prosecution, Warden T. B. White was followed by five guards and ten prisoners.

The defense had no witnesses. All O'Neil could do was call Panzram to the stand. "You and the judge," Panzram said, "wouldn't let me be my lawyer, so go ahead. I have nothing to say."

The jury did—forty-five minutes later—and gave the judge a sealed verdict read the next morning: guilty of murder, with no recommendation for mercy. Panzram was remanded back to Leavenworth until "the fifth of September, nineteen thirty, when between the hours of six to nine o'clock in the morning, you shall be taken to some suitable place within the confines of the penitentiary and hanged by the neck until dead."

Panzram was delighted and shocked the courtroom with these words: "I certainly want to thank you, judge. Just let me get my fingers around your neck for sixty seconds and you'll never sit on another bench as judge."

Panzram shared the "good news" with Lesser. For once in Panzram's life, justice was carried out: "They gave me justice. This is the one and only case that I actually know of where law and justice were synonymous. I believe that I know what justice is, and justice is what I have been wanting and trying to get all of my life but what I have never got until now, and I don't get that until the fifth of next September."

Now that death was near, Panzram wanted Lesser to supply him with reading materials, namely, the *Forum*, the *Atlantic Monthly*, the *Pathfinder*, the *Mercury*, and *Psychiatrist's Review*.

With hanging set for September, concerned parties went into motion: prison authorities to ensure that Panzram did not cheat the hangman; prison authorities and the marshal to ready the mechanical arrangements; Panzram himself to guarantee that he would be killed; anti–capital punishment groups to block the execution.

Depravity

Panzram was guarded carefully; in fact, one more guard was added to keep watch. Perhaps it was fear of another trial or commutation of the death sentence. Panzram was worried that he might be spared and turned his mind to suicide.

The Birdman was willing to help, speaking in loud tones to the guard (e.g., opening veins, cutting arteries). Interestingly, *Killers* speaks of Stroud's being convinced that Panzram was not the murderer he boasted of and he had no desire to die:

"Despite his desperate outlook, Stroud was a tenacious liver of life. In common with most persons, he was unable to accept the idea of a sustained desire for one's own death. Not knowing Panzram, Stroud believed that Panzram's hunger for his own execution had to be a bluff."

On June 20, Panzram wrote a letter to Lesser informing him of his planned suicide that evening. "Tonight I die and tomorrow I go to a grave. Farther than that nobody can drive me. I am sure glad to leave this lousy world and the lousiest people in this world, but of all the lousiest people in this world, I believe that I am the lousiest of 'em all."

When one guard went off duty, Panzram ate a poisonous plate of beans and cut a deep gash in his leg. The night guard heard the retching of the prisoner and saw blood. He called for help; the hospital trusties rushed in, and pumped Panzram's stomach, foiling the suicide attempt.

An unanswered question: how could such a clever fellow like Panzram be so clumsy?

Kansas had not had an execution since 1970. As the day neared, civilian workmen would have to wield hammers and saws to construct the scaffold. Technical requirements needed to be met. A qualified hangman needed to be retained. The anonymous hangman worked from Panzram's height and weight and concluded that a drop of seven feet, eight inches would do. Drops had to produce a force of twenty-four hundred pounds on Panzram's neck.

Others had plans to thwart the execution. One day a small delegation of Kansans flocked to the visiting room of the isolation building. The

Society for the Abolishment of Capital Punishment wanted Panzram to sign a commutation petition for President Hoover's signature. Panzram responded, arguing against the supposed inhumanity of the punishment and his supposed insanity:

"I do not believe that being hanged by the neck is a barbaric or inhuman punishment. I look forward to that as real pleasure and a big relief to me. I do not feel bad or unhappy about it in every way ... when my last hour comes, I will dance out of my dungeon and on to the scaffold with a smile on my face and happiness in my heart ... I believe that any person who is sober and sane and who is not blind and who is able to read and understand the English language as I am here writing, he or she should be convinced that I am perfectly sane in every way and therefore responsible for my acts."

Not leaving anything to chance, Panzram wrote to President Hoover that he not step in and block his death wish:

"I believe that I am within my constitutional rights when I refuse to accept a pardon or commutation from the death penalty to a sentence of life imprisonment, either in prison or an insane asylum.

"I absolutely refuse to accept either a pardon or a commutation should either one or the other be offered to me."

Birdman Stroud did not give up his plan for Panzram's suicide. He arranged for shaving blades be dropped into Panzram's cell. Panzram was not moved.

On the eve of the execution, reporters from Topeka's *Daily Capital* came to Leavenworth, hoping to get a quote or two from Panzram. "Does Panzram have any regrets?" a reporter queried a guard.

"Yeah," answered Panzram. "I regret I won't be able to read the end of this magazine story. It's continued next issue."

Stroud wrote of Panzram in his lengthy study of the penal system. "He walked the floor of his cell, singing a pornographic little song that he had composed himself. It was not much of a song either from the point of view of melody or lyrics, but it undoubtedly expressed, in not too polite terms, the deepest craving of his heart. The principal theme was, 'Oh, how I love my roundeye!'"

The warden and his party came to Panzram's cell at dawn. Upon seeing two clerics in the assemblage, Panzram roared, "Get 'em out. I don't mind being hanged, but I don't need any Bible-backed hypocrites around me. Run 'em out, Warden, or you're going to have one hell of a time getting me out of this cell."

The hangman stared at Panzram. "Anything you want to say?"

Supposedly, Panzram spit at the executioner and then roared, "Yes, hurry up, you Hoosier bastard. I could kill a dozen men while you're fooling around."

At exactly 6:03 AM, September 5, Panzram emerged and sprinted up the thirteen steps to the platform. The trap doors swung open; Panzram dropped five and a half feet down. He was pronounced dead at 6:19 AM by Dr. Justin K. Fuller. The cost of the execution: $111.28.

In his book, *Man Against Himself*, famed psychiatrist Dr. Karl Menninger gave a brief review of the hanging:

"On the day of his execution, he ran eagerly forward, climbed to the gallows with alacrity, urging his executioners to hurry the thing up and get it over with. It was remarked by everyone how eager he was to die. His execution was, in essence, a suicide, a direct accomplishment of what he had indirectly sought for all of his thirty-eight years."

Other jurisdictions across America had wanted Panzram, but Kansas came first. They now received word that the matter was at end. The Oregon State Penitentiary in Oregon received a letter sent to other institutions:

"Our records revealed the subject was wanted by your department at the expiration of his sentence.

"I regret to inform you that this subject died by a legal execution (by hanging) September 5, 1930."

The death of Panzram put an end to these requests. However, his death brought to the fore the *Confessions*—and eventual book—and a thorough analysis of the Panzram personality. All this analysis was the result of the friendship developed between Lesser and Panzram.

The Panzram case involved great thinkers of the day: Prof. Sheldon Glueck, Dr. Benjamin Karpman, and Dr. Karl Menninger.

Prof. Glueck spent decades at Harvard University Law School as a writer with a specialty in criminal law and anti-social behavior. He never met Panzram but read *Confessions*. "Of all criminal autobiographies," he wrote Lesser, "it is unquestionably the most striking, and in many ways the criticisms he makes of the existing penal system are justified."

Panzram may be a good read, but much more is needed, insisted Glueck. "Merely to classify him as one type or another of offender or psychopath is not an illuminative process; he should be studied by a skilled psychiatrist over a long period of daily contacts."

Glueck never had that chance; neither did Dr. Benjamin Karpman, a noted psychiatrist-criminologist. Lesser had often attended Dr. Karpman's lectures after meeting him early in the guard's career. Lesser renewed contact with Karpman after the Warnke murder. Karpman asked Lesser to put forward some questions in his correspondence with Panzram.

Karpman wanted to know whether Panzram got personal joy out of his sadistic crimes. Panzram responded:

"You asked me why I had done it. I had not one good reason for doing it, but about forty-seven reasons, and each one of them was a good reason. Good enough for me anyway ... You asked me if I get a kick out of killing people. Sure I do. If you don't think so, you do as I had done to me: five or six big huskies walk in on you and let 'em hammer you unconscious, then drag you down in a cellar and chain you up to a post and work you over some more, and then if you feel like forgiving and forgetting all about it, write and tell me about it, will you?"

A week letter, in October 1929, Panzram went back to this theme:

"As for the kick I get out of it, I meant figuratively and not literally. Whatever possessed you to think that me or anyone else had a sexual-like feeling when we commit a crime like a murder or arson? That's

Depravity

the bunk. I myself have intelligence enough to know the feeling, but I haven't knowledge enough to explain it so that you could understand it. The only way I know of for you to find out just what sort of a kick I get out of it is for you to do as I done.

"Experiment: go buy yourself a box of matches, or go get an ax and bop some guy on the back of the neck. It's easy when you know how. Besides, you put 'em out of all their misery when you knock 'em off."

Ask Panzram about his parents and schooling, pleaded Karpman.

"I went to school but never learned anything," wrote Panzram. "I learned to become a first-class liar and hypocrite and the beginnings of degeneracy. I also learned how to sing hymns, say prayers, and read the Bible. I learned so much about the Christian religion that I finally came to detest and hate anything and everybody connected with it. I still do.

"My father was no good and mother was very little better. Father pulled his freight when I was seven or eight years old, so you see I know a little about him and none of that good. Mother was too dumb to know anything good to teach me. There was little love lost. I first liked her and respected her. My feelings gradually turned from that to distrust, dislike, disgust, and from there it was very simple for my feelings to turn into positive hatred towards her."

Karpman suggested that Lesser contact Dr. Karl Menninger, who was developing a career as a brilliant and articulate psychiatrist near Leavenworth. Menninger was taken aback by the power of Panzram's insights into his own sadism. This obsessive interest in Panzram endured throughout the psychiatrist's career.

Before trial for Warnke's murder, the court requested that Dr. Menninger evaluate Panzram's sanity. The psychiatrist spoke to the prisoner for fifty minutes. "The doctor saw deep into a human psyche in ways he had never seen before," wrote Gaddis and Long. Menninger noted that the psychological factors seen in Panzram were noted by Panzram himself in *Confessions*.

Menninger writes of Panzram in his 1938 bestseller *Man Against*

Himself. Menninger gives Panzram the name John Smith, with numbers 31614, the actual Leavenworth number:

"They are, in short, proof that hate breeds hate, that the injustices perpetrated upon a child arouse in him unendurable reactions of retaliation which the child must repress and postpone but which sooner or later come out in some form or another, that the wages of sin is death, that murder breeds suicide, that to kill is only to be killed, that there is no real atonement but suffering and that bitter suffering bears no fruit."

Menninger called Panzram "one of the most extraordinary individuals, sane or insane, criminal or non-criminal, that I have ever met."

The psychiatrist elaborates, "I have never seen an individual whose destructive impulses were so completely accepted and acknowledged by his conscious ego. He outlined to me in detail a plan he had conceived for bringing about the destruction of the entire human race, a plan which was by no means absurd in its conception and compares favorably with the ingenious devices patented by inventors pandering to the munitions manufacturers who are proud of their devices for increasing official murderousness."

Reading *Confessions* gives one an "emotional thrill," observes Menninger. Panzram gives readers "an incongruous picture of stark reality which produced an effect comparable to that of gazing into the interior of a human body torn open in some horrible accident, with all the vital organs laid bare, the person retaining consciousness with a superhuman ability to endure pain so that he could calmly discuss the accident and his approaching death."

The study of Carl Panzram will not offer a key to understanding all serial killers. For one thing, many serial murderers were motivated only by greed; others were only driven by revenge on certain individuals; others flourished only by lustmorde.

However, the story of Carl Panzram shows the intelligent side of the serial killer and the disastrous parenting and schooling experience that would be translated into the tragedy of a lifetime.

SECTION III—

THE VENGEFUL KILLER

BELA KISS
Vengeance in Oil

The story of Bela Kiss has fascinated students of mass murder. He sought refuge from sex crimes in the Hungarian army and the French Foreign Legion. What is most intriguing, however, is his having escaped justice.

Designated among "the ones who got away," Kiss has become immortalized in recent years. Perhaps the Hungarian-born cuckold has become an exotic personality because Transylvania was the home of Count Dracula, and the birthplace of Bela Lugosi and mass murderess Countess Elizabeth Bathory, who claimed some six hundred victims between 1610–1614.

The legend of Kiss has produced a scenario for a play by French surrealist poet Antonin Artaud, a comic book, a dramatization on radio, a Swedish metal band with his name, and a death metal band that has recorded a song about him.

Because Kiss has never been brought to justice, much of his early years and any psychological profile relating to his crimes are not known. In short, his life, before and after his murder rampage, remains uncertain and speculative.

In 1912, the forty-year-old Kiss moved into Czinkota, a picturesque village outside of Budapest, with his attractive wife, Marie, fifteen years his junior. They purchased the only impressive house in the community. The large, imposing home was on the outskirts of the village.

Nothing of any consequence ever seemed to happen in Czinkota. However, Bela made a quick, positive impression. Although short and somewhat chubby, he was still a handsome fellow with a handlebar moustache, who also sported a broad-brimmed black hat. Kiss aficionados insist they see a facial resemblance to actor Burt Lancaster.

The Kisses seemed an ideal addition to the community. Marie Kiss combined a gorgeous face with a statuesque figure. Added to the fairytale setting was a magnificent home with a stunning red automobile. A tinsmith, Kiss adjusted well to his surroundings. Reserved and introverted, Kiss struck citizens as conscientious and hardworking. No one paid much attention to his interest in the occult, especially astrology, even though he was known to tell fortunes.

Above all, the Czinkota community raved over his apparent kindness. He was seen in the evenings in his roadster doing good deeds, at times bringing food for needy neighbors or delivering medicine to the sick. The Kisses employed two village girls as servants during the day. Financially, how did the tinsmith do this? No one knew, but they were so thankful that the Kisses lived amongst them.

When did the idyllic life of the Kisses turn sour? The consensus seemed that it was not long after their arrival in Czinkota. When the red car was not seen outside the home at times for several days, it seemed certain that Bela Kiss was away.

Soon after the Kisses came to town, Constable Adolph Trauber, who had heard about the exemplary Mr. Kiss, visited their home. "Can I be of service to you?" asked the constable.

"That's very nice of you," responded the tinsmith. "At times I am away on business. I would be very appreciative if you could keep an eye on my property."

"Certainly," an agreeable constable promised. Trauber and Kiss quickly became close friends. The constable looked at Kiss as the village hero, an arrival that the community had never experienced.

Trauber was a conscientious watcher over Kiss's property, but did not do an effective job in watching Marie Kiss. Bela Kiss was indeed reminiscent of the cuckolded carpenter of Chaucer's "Miller's Tale." The major difference, of course, is that Alison and her lover Nicholas were not killed by the carpenter. The tinsmith avenged the insult.

Apart from his age and figure—albeit he was not ugly—Bela Kiss could not compete with Marie's lover, an artist named Paul Bihari, tall, slender, dashing, and Marie's age.

The affair began around February 1912, and the offended Bela found out sometime that spring. The available information takes the reader to Christmas 1912. The two servants, still in the Kiss's employ, reported for work and found their employer saddened with his head in his arms.

"Why are you so sad, Mr. Kiss? Christmas is almost here."

"My wife has left me for another man, an artist," he told the girls, as he flashed a letter before them. "I am sorry that I won't need your services anymore. I want to be alone in my sadness."

So Bela Kiss remained secluded in his large mansion as the holidays came and went, and as the winter approached.

Nothing much ever happened in Czinkota, so the gossip was exciting. All wondered, how would the triangle of the Kisses and the artist play itself out?

As the wintry days continued, the villagers remained inquisitive. One evening they noticed a wagon arriving at Mr. Kiss's door and leaving two large metal drums. As far as they knew, the story had ended with Marie Kiss abandoning her husband for the handsome artist.

All had forgotten Bela except the constable. Assuming that Marie had run away, Mr. Trauber was concerned that he had not seen his friend for a long time. He paid his friend a visit. He hammered at the door, but no one responded. Trauber broke the lock and entered the gloomy residence. He was startled to find Bela, who looked famished, in torn clothes. The house was dirty, in shambles. Since Marie left, Bela had obviously not cared for himself or for his house.

Greeting his friend, Bela said, "I have nothing to live for, Adolph."

"That's nonsense," reasoned the constable. "To start, we will find someone to care for you and straighten out this home."

The constable was good to his word. "I am the widow Kalman," a woman told Bela the next day. "Mr. Trauber sent me."

The advice was great, or so it seemed.

The color came back to Bela's face. Once again, he was robust. He was reserved, as in the past, but he was cheery among people. It was a rebirth as spring came to Czinkota.

On a delightful spring day in April 1913, Czinkota was in its glory. With much graciousness, Bela Kiss thanked the widow for her devoted care. "You have nursed me back to health," he said, "and my home has been restored to its beauty. Now that things are back in order, we will do things differently. Since I can now take care of myself, I would like you to come each morning and return home in the evening." In fact, that was the arrangement before Mrs. Kiss had supposedly run off with the artist.

At first insulted, widow Kalman was pleased upon learning of the prior arrangement. However, she thought Bela Kiss's behavior was a little strange. The upstairs closet was always locked, and she was told by him not to clean in there.

After their new arrangement, Bela left town and came back with a woman, whom Bela called Madame. She was a buxom blonde in her late fifties. Not long after Madame got settled in the house, neighbors noticed a wagon that pulled up and dropped off another metal drum, joining the other two deposits in the Kiss upstairs closet.

The nest day, Kiss greeted the widow Kalman. "You have worked with much devotion," said Kiss. "Why don't you treat yourself to a vacation at my expense?" The employee accepted.

"Where is Madame?" asked the widow upon returning from holiday.

"Oh, she left," matter-of-factly answered Kiss.

Sensing some uneasiness in the widow, Bela invited her to his study. "I must tell you," he said candidly, "I like women, and I intend to satisfy my pleasure. And I must tell you that more will be coming here in the future. If that troubles you, I would understand if you left. However, I would really like you to say and take care of my house." And he added, "There will be other vacations for you in the future."

The widow felt that Bela was a charming fellow, and women or no, she would still work for him.

The next day Bela came back with a bigger Madame, about six feet and three hundred pounds. "Madame will be with us for a long time," Bela proclaimed.

It was time for the widow's next vacation, so following schedule, a wagon drove up with steel drum number four.

"How is Madame?" a cheerful Kalman inquired after returning from vacation.

"She has left," said Kiss. The widow accepted the news and continued her house chores.

Two Budapest widows had disappeared in recent months, so the constable thought he could renew his dormant friendship. After all, he had a key role in the restoration of Bela's health. Certainly, his friend wouldn't mind sharing any news or thoughts about the missing.

Bela had entertained two women; two women had disappeared. But the police had the name of Hofmann as the enticer. And both victims had withdrawn their life savings before their disappearance. At this point, no one had linked Kiss to Hofmann.

Trauber and Kiss embraced. "How about some wine?" asked the hospitable Kiss. They toasted each other's continued good health and smoked choice cigars offered by Kiss.

The conversation was delightful, giddy. "You know " said Kiss, "women should not be so gullible as to trust strangers and leave fortunes to them. Perhaps out of arrogance or near drunkenness, Kiss said to the constable. "I have something that I have wanted to show you for a long time." He escorted Trauber upstairs and opened the closet. As he banged on the drum, he told the constable, taking the cover off. "Look inside."

"Obviously, petrol," said Trauber.

"Yes," said Kiss. "I had an associate who had debts piling up and had little money. 'Would you take petrol?' he asked. War clouds are hovering over Europe," Kiss told Trauber. "The world will be at war, and what could be better than petrol?"

Kiss then tapped the other three drums. "They also have petrol. You are my good friend," said Kiss. "I can trust you. Take the keys to this room. One doesn't know what can happen in wartime. I don't want my former wife and her bastard lover to get their hands on these barrels."

As they returned downstairs for more good cheer, Trauber assured Kiss that nothing would happen to him.

And war did come to Europe. At the start of the war, Kiss continued with the usual scenario: his car returned from Budapest with middle-age women, and with widow Kalman on vacation, drums continued to arrive at his door.

No one suspected Kiss. After all, he was the noble Hungarian patriot. He was the voluntary recruiting officer. Because he was very conscientious in this effort, no young healthy Czinkota citizen dared avoid military service.

However, Kiss's day came too, in late 1914. He was sent to the front without much notice. In fact, he had no time to take care of affairs at his home. All he could do was put bars and padlocks on the doors and windows of his villa.

As 1914 turned into 1915, the patriotic neighbors wondered how their heroic citizen was doing on the front. "He's dead," announced a saddened Adolph Trauber to the townspeople. "He died in the front lines fighting for his countrymen."

Trauber felt a personal tragedy. He called together the villagers for a ceremony at the village square and inscribed the name of Bela Kiss on the roll of honor.

It wasn't long after this poignant memorial that government agents intensified their search for petrol to bolster the war effort. "Constable

Trauber," they asked. "Perhaps you can help us. You know this village well. Can we find petrol?"

Quickly, Trauber recalled his visit to Kiss months ago. "You're in luck, gentlemen," he happily said. "My friend has some drums in his apartment."

The excited group went to the deserted gray house. "Here," announced the constable, opening the locked upstairs door.

"My God," exclaimed an official, looking into the drum. He was nearly speechless, inviting an accompanying soldier to examine the drum. He, too, could not speak.

What they found was the body of a woman pickled and preserved in alcohol. When the initial shock subsided, the search party discovered seven drums—all in the closet. All victims had been strangled before being preserved. Five victims were middle-aged women, all naked. The other two were Marie Kiss and lover Paul Bikari. The victims were tied with ropes into a doubled-up position so that they could fit inside the drum.

The riddle of Mr. Hofmann was also solved. The house was filled with letters and cards addressed to Mr. Hofmann.

The correspondence had been solicited by Bela Kiss, who had placed the following advertisement in the newspapers: "Lonely Widower Seeking Female Companionship."

Trauber suspected that there might be more drums and asked for a search of the neighborhood. Detective Nagy was dispatched from Budapest to handle the case.

Nagy searched the entire village. Farmers came forward and told detectives of finding skeletons when they ploughed fields near the Kiss villa. This confirmed Nagy's suspicion that more drums were out there. In fact, Nagy contacted the supplier of the drums, who told him that he had delivered more than the seven drums in the villa.

Now that Kiss was the serial killer, how could he be apprehended? The initial war report had Kiss assigned to Serbia, where he was wounded and died in a military hospital. However, later reports surfaced that Bela Kiss had been spotted in Budapest.

Nagy decided to find out for himself. He went to the Belgrade hospital where Kiss supposedly died. The deceased was not a middle-aged Kiss, but a much younger, tall, blond, blue-eyed Nordic specimen.

Obviously, Kiss had switched identities with the critically wounded soldier. When the soldier died, Kiss took the youth's identity and was discharged at the end of the war.

With the confusion at war's end, Bela Kiss disappeared into Hungarian society. At that point, it would seem the books were closed on Bela Kiss, murderer of twenty-four.

However, sightings were reported across the globe. One report claimed that Kiss was seen in the streets of Budapest. So the police continued their search for Kiss. A deserter of the French Foreign Legion went to the police station with a tale of a fellow legionnaire he believed was Kiss. The suspected legionnaire gave his name as Hofmann and boasted of his skill with garrote, a method of execution with an iron collar tightened by a screw.

The Legion deserter found Detective Nagy and also told him that Hofmann entertained in the desert with stories of how he had lived and strangled women in Hungary. Nagy contacted the French Foreign Legion, but Bela Kiss was nowhere to be seen.

Without delay, the police also went to the unit to question Hofmann; however, the supposed Hofmann was no longer in the unit and left no traces of his whereabouts.

The story picked up again in 1932. A New York City homicide detective, Henry Oswald, was sure he had seen Bela Kiss coming out of the New York City Times Square subway station. Oswald was no ordinary detective. His extraordinary memory for faces earned him the respect of fellow detectives as well as the nickname "Camera Eye." So no one made light of Oswald's claim. Unfortunately, the usual large Times Square crowds prevented the detective from following the suspect.

Nevertheless, many Kiss hunters felt that the Hungarian was still at large.

One additional sighting placed Kiss in New York City as a janitor.

Depravity

The police followed up on the tip and visited the house where Kiss was said to be working. The janitor disappeared, and one cannot be certain that the individual was Bela Kiss.

That was the last credible sighting. Many serial killer watchers and other criminologists are convinced the Hungarian serial killer immigrated to America. Wherever he was or may be—he would now be over one hundred years old—he has never been apprehended.

What Kiss watchers talk about are the following: how many did he actually murder? Beyond his wife and artist lover, what were his motives?

The police set the number at twenty-four, based on the findings of the barrels. However, since he has been at large for such a long time, why should the number be limited to twenty-four?

David Everitt writes in *Human Monsters*, "Despite all this alleged globetrotting by Kiss, no other murders were ever attributed to him."

Criminologists have pointed out that the majority of serial killers began their murder sprees while in their twenties or early thirties. Bela Kiss is different. The Hungarian began his notoriety at age forty. Because the revelations came out during World War I, investigators could not place undivided attention on Bela Kiss. Therefore, the investigation was not complete, and revelations of his life were not forthcoming.

Because all the victims—except for the artist—were women, should one conclude that he was tapping into a hidden rage against women? Was his mother overly loving, or negligent, abusive, or repressive? We do not have the answers. We also are uncertain whether he considered women inferior. Did he transfer his hatred of his immoral wife to other loose women?

Or perhaps the cuckolded tinsmith was crushed. His ego needed some soothing. The ability to kill and baffle the police was the perfect remedy, so he felt. If that was what he needed, he then proclaimed, "I am above the law," and confounded his hunters with disguises from the Foreign Legion to the sidewalks of New York.

Into the Kiss mix, one needs to place his drive for money. Having lured them, charmed them, and told their fortunes, he then convinced the victims to turn over their fortunes to him. And once possessed of this, he no longer needed them, so he killed them.

Beyond the motives, was there anything special about the preservation of corpses in barrels? The victim is like a prize or trophy for the murderer, who feels the need to celebrate his taking home the prey. Referring to Michael Newton's encyclopedic *Hunting Humans*, Harold Schechter and David Everitt observe in *The A to Z Encyclopedia of Serial Killers*:

"Like big game hunters who commemorate their feats by bringing home a trophy of their kill—a set of antlers, a stuffed head, or a prize pelt, the serial killer often does the same thing, removing an item from his victim and preserving it as a precious keepsake … The most hideous trophies of all, of course, are human body parts."

For Bela Kiss, preserving his victims in barrels was his expression of celebrating his achievements.

With the case remaining a riddle, the legend or mythology of Bela Kiss has sprung up. The Hungarian serial killer has been immortalized in *Thirty-Two*, actually a scenario for a silent movie. The writer is Antonin Artaud, a French surrealist, poet, actor, and playwright.

Bela Kiss has been transformed into a medical professor. After attending one of his lectures, a young student seeks him because she wants to relate her story of misery. She got mixed up in an affair. The man has left, and she is pregnant and needs an abortion.

Obviously not the Kiss story, the similarity is sexual immorality. Out of apparent sympathy for the woman, the professor invites her to his home. She notes thirty-two large barrels in his home. The frightened woman runs out in haste. When the investigation was completed, the detectives turned up seventeen additional drums all around quaint Czinkota—twenty-four bodies. All were women except for the lover. The detectives also uncovered female clothing and jewelry in the Kiss villa. Pawn tickets for the same were scattered throughout the house.

As in the Bela Kiss story, the Great War engulfs Europe. The professor, like Kiss, is called to service. They also learn that he has died in battle. And, like the Kiss story, officials recall his hoarding petrol in his home. When they come to the house, they open the canister and find a woman strangled with a silken cord.

The Artaud scenario also deals with the supposed death of Kiss. At the end of the scenario, the police superintendent, the mayor, the professor, and the girl visit a hospital on the war front in Turkey. They have heard that Kiss, Monsieur D, is mortally wounded. But they are disappointed because it is not the Monsieur D they are looking for:

> The doctor comes up, draws back the blankets. They lean over.
>
> A large dark man with thick lips, his face covered in marks, is revealed, bearing no resemblance to the original young man.
>
> He is evidently another man.
>
> The visitor explains that the doctor is mistaken.
>
> The doctor shakes his head.
>
> He affirms that this is indeed Monsieur D ... He shows them the other beds.
>
> The ring of beds appears on the screen with the invalid's name written at the head of each bed. It is obvious that the invalid is D ...

How did the professor's student feel that her hero had slipped away? This is answered in the last line, "The girl's face, amazed and happy."

In decades past when radio thrived on mystery stories, one program, *Unsolved Mysteries,* presented a dramatization of the Bela Kiss story titled "Bela Kiss: Mystery Man of Europe."

All programs of that day began with this disclaimer: "Out of deference to persons who may still be living, characters' names in some of these true unsolved mysteries have been changed." But the dramatization went way beyond name changes.

The narrative is preceded with a fascinating quote from the *Rubaiyat of Omar Khayyam,* which the audience told is most applicable to the Kiss case:

> "The Moving Finger writes; and, having writ,
> Moves on: nor all your Piety nor Wit
> Shall lure it back to cancel half a Line,
> Nor all your tears wash out a word of it."

The listener is told that the year is 1914 and the action begins in Budapest in the office of the chief of police. A woman enters. "Her face is white, terror stares from her eyes, and her hands tremble as she tears her tiny handkerchief to pieces."

She tells her tale of woe: "Oh, Chief, you must believe me ... someone will be killed if you don't believe me." Clearly, the distressed woman fears the police chief will dismiss her as a raving lunatic.

Rather calmly, she relates her meeting a charming gentleman who promised to tell her fortune. After fortune telling, the gentleman invited her to his home, and then tried to strangle her. She miraculously escaped, but the radio audience is not told how.

The woman escaped death; no one did in the actual Kiss saga. Bela Kiss lived in a magnificent villa. The radio character had his abode in a castle.

However, similarities follow. The radio slayer is drafted into the Hungarian army of World War I and is thought to have been killed in action, and true to the real-life story, the military needs gasoline and come to the Kiss home-castle looking for petrol. They find the same atrocities—preserved in alcohol. The total of murders—all unsolved—now has mushroomed to three hundred.

And there are other changes. Cited is the figure of one hundred sixty pawn tickets belonging to the murdered, when the officials come to the Kiss home. Sightings are reported of Kiss, despite hospital information of his death.

The program tells the audience that the following information was supplied by the chief of police in Budapest and had never been published in American newspapers. The nurse of the hospital is interviewed by the police and insists that she treated the deceased Bela Kiss, who was a twenty-year-old lad. Refusing to accept this, the police, several days later, drive to the Kiss mansion. The police plant an ad: a rich woman seeking company of attractive man. Bela Kiss has answered the ad.

Kiss comes and, suspicious, he drives away in a taxi. The police follow and shoot him near the river, but he disappears into the Danube, never to be seen again. All this "provides a solution for a fifteen-year-old mystery."

From drama to radio to the comic book. The author is Jay Stephens of *The Land of Nod Rockabye Book*. In Norse legend, Nod is the imaginary realm of sleep and dreams. The villain of the comic is Bela Kiss.

In the *Comics Journal*, the reviewer had high praise for Stephens. "If Hanna-Barbera dealt with existential angst and deconstructionalism, the end result would probably resemble *The Land of Nod*, the new comic from Jay Stephens."

The child in the story is Melanie McCay, who changes herself into superhero Jetcat, a la Clark Kent and Superman. In the story, a collection of villains seek to enroll members for their Jetcat Haters Society.

The Society is successful in signing up Bela Kiss. He is depicted like the Hungarian serial killer: short and stocky. But Stephens embellishes the image into a monster with a Frankenstein-like flathead with a Dracula-like cloak.

The other club members insist that Kiss change his name to something more menacing. Kiss is outraged and rebuffs all attempts to rename him.

A commentator in the online journal *The Wacky World of Murder* chanted the praises of Bela Kiss, now known "The Mystery Man of Europe" and "The Monster of Czinkota." "Bela Kiss is definitely my number-one Hungarian. The pickling was really inspired, although it kept the identities of the corpses easily recognized, and I love originality. Kiss also had a great name. A serial killer called Kiss—how cool is that. You just can imagine the papers—"The Kiss of Death."

"Anyway, I have always rated the guy very highly, and the fact that he got away with it, that just puts him into almost legendary status. A great murderer, who like most European Killers of the early 1900s, is highly underrated by today's media."

In the Crime Library, Denise Loe ties Bela Kiss to his forebears Count Dracula and Countess Elizabeth Bathory. Bela Kiss "has become a blood drinker in some legends. In these folktales, the corpses found in the barrels were drained of blood. Indeed, in rural lore, Bela Kiss is believed to be a genuine member of the undead. Some fear that he still walks by night stalking fresh victims."

The music world has also been bewitched by Bela Kiss. A Swedish metal band was attracted to the Hungarian and goes by the name Bela Kiss. A death metal band, PUS, cut a song, "Lady-Killer (Bela Kiss, Never Get Caught)" about the Hungarian:

> My wife was unfaithful for the last time. I stopped it by strangling her a hard strangulation with a [expletive] garter, emotionless and artistic way to kill picking up ladies from the magazines, luring them, misleading them, killing them. I will tell you all about your future, something chafed your neck, now you're dead.
>
> Hatred, vile, sanction, undressed corpse I will force you into the barrel, pure alcohol for you darling. You're not even worth a blow job.
>
> Die!
>
> I am a gentleman who has a problem with hate, and that's why you die when the night is late, you stupid [expletive], you're all the same strangling rich [expletive], brings me the fame.
>
> Guess where I'm now, didn't die in the war, didn't leave you any clues, just rotted [expletive] whores.

ROBERT HANSEN

Hunting Women in Alaska

In *Serial Murderers and Their Victims*, Eric Hickey notes that Robert Hansen is "considered to be Alaska's worst mass murderer in history." That dubious distinction is not remarkable because, in his study of serial murderers from 1800–1895, Hickey charted the distribution by frequency into five groups. Alaska is in the group with the fewest number of cases. Of course, that fact needs to be evaluated in view of Alaska's relatively small population.

What makes the case noteworthy is that his serial killer career stretched out over ten years and the numbers of victims—not fully certain—might place him among the most notorious serial killers in American history.

His case also offers a fresh perspective in serial killer history when available psychological profiling on the suspect set a precedent as a basis for issuing search warrants in his home.

The story of Robert Hansen has added fascinating perspectives. He cleverly exploited the findings and evaluations of psychologists and psychiatrists to advance his killing spree. He skillfully positioned his status as respectable community member and family man to challenge and slam down charges by the lowest members on the social scale.

The serial killer has often been described as stalker or hunter. No one fit the role better than Robert Hansen. A world-class hunter, he stalked and hunted his victims, flew them into the Alaskan wild, released them, hunted them, killed them, and brought back relics as trophies.

Robert Hansen, not unique in these respects, stands as a model for the serial killer who chooses the vulnerable in society as victims. He is also a striking example of the serial killer's response to an earlier humiliation.

And like other serial killers, the roots of criminality can be traced to his upbringing. Robert Hansen was born in 1940 in Pocahontas, Iowa, son of a Danish immigrant who followed the family's trade as baker. Pocahontas was a small town one hundred fifty-five miles from Des Moines. As a town that attracted many immigrants after the Civil War, the town—with a population little more than two thousand—took the name of the Indian princess who acted on behalf of the Jamestown settlers making new arrivals welcome in their surroundings.

Robert Hansen's father, Chris Hansen, married a girl, Edna, from nearby Ringstad, and they worked together in the family bakery. Business flourished. In *Fair Game*, Bernard Du Clos details the community's view of Chris Hansen: "hardnosed authoritarian figure ... an 'old world father,' very religious and very strict." The father was a hard worker, and he enforced that ethic in his household. Robert started working at the bakery at an early age, not unlike other neighboring youth who toiled on Iowa's farms.

The youth was quite displeased, as reported by Du Clos: "When I was a young boy, I worked at my dad's shop and I'd get maybe thirty-five to forty-five cents. When I got to be a sophomore, junior, senior ... I wouldn't even get a dollar." Moreover, the father was rarely satisfied with the son's work and often called him worthless.

The son also had to deal with his dad's obstinacy. Robert was born left-handed, and the father—and mother—wanted him to do things with the right hand, so they forced him to that position. He had a stuttering problem, and psychologists said that being forced to switch hands might have aggravated that problem.

Because of speech problems, the youth was especially unhappy during junior high and high school days. He was often embarrassed and humiliated when he had trouble communicating with teachers and classmates. "All through high school," he said, "I knew there was a possibility that I would have to say anything in class or make a comment, I would literally break out in sweats, and, of course, getting excited made my stuttering worse ..." Beyond the speech impediment, Hansen was not a particularly good-looking youngster. Unappealingly skinny, he had an acute case of acne that left him permanently scarred. As Clifford Linedecker writes in *Thrill Killers*, Hansen was "the skinny stutterer with the pimply face [who] was virtually shut out of the dating game during his teenage years." This social rejection brought a "deep-seated hatred for young, beautiful women."

As Du Clos adds, perhaps the results would have been different if Hansen had found a way of dealing with this difficulty:

> Worst of all was when the girls made fun of him on the playground or in the halls. Perhaps if he'd been able to face their jokes and laugh along with them, their taunting might have stopped. But he wasn't and his subsequent feelings of rejection and inadequacy took hold of him with an anger he couldn't control.
>
> Robert Hansen never did learn to control those feelings and anger. Ultimately, they led to his aberrant desire to control women by raping and murdering them.

Even without those problems, Robert Hansen would have had problems socially. His parents were religious, he had little money, and extra time was put in the bakery. And although he took part in the boys' chorus, mixed chorus, and pep club, he was understandably looked at as a loner.

To fill in the void of socializing, he spent his spare time in fishing, hunting, and archery.

His schoolwork was average, as was his IQ of 91. The fact that his school performance was not exemplary could be attributed to a rigorous work schedule in the bakery. He graduated in 1957, with his yearbook photos displaying the misspelled name "Hanson" and his favorite quote: "Worry never made men great, so why should I worry?"

After working in the family bakery, he enlisted in the Army Reserves and took basic training in Fort Dix, New Jersey. On his own, he had his first sexual activities there—with prostitutes—and later during active duty. When back in Iowa, Robert Hansen moved into his own apartment. During his first encounter with the law—in 1961—he was described as "being different," associating with those years his junior.

He would have high school boys over to his apartment to talk about guns, hunting, and who or what he didn't like in Pocahontas.

Interestingly, as much as Edna Hansen was withdrawn and subservient to her husband, Du Clos makes the case that she was to blame for the son's hatred of women:

> Chris Hansen was a hard-nosed strict authoritarian. Edna Hansen may have been just the opposite, causing Robert to seek sanctuary with his mother. Studies of serial killers have shown that such a parenting situation can contribute to the development of a resentment toward women in the male child because of his overdependence on his mother. As a male, he resents that he is so dependent on her—thereby being deprived of his father.

Some six months after returning from the army, Robert Hansen was in trouble with the law. Pocahontas Police Chief Marvin Wiseman recalled a troubled Hansen, who was showing off his skills with bow and arrow and flaunting a knife. "He became the ringleader of a group of younger kids," writes Walter Gilmour and Leland Hale in *Butcher, Baker*. "They didn't have much use for the 'Poky' Police Department." Hansen and friends had been suspected of blowing up a tractor.

Hansen hired an assistant at the bakery, a sixteen-year-old son of a jeweler. In December 1960, Robert and the employee burned the school bus garage. The school's seven buses were destroyed, as was the garage itself. The loss was estimated at eleven thousand dollars. One fireman was injured. The investigation determined arson but could not point to the arsonist although Robert Hansen was rumored to be the culprit.

In the midst of all this, Robert Hansen married Phoebe Padgett, daughter of the town chiropractor. However, his employee felt a twinge of conscience and called the police in March 1961. He told police that Robert had often spoken of burning the school barn as a way of getting even with the school superintendent who had disciplined him while he attended the school.

The grand jury was solid, so Hansen waived a trial and pleaded guilty. "I guess I burned down the barn," he said, "because I hated the school with a divine passion. I do whatever I could think of to get back at that monster school that did Bob Hansen a personal wrong." The sentence was three years at the state correctional facility at Anamosa. With that, his marriage ended.

He became adept at "playing the system." He worked for a staff counselor, helped inmates who couldn't read or write, and gave religious "counseling" to other inmates. One immediate benefit was that one of the counselors later arranged speech therapy sessions for him at the University of Iowa, which improved his speech.

He served twenty months of the sentence, paroled because of good conduct. The negative psychiatric workup on him showed an "infantile personality," translated into an obsession about getting even with people.

Upon parole, Hansen worked at his parents' resort in Minnesota, doing such jobs as painting cabins and boats. His new life also brought his second marriage, to Gloria Deacon, who was cleaning cabins at the resort. Her parents were the motel operators in Pocahontas.

Hansen returned to the baking trade, hired by Cox Bakeries in Moorhead, Minnesota. Because the position involved continued travel among the chain's thirty-two shops in the Midwest, the couple decided to move to Minneapolis. He was hired as foreman and cake decorator in a local bakery.

Suspicion fell on Hansen. The bakery was filled with all sorts of goodies—not pastry: bicycles, radios, sporting goods, and the like. One employee peeked into Hansen's car and noticed the goods. One day, in 1965, Hansen was caught in the act, stealing fishing equipment from a Bloomington sporting goods store. His employer paid for the goods.

Several weeks later, the boss caught Hansen in the act of going through drawers and gaining entry in the shop by breaking the lock. Rather than face charges, Hansen told the owner that he was leaving for another position. The boss wished him well and advanced his departure. Other episodes of theft—without jail sentences—occurred. Many studies of serial killers have linked kleptomania to serial killers. Robert Hansen would not be an exception.

As noted, Du Clos accents Hansen's pathological frugality. It was an aversion to payment, "but mainly it was just for the thrill of it all. When he shoplifted, he'd come close to ejaculating in his pants—it gave him the same satisfaction he got with a prostitute."

Now a graduate of the University of Iowa, Mrs. Hansen and her husband loved the wide-open spaces, so they agreed that Anchorage, Alaska, would be their next move.

Anchorage was experiencing growth that would see a doubling of population to more than two hundred thousand within fifteen years. People with skills and a degree were in demand. Hansen was hired as baker and cake decorator at a local bakery; Mrs. Hansen was hired as a teacher. They went from apartment dwellers to homeowners of a duplex. Mrs. Hansen spent much time with the Lutheran Central Church. They hiked, climbed, fished, and relaxed with many other outdoor activities. In short, they were known as a very respectable couple.

Hansen's new pursuit would change his life as well as those around him: archery and bow hunting.

He joined the Alaska Archery Association and Black Sheep Bowmen. Over the next few years, he entered the Pope and Young record book, for bringing down a fourth-ranked mountain goat on the Kenai Peninsula; for killing a thirty-third ranked Barren Ground caribou at the Tyohne River; for shooting a third-ranked Dali sheep.

Accomplished hunter, successful baker, and happily married, Robert Hansen added to his highly favorable profile with the birth of a daughter in 1971. He took a second job at a bakery and moved to a larger house.

That year also marked his great hunting feat: the biggest Dali sheep ever seized by a bow. To his list of achievements he added a second-ranked Barren Ground caribou.

However, Hansen was launching his criminal career in Alaska. He was arrested on charges of abduction and attempted rape of a real estate secretary and later the rape of a prostitute.

The assault on the secretary brought another psychiatric session for Hansen, the first since he was in an Iowa prison. It "seemed like a bad dream," was his response to the police concerning the rape. And psychiatrists came to the rescue because Hansen was able to manipulate the professionals.

Hansen was examined by Dr. J. Ray Langdon, a psychiatrist at the Alaska Clinic in Anchorage. In his report, Dr. Langdon spoke of Hansen's mental illness and loss of memory and sought to link his criminality to the mental illness. "His compulsive actions have psychological causes," said the report. Langdon also included a military service note that Hansen "worked on an Army firing range." Most important were references to the teen years, when Hansen "fantasized about all sorts of harmful things to girls who rejected him."

Hansen's case was also aided by the Reverend Albert L. Abrahamson, pastor of Lutheran Central Church. No information or testimony changed his opinion about Hansen. He still subscribed to the "peacefulness of the character" of Hansen.

The judge went along with the psychiatric report. While it was a five-year sentence, it was subject to a review by the parole board, which resulted in release after six months. "I believe you have a mental illness and one which makes you, under certain circumstances, extremely dangerous to others in the community. I think this condition requires psychiatric therapy and I'm told by the doctor that it's the condition which he has apparently diagnosed or ... your condition is one that may be treatable ... I recommend as well that you be allowed a release to follow your employment or your work because I'm told you are a good worker and I believe that you're not a danger to the community. As long as you're subject to close supervision, I think that the danger to the community and to the others in the community will be minimized."

In 1976, Hansen was convicted of larceny for shoplifting a chainsaw. The psychiatrist could not help Hansen, for Judge James K. Singleton called Hansen "dangerous." As a third-time felon, "His sentence should be near the maximum range permitted for this crime." Hansen was sentenced to five years at Juneau Correction Center. But the State Supreme Court now came to Hansen's rescue. The sentence was too harsh, it ruled. After one year in prison, he was placed on probation.

His mental illness and continued treatment dictated that decision. "We agree," said the court, "that Hansen's prior record did compel some term of incarceration rather than straight probation. However, the particulars of this case—the clearly diagnosed mental illness; Hansen's amenability to treatment; the linkage of the mental illness to past antisocial behavior; the definite, prescribed course of treatment to mitigate the possibility of future criminal behavior; the stable home and work environment; and the factor that the monetary value of the property stolen was relatively low lead us to conclude that the court below was clearly mistaken in imposing a five-year sentence."

These arrests covered the deadly activities that Hansen was practicing in Anchorage. The pipeline boom in the '70s filled Anchorage—and other Alaskan cities—with a young transient population. They were all out to make a buck. Many were strippers and prostitutes. They were the most vulnerable in that society. When they filed charges of attempted rape, for example, or even rape, would the police believe those who were of the Tenderloin district or the respectable Alaskan citizen? And to aggravate the situation, the major operator in the district was Seattle Mafioso Frank Colacurio.

The plight of these transients was related by a former dancer to

Depravity

Du Clos: "What you had was a very scared, transient girl whose only friends were other dancers and the creeps that came into the bars. She didn't have anybody to turn to ... she was confused, in a game that was over her head."

One avenue of escape was accepting money, often three hundred dollars, from those who sought sexual favors. Ideally, the customer should not be vicious or look vicious. Foolish or stupid would do well. In the slimy world of Anchorage, Hansen could find all the victims he wanted. And the girls saw him as the perfect client. As one rape victim reported, "He sort of looked like the perfect dork."

For Hansen, these were the dregs of society. He wanted to avenge his early life of rejection by women. These women did not serve society in a useful way, reasoned Hansen. According to Robert Hale in *Serial Murder*, Hansen felt "internally justified in releasing his naked prey into the Alaska wilderness before hunting them down with a rifle." Hansen looked at these victims as inhuman. The world would function better without their presence.

According to his eventual confession, in 1984, Hansen hunted or preyed on victims, resulting in seventeen murders and thirty rapes. And there well may be many others not confessed to.

Hansen might ask for a date, perhaps posing as doctor or attorney. Or he would say he was a photographer who wanted to take a few nude poses.

John Douglas, the FBI agent, whose serial killer profile would prove critical to resolve the Hansen case, noted the Alaskan locale and aircraft as unprecedented:

> Hansen was able to adapt his fantasy of total domination of his victims in a way he couldn't have done, say for instance, in New York City. There, he would've been limited to the back of a van or something.
>
> In Alaska, he had the tools ... the aircraft to take his victims to isolated areas where no one was around for miles. He could

turn them loose if he wanted to, and hunt them down like wild animals.

I've never seen that in another case.

Many selected were taken by airplane to the wilds outside of Anchorage. They were forced to perform to the dictates of Hansen's private fantasies.

"If they came across with what I wanted," he told police, "we'd come back to town. I'd tell them if they made any trouble for me, I had connections and would have them put in jail for being prostitutes." On the other hand, those who resisted or demanded money after sex would be murdered, often stripped naked, allowed to run, stalked, and killed, either with a hunting knife or big game rifle. No witnesses ever stepped forward because the murder scenes were so isolated.

Many missing persons came from Tenderloin, but it was first in 1980 that Anchorage officials started piecing matters together: all the missing were either prostitutes, topless dancers, or barmaids. Before disappearance they had been offered money for a "date" by a stranger.

The fortunate ones were taken beyond the center of Anchorage (e.g., Chugach State Park), raped, and let go.

If the girl went to authorities, he would play the "whom do you trust" game or came up with a tale. Du Clos relates one confrontation with parole officer Wayne Burgess:

"Hansen admitted being with the woman, but with a stutter said, 'I thought it was a date, then she asked for money, and I refused to pay. So, she gets mad and hollers rape.'"

Those who did not survive included Paula Golding, a topless barmaid whose remains were found in 1981. They met at an arranged time before noon. Hansen seemed quiet, polite, and harmless. That changed when they arrived in the Muldoon section of Anchorage. Suddenly, he pulled her blond hair back, put a gun at her head, and said, "All right. You'll do just what I tell you. I'm good at this … done it lots of times before." He then handcuffed her hands behind her back, having forced her onto her knees.

Hansen then headed for the airfield.

"Just don't hurt me. I won't make trouble," Golding pleaded. She was put aboard the plane and forced down behind the pilot's seat. They landed alongside the Knik River, scene of many of the killings.

He took her into a shack and uncuffed her. She slapped and screamed at Hansen, "You're going to kill me." His denials did not help her mood. Unfortunately, she began to run. Now it was a hunt; Paula Golding was the prey, as Du Clos narrates:

> Robert got his rifle and went after her; he caught up and snagged her by the shirt; it ripped down the back as she stumbled to her knees.
>
> "Don't make things worse!" he whined with a stutter, feeling he was losing control.
>
> Hysterical, the woman kept slapping at him, screaming that he was going to kill her.
>
> Hansen wasn't going to say any more. He released his grip, allowing his prey to stumble away as fast as she could.
>
> Paula Golding could see the sandbar and the river beyond as she reached the edge of the woods. The .223 bullet burst her heart before the sound of the rifle reached her ear.

The first signs of a killer at large came in 1980 when construction workers found a decomposed body buried alongside a power line outside Eklutna. Forensic experts said that the body might have been dead about a year. With no identification, she was called "Eklutna Annie." Officials are not convinced that this was Hansen's first victim.

Hansen gave details at his confession. She was a topless dancer or prostitute, he recalled. He took her out of town and when she refused to get out of his car, he told her, "If you do exactly what I tell you and don't give me any problem whatsoever, there's going to be no problem … you won't get hurt in any way, shape, or form."

She tried to run away and pulled a knife from her purse, Hansen claimed. He overpowered her and used her knife to stab her in the back. Other corpses were shortly discovered: Joanna Messina near Steward and Sherry Morrow beside the Knik River.

These unfortunates were not only victims but trophies for Hansen. Along with remembrances of his legitimate hunts, Hansen had—like other serial killers—trophies from human hunts, jewelry and other valuables. One of the most striking was a fish necklace custom made for victim Audrea Altiry.

Adding to the low priority attached to the victims and the psychiatric file on Hansen, the case was hindered from the start by the incompetence or lack of professionalism by authorities. When an officer of the Anchorage Police Department took his findings to the state troopers, he was chewed out for wasting their time. "We have no time," the officer was told by state troopers, who sought to complete documents to search Hansen's property.

Hansen continued to prosper. He opened another bakery, with thirteen thousand dollars in an insurance settlement for a faked burglary of his home. The stolen items were his hunting trophies. When the fraud was exposed, trophies found in his backyard, he matter-of-factly said that he forgot to tell the insurance company.

"Why take them out to the wilderness?" thought Hansen. "I can take my hunt home." He came up with a "summer project." To facilitate these plans, he sent his wife and children on a European vacation.

He placed ads in the local papers before his family left the first week of June, seeking women interested in "joining me in finding what's around the next bend, over the next hill." Some thirty responses were received. He later said, "I wanted to find someone to be close to, a warm relationship, a close friend—noncommercial. I wanted it to be relaxed, not have to be scared the whole time."

Perhaps this might have been an attempt by Hansen to come to terms with past social rejections. Maybe he would turn a new direction:

"When I was a teenager, my face was always one big yellow pimple.

Consequently, I never had any girl interested in me. I'd ask a girl out, and she'd say, 'Well, no, I'm sorry. I've got something else planned.' I heard that so doggone many times.

"It's hard to explain what it's like to always be wanting, to see others go out on dates. I was just seeing everybody else get theirs."

"He didn't start out hating all women or his victims," writes Du Clos, "but rather he felt he was falling in love with them. He wanted their friendship—he wanted them to like him. But in his own mind he would classify them as either 'good' or 'bad' women."

He interviewed several respondents, dated several, but had sex with none. Nevertheless, nothing had changed. He would continue hunting.

His first target in mid-June was a seventeen-year-old prostitute, Cindy Paulsen. He took her home and assaulted her sexually. He then forced her into his car. They headed to Merrill Field.

"I'm gonna load my plane. Stay down and don't move—if you try anything, I'll kill you."

As soon as she saw him loading the plane, she ran and fled to safety. The terrified victim was still handcuffed. "I really want to help," she told the police, "but am I going to get into trouble? I mean, because I am a prostitute."

A reassured victim continued, "But if I don't help, I'm afraid he's gonna hurt somebody else. He's killed other women. I just don't know what I should do."

By the time the victim was taken to the police for questioning, Hansen had already crafted an alibi with friend, John Henning. They had been together the entire period of the alleged rape.

But the reluctant Paulsen agreed to give testimony in September 1983, and that turned the case. Faced with lying under oath, Henning withdrew the alibi.

FBI profiler John Douglas was brought into the case. In an article for *Biography*, Marjorie Rosen calls him "the most famous FBI agent since Dick Tracy." He was a central figure in the investigation and conviction of Atlanta child murderer Wayne Bertram Williams. When Jodie Foster received an Academy Award for *Silence of the Lambs*, she thanked Douglas.

Of relevance for Hansen, it was his profile that became the basis for search warrants for Hansen's home—a first in criminal procedures. Having studied details of the murders and listened to the story of Cindy Paulsen, Douglas constructed a profile of Robert Hansen, the forty-three-year-old Anchorage baker.

In October 1983, Sergeant Glenn Flothe presented Judge Victor Carlson with a forty-eight-page affidavit: the result—eight search warrants executed against Hansen. The police searched his house, cars, and plane. The mementos (i.e., trophies) of victims were found, as were a .223 caliber rifle and an aviation map with massive details relating to the murder sites. Two of the marks were precise locations near the Knik River. The Morrow and Golding bodies had been recovered there. He was arrested and charged with insurance fraud, theft, weapons offense, assault, and kidnapping. Hansen's bail was set at five hundred thousand dollars.

The hunter was trapped. No friends, no psychiatrists could come to his rescue. He hoped to avoid the disgrace that would befall his wife and children in protracted legal proceedings. In February 1984, he signed an Agreement of Understanding with the State of Alaska. He would confess, and lead police to the bodies of seventeen victims. Hansen showed investigators asterisks on a map. Four marks on the map would lead to Eklutna Annie, Joanne Messina, Sherry Morrow, and Paula Golding. Although the bodies of seventeen victims were eventually found, Hansen would only be charged with the five murders the authorities were aware of.

The confession amazed Flothe and prosecutor Frank Rothschild. They listened to details of the modus operandi:

> I pull out the gun ... "Look, you're a professional. You don't get excited. You know there is some risk to what you've been

doing." [Hansen told the victim] "If you do exactly what I tell you, you're not going to get hurt. You're just going to count this off as a bad experience and be a little more careful next time who you are gonna proposition or go out with, you know."

I tried to act as tough as I could, to get them as scared as possible, give that right away, even before I started talking at all. Reach over, you know, and hold that head back and put a gun in her face and get 'em to feel helpless, scared and face the seat on the knees on the floorboard. That way, they were down, they wouldn't start anything there.

The bodies of victims were spread out over hundreds of square miles in the Alaska wild. Hansen was taken by helicopter to the sites on his map. He identified twelve burial sites.

"Why did you keep the map?" Rothschild queried.

The hunter responded, "Ah, it was kept for … one night I was sitting at home and, ah, there was some marks on the map that didn't have any correspondence to, ah, these girls. And I was looking at places that I had some bear stands and for some reason or other I just started correlating where the people were to my bear stands, for some reason."

At the end of February 1984, the court proceedings were heading to a close. Hansen was relaxed and, like other serial killers, showed no remorse.

The search orders, noted Trooper Wayne Von Clausen, meant "we could ask Mrs. Hansen questions, but we couldn't answer any of hers. That made it easier for us … but you had to feel for the woman. She couldn't believe all that was happening to her and the kids."

The defense attorney was thwarted in his attempts to seal documents and close hearings. He was also turned down when asking for a delay to review documents and investigation of victims' backgrounds.

Superior Court Judge Henry Keene ruled that all searches were proper and that all seized evidence would be admissible.

The prosecutor made his closing statement:

Before you sits a monster, an extreme aberration of a human being who walked among us for seventeen years serving us doughnuts, Danish, and coffee with a pleasant smile. His family was a prop; he hid behind decency.

The hunter who kept trophies on the wall now has trophies scattered throughout south central Alaska. And while he doesn't talk about or admit to it, it's obvious from looking at where things started and where women ended up, he hunted them down. He'd let them run a little bit, then he enjoyed a hunt, just as with his big-game animals. He toyed with them. He got a charge out of it. We don't think for a moment that he told us the whole story ...

Hansen had nothing to say before sentencing. Judge Keene sentenced Hansen to 461 years without chance of parole. He was first sent to the maximum security facility in Lewisburg, Pennsylvania. In April 1984, as Hansen was flown to Oklahoma for processing into the federal penal system, the police hoped that Hansen might tell then about other missing people.

"No," snapped Hansen, "The book is closed ... I can't see anything in it for me."

In 1988, he returned to Alaska as one of the first prisoners in the new Spring Creek Correctional Center in Seward. His ego was crushed with the loss of his trophies. The 1987 edition of the *Bowhunting Big Game Records of North America* eliminated Hansen's name from all the categories of Pope and Young records previously held by him. This was an about face from a statement after his sentencing that Hansen would keep all his records since "his crimes were an issue apart from his accomplishments as bow hunter."

Hansen also lost his family. The Hansens could not stay in Alaska, for the children were harassed at school. Mrs. Hansen filed for divorce and left Alaska.

His hometown of Pocahontas, Iowa, shook off association with the serial killer with the onset of other problems, noted Du Clos: "The shock and embarrassment of Hansen's crimes had mingled with the more immediate concerns of a bank failure, personal bankruptcies, the effects of agricultural chemicals on the ground water supply, and business failures attested to by vacant commercial buildings."

Before transfer to Seward, Hansen's cell was searched. A cache of stamps and aviation maps of southeast Alaska were found. His prison life has not been inactive. He has written several humorous short stories and plans an autobiography, which has attracted two publishers seeking rights.

The story also maintained currency with the announcement in February 2003 by Alaska state troopers that they are intensifying attempts to identify Eklutna Annie, who was found dead in July 1980.

Readers of serial killer narratives will be struck by the stories of Robert Hansen, the hunter, and the hunted—the prostitutes and topless dancers. What most readers won't know is that most of the hunted might have had different lives if the hunter had been compelled to adhere to the required, supervised lithium and psychotherapy program.

The unpunished criminal was society for not having controlled Robert Hansen. Judge Keene's final words to the court indicted society:

"There are no words which can adequately describe what we have seen here today, and what the defendant has admitted to ... I can't think of a bigger indictment of society than what we have here. This gentleman has been known to us for several years. Yet, we've turned him loose several times knowing that he had the potential to kill."

LUCIAN STANIAK
The Red Spider

The Red Spider, Lucian Staniak, has fascinated serial killer watchers. Artist, translator, and student of Polish literature, Staniak exemplifies the phenomenon of intelligent serial killer. Colin Wilson and Damon Wilson, in *The Killers Among Us*, called Staniak an illustration of the "high IQ killer."

Staniak personifies "a new level of motivation in serial killers. The desire to violate is less than compulsive, but they use their intelligence to justify it, asking themselves—in an almost philosophical spirit— 'Why not?'"

Lucian Staniak has also attracted interest as a modern-day Jack the Ripper; however, much differentiates the two, as will be noted.

Hickey has examined serial killers from an international perspective. In his *Serial Murderers and Their Victims*, Hickey places Staniak in his list of serial killers from 1430–1987. Hickey ranks Staniak second among serial killers, with thirty-plus attributed to Carl Denke. Born in Silesia, Germany, now Ziebice, Poland, Denke hanged himself in prison in 1924, so all information is not available. In the list of sixty-four, the only other Pole is Pawel Alojzy Tuchlin, whose victims totaled nine-plus during 1984–1985.

The serial killings of the twenty-four-year-old Staniak began in the summer of 1964. Poland was preparing to celebrate the twentieth anniversary of the liberation of Warsaw from the Axis by Russian troops. A large parade was planned for Warsaw on July 22, with smaller celebrations scheduled throughout the country.

The planned festivities hit a sour note on July 4. Marian Starzynski, editor of *Prezeglad Polityczny*, the Polish version of *Pravda*, received an anonymous note. It was written in a strange red ink, in a spidery style of writing: "There is no happiness without tears, no life without death. Beware. I am going to make you cry!"

The editor was convinced that he was targeted for death, and demanded police protection. When the 22nd passed without incident, Starzynski breathed a sigh of relief.

However, the action was not in Warsaw but in Olsztyn, some one hundred fifty miles to the north. On the day of the festivities, seventeen-year-old blond Danka Maciejowitz did not return home from a parade organized by the local school of Choreography and Folklore.

The next morning, a gardener working in the Park of Polish Heroes discovered the corpse concealed in shrubbery. She had been stripped naked and raped; the lower part of her body was disemboweled.

As a follow-up, Staniak penned a note to the Warsaw newspaper *Kulisy*. Like the previous missive, this note was in red ink: "I picked a juicy flower in Olsztyn, and I shall do it again somewhere else, for there is no holiday without a funeral." Police experts examined the ink and determined that it was artist's paint dissolved in turpentine.

However, the elements were not uncommon, so the police had no clues. There were no samples for comparison. The corpse of Danka Maciejowitz offered no leads. No suspects were available. Warsaw's police could only wait with anxiety to see if the killer would fulfill his threat.

While there were no suspects, a newspaperman looked at the spidery script, the crimson ink, and tightly spaced handwriting and dubbed the at-large killer the "Red Spider."

Like other serial killers, the Red Spider needed to correspond with the authorities or with the police. Jack the Ripper signed more than three hundred letters sent to the London press. The BTK Strangler berated authorities, "How many times do I have to kill before I get my name in the paper or some national attention?" Son of Sam, David Berkowitz, wrote to New York columnist Jimmy Breslin, among others.

According to Michael Newton, the letter writing gives the killers "peripheral involvement in the manhunt" and may "generate sufficient thrills."

Lucian Staniak made good on his threat, although some six months later.

On January 16, 1965, *Zycie Warsawy*, a Warsaw daily, published the photograph of an attractive sixteen-year-old girl, Aniuta Kaliniak, who had been picked to lead a student parade through Warsaw on the 17th. In order to get to the parade, she walked from her home in Praga, an eastern suburb of Warsaw, and crossed the bridge spanning the Vistula River. Exhausted after the parade, the teenager hitched a ride from a lorry driver. He dropped the parade leader close to her home at a crossroads.

Most parents in Western countries, such as the United States, would strongly advise their children never to thumb a ride. Either the teen spurned such likely advice, or crime, especially sex crime, was not an important concern in Poland.

It proved fatal. She was dropped off within two blocks of her house, but she never made it home. A search party went out looking for Aniuta; they were unsuccessful until alerted by the police, who had received a note from the Red Spider directing them where to look for the remains.

On January 18, the searchers found the body in the basement of a leather factory opposite her house. The police concluded that the killer had carefully planned the murder: had stalked her, hid in the shadows of walls of the factory, and ambushed her. Without allowing her to cry out for help, the killer strangled her, dropping a noose over her head.

After killing her, the Red Spider removed the sidewalk grate, thereby gaining entry to the factory basement. He raped her and left a six-inch spike sticking in her sexual organs.

The Red Spider next struck ten months later, on November 1, 1965—All Saint's Day. He found another site: Poznan, one hundred seventy-five miles west of Warsaw. The chosen victim was attractive Janka Popielski, a young blond hotel receptionist. She was at the train terminal that afternoon, hoping to get a lift to a nearby village, where she planned to join her boyfriend.

Tragically, the terminal was empty on this religious holiday—except for the killer. The Red Spider overcame her as he applied a chloroform-soaked bandage over her nose and mouth. He then dragged her behind a packing shed filled with crates. He removed her skirt, stockings, and panties and raped her.

The Red Spider was not finished. He killed her with a screwdriver, mutilated her, and stuffed her body into a packing case. No directions were given the police, but they found her body an hour after the gruesome acts. The acts were so horrific that the police offered no details about the mutilations.

Acting quickly, the police acted to capture the killer, who would be a man with bloodstained clothes. All trains and buses leaving Poznan were stopped and searched but the police came up empty, frustrated again.

But the Red Spider had another message, this one received on November 2 by a Poznan newspaper *Courier Zachodni*. As expected, it was in red ink. This time the killer revealed his literary side with a quote from *Popioli*, an epic novel written in 1928 by Stefan Zeromsky: "Only tears of sorrow can wash out the stain of shame; only pangs of suffering can blot out the fires of lust."

With three revolting, unsolved murders committed, police, detectives, and anxious citizens sought to piece together a reasoned modus operandi of the Red Spider. The locale varied in Olsztyn, Praga, and Poznan. Two of the three murders were committed on national or religious holidays. In his sadistic acts, he echoed the Boston Strangler, Albert DeSalvo, whose crime rampage preceded the Spider's by a few years. In one of his narratives, he told police:

Depravity

"Then I took this fork and stuck it into her right bust, and I left it there. I covered her with a sheet. It was bloody."

Others compared him to Jack the Ripper, the sadistic Englishman of the 1880s who disemboweled many of his victims. The important difference was that all Staniak's victims were mere women. However, Jack the Ripper's victims were clearly prostitutes.

Jack the Ripper, or Kuba Prozpruwacz, as he was known in Polish, did not focus his attacks on national holidays. While Staniak committed his murders over a three-year period, the Ripper operated in a ten-week span.

The Red Spider's note, apart from an artistic touch, revealed a well-read killer. This was especially true in his quote from Zeromsky, the most popular Polish novelist of the first quarter of the twentieth century, author of *Popioly*, which has been called the *War and Peace* of Poland. He accented social justice in his writings and articulated a fervent Polish nationalism, perhaps related to the Spider's penchant for activity during holidays.

Perhaps most relevant are his descriptions of savage brutality and rape in *Popioly*, which deals with the Napoleonic Wars.

The imagery is present in other writings, among them *Dream of a Sword*, written in 1905, the year of a Socialist revolution in Russian-occupied Poland:

> Even if your cause were lost, she [Polish Muse] will keep her faith in you. She will see and bear in mind your days and nights, your pains, efforts, toil, and death. She will lay your head, bashed by the butts of the soldiery, on a pillow of the most wondrous verse ... With a cloak of dignity, woven of the most wondrous colors of her art, she will cover your naked body that knows no belt of gold or robe of red, when the people of Lodz dig it up from the common pit, to give it the only thing the people can give, a pinewood coffin.
>
> Into your hands grown stiff, hands that are powerless only

in death, she will lay her golden dream, the dream of so many generations of the young, the dream of a knightly sword.

As Poland wondered, the Red Spider remained quiet, until May 1, 1966, May Day, also celebrated as Labor Day and the Communist Party's national holiday. Lucian Staniak was marking the day in his unique manner.

The setting was the always peaceful suburb of Zoliborz in northern Warsaw. As the holiday neared its close, seventeen-year-old Marysia Galazka went out looking for her cat. She did not return. Her father went to look for her. He did not have to look long or far. She was in the tool shed behind the house, vulgarly mutilated. The entrails were draped across her thighs. The autopsy showed that the killer had raped her before disemboweling her.

The Warsaw police turned to Major Ciznek of the homicide squad and appointed him to head the investigations. Apart from the murders described above, Ciznek examined the country's crime record since April 1964, and found fourteen other homicides that reflected the modus operandi of the Red Spider. All the other murders, however, were not accompanied by spidery writing.

Almost all were not committed on holidays. The Poznan district was the favorite setting, with five of the fourteen murders; two occurred at Bydoszcz; the others, at Bialystok, Kielce, Lodz, Lomza, Lublin, and Radom.

The major came up with what he considered a clever deduction as he charted the murders on a map. All the crimes were committed within four hundred kilometers of Warsaw. All the crime scenes lay south and west of Warsaw, in towns connected by direct rail transportation to Katowice and Kracow.

Therefore, Warsaw was logically the home of the Red Spider since the killings took place all around it. Katowice and Kracow had not witnessed killing because the Spider did not want to hit too close to home. Warsaw, Katowice, and Kracow are all large cities. How would one find the Red Spider without solid clues?

The major had ample time to resolve the puzzle. Seven months passed, and the next murder was indeed a holiday: Christmas Eve 1966. Three soldiers boarded a train in Kracow headed for Warsaw. Deciding to avoid a third-class ride, they headed for a reserved compartment and in disbelief discovered a mutilated corpse on the floor. Her leather miniskirt had been cut to pieces, as had her abdomen and thighs.

The soldiers notified the train conductor, who ordered the train to head nonstop to Warsaw. All passengers were examined before leaving the train but none showed bloody hands or stained clothes. No clues—again.

But the Red Spider had left his imprint. The police found a letter dropped into the post slot of the mail van before the train departed Kracow. "I have done it again," read the brief notification.

The victim was seventeen-year-old Janina Kozielska. Upon further investigation, detectives realized that fourteen-year-old Aniela Kozielska had been butchered in Warsaw in 1964. This was Janina's sister.

Major Ciznek now ruled out Kracow as the home of the Red Spider. The two murders had to be connected, and if he could find the murderer of the sisters, he would have caught the Red Spider.

As the police gathered details about this train ride, they learned that the first-class compartment had been booked over the telephone by a man who gave his name as Stanislav Kozielski, almost exactly the name of the murdered. When ordering, Kozielski had said that that his wife would pick up the tickets. In fact, she did pay for them in cash—1,422 zlotys, about twenty-five pounds, or eighty-five dollars.

The conductor told police that he had shown her to the compartment. She told the conductor that her husband would shortly arrive. When he arrived, the conductor checked the "husband's" ticket, but he could not remember his face.

It was clear to the police that the victim knew her killer, well enough to travel with him and pose as his wife. And she paid for the tickets too.

From the information received, she had been murdered within ten minutes of arrival on the train. The murderer then quickly left the train.

Major Ciznek went to the home of the shocked parents, who could give them no help in suggesting a potential killer. But they did tell the major that the sisters had at times worked as models at the Kracow School of Plastic Arts and the Art Lovers Club.

The trademark of the Red Spider, thought the Major, might be the lead they needed. The killer's red ink was made of artist's paint dissolved in turpentine and water.

The investigative team headed for the Art Lovers Club and went through the list of members: 118. The membership list featured very respectable citizens: physicians, dentists, government officials, journalists, and community leaders. "Is there anybody from Katowice?" Ciznek asked his investigative team.

They found only one—but that would be enough. The member was Lucian Staniak, a twenty-six-year-old translator who worked at Poland's government printing house. The police learned from the club's director that Staniak traveled often on business and used an *uglowy* billet. This special ticket enabled the user unlimited railroad travel throughout Poland.

"We want to see Staniak's locker," Ciznek ordered the director. Perhaps they could now break this case. Upon opening the locker, the detectives found an assortment of knives used for smearing paint on canvas.

"Staniak daubed the paint on canvas with a knife blade," the director told detectives. "He liked to use red paint. Here is one his paintings called 'The Circle of Life.'"

That painting showed a flower being devoured by a cow. The cow was eaten by a wolf. The wolf was shot by a hunter. The hunter was

Depravity

run down by a female motorist. The woman lay in a field with her abdomen ripped open, with flowers sprouting from her wound.

The case was solved, Ciznek announced to his squad. All that remained was to find and arrest the Red Spider. Ciznek phoned the Katowice police on January 31, 1967. They headed for Staniak's home at 117 Aleje Wyzwolenia. They tried the door, but no one was home.

A month had passed since the murder of Janina Kozielska. The Red Spider was anxious to be active again. While the police hunted Staniak, he was searching for another victim.

That morning Staniak had taken the train to Lodz, looking for one more victim—his last. He chose eighteen-year-old Bozhena Raczkiewicz, a student at the Lodz Institute of Cinematographic Arts. He walked her to the Lodz rail station at around 6 PM. They entered a shelter at the station for overnight travelers who sought refuge from inclement weather.

He stunned the victim with a vodka bottle, and following his past script cut off her skirt and panties, and then slashed her to death with his knife. The time of the murder was between 6 and 6:25 PM.

In rushing to flee the crime scene, Staniak left his fingerprints on the broken bottle's neck. The atrocity committed; Staniak spent the evening in Lodz and then took a train homeward to Katowice. The police were waiting at the depot and brought him in for questioning.

When he realized that there was no way out, Staniak fully confessed to twenty murders, although only six slayings were clearly linked to the Red Spider. In fact, the final charges brought against Staniak detailed only six homicides. According to Radom.net, a Polish serial killers Web site, some have theorized that Staniak was coerced into confessing to fourteen murders that were still unsolved.

Having received the confession, detectives consulted with psychologists to determine a motive. Before Staniak was brought in, theories had focused on a killer who was "morally absent" and a "sexually frustrated pervert." It was also suggested that the killer, especially as seen through his notes, was actively seeking notoriety.

Actually, the initial foray into crime was totally unrelated to those theories. One day, in the sixties, his parents and sister were crossing an icy road. They were hit by a speeding car that skidded on the ice. The hit-and-run driver was the young, attractive wife of a Polish Air Force pilot. The driver escaped the net of justice, so Lucian Staniak decided to take justice into his own hands. His targeted victims would be any woman that bore a resemblance to that killer driver.

Why didn't he do the obvious: kill that reckless driver? He reasoned that such a murder would be traced to the grieving son and brother.

He gathered his would-be victims from newspaper photos. Why did he persist in his rampage? How many victims were needed to satisfy the Red Spider's thirst for revenge?

Having felt self-gratification after the first murder, Staniak looked for other victims for sport and the thrill. Other theories determined that Staniak seemed to glory in being perceived as notorious and deviant.

Elliott Leyton found nothing unusual about Staniak's explanation of his crimes. As he writes in *Modern Multiple Murder*, Staniak's explanation "is curiously familiar to us, for it possesses the distinctive mixture of bizarre pseudo-rationality and apparent insanity that multiple murderers customarily deliver to us and to the authorities. We do not know enough about his life to speak with any certainty about what created him. We can only note how similar in feel and texture the case is to our own."

How was it possible for the Staniak case to drag on for three years? Clues existed; there were scrawled notes from the Red Spider. According to Radom.net, Poland was preoccupied with the building of a Communist state and looked at serial murders as a phenomenon of the West:

"During the 1960s in Poland, the newspapers were filled with articles devoted to praising the architects of People's Poland. The dark aspects of life were bypassed, or at best dealt with superficially. To the leaders of Poland, everything about socialistic Poland was good. Evil was to be found only in imperialistic nations."

Depravity

In *Modern Multiple Murder*, Leyton wonders whether the trebling of the rate of multiple murders in the United States in the seventies and the quadrupling in the early eighties was "a consequence only of the predatory nature of capitalism." Such a conclusion is not warranted, according to Leyton.

Writes Leyton: "The structure of humiliation and deprivation coalesce around any stratified and hierarchical industrial system, whether it be capitalist or Communist, and neither system appears to hold any monopoly on alienation and exclusion, dehumanization and depersonalization." Leyton cites the studies of Russian criminologist Valerie Chalidze, who studied multiple or serial murders in the sixties and found that they were not as common as in America but still "fairly common."

Because of the lack of concern with sadistic crime, the police were unable to deal efficiently with the Red Spider phenomenon. The police were uneducated about serial killers. "Their main concern was with the enemies of the system," observed Radom.net. "Indeed, it was the deceitful atmosphere that made it possible for the murderer to operate for three years."

The Red Spider was sentenced to death. As a result of a psychiatric examination, he was declared insane and was committed to an insane asylum in his home town of Katowice. He has made no further comments on his case. The "exact location of his confinement" is unknown, according to the Radom Web site.

The fourteen other murders first charged to Staniak remain unsolved. The Radom Web site ends on a strange note: "In principle, it is not known whether Staniak killed anyone. The guilty party was tracked down and punished. The case was closed."

The case was also closed by the Polish media. Nary a story appeared in the press during his rampage. An examination of Poland's *Biblioteka Narodowa*, Poland's *Readers Guide To Periodical Literature*, for 1967–68 found not one single entry on Staniak or on the case.

Wojciech Siemaskiewicz, a Polish specialist at the Slavic and Baltic

Division of the New York Public Library, found almost no Polish reference materials on Staniak. He feels that authorities want to "fully" close this case.

We e-mailed the head of the Warsaw police, Pawel Biedziak, asking if the archives provided any information on Lucian Staniak. We received no answer.

However, in 2001, the Muza publishing house of Warsaw published a book on serial killers, including Staniak, titled *Seryjni Mordercy*.

SECTION IV—

SADO-SEXUAL CRIMES

HENRY LEE LUCAS AND OTTIS TOOLE

The Tag Team from Hell

Duo serial killers are uncommon but not rare. However, Henry Lee Lucas and Ottis Toole offer a deadly combination in which the career of one partner, here Lucas, was already well advanced but sunk to new hellishness with a crime associate.

Together and individually, Lucas and Toole stand apart from other serial killers. They have been described as "The Tag Team from Hell: the Sadist King and the Generalissimo of Pain." In short, they were the "consummate killer couple."

Some consider Lucas America's most prolific serial killer, but some call him America's most "controversial" murderer whose confessions were false. He also has the distinction of having his sentence commuted by President George Bush, then Texas governor. This was the first and only time the governor did so for a death row inmate. Lucas is among the first of the "wandering serial killers" or "recreational killers," described by *Washington Post*'s Cynthia Gorney as those who kill by "drawn-out wanderings," as distinct from the "sudden apocalypse of a gunman" who mows down victims in crowded settings. Lucas was convicted of murders in twenty-six states.

In the words of partner/lover Lucas, Toole was one of "the worstest killers in the world." The story of Toole accentuates the vulnerability of children. That was brought to world attention by Toole's kidnapping and murder of a six-year-old in front of a Florida department store.

Damned from the womb, Lucas was born in 1936, the youngest of nine children, in Blackburg, Virginia. According to Max Call, in *Hand of Death*, the mother was bitterly disappointed with his birth. "It's a damned boy! Why couldn't he have been a girl! In a few years, a daughter could be turning a few tricks of her own. A lot of men like to be entertained by a mother and her daughter. She'd be earning money before she was six."

He was reared in a dirt-floor cabin in the woods outside of Montgomery County. A half–Chippewa Indian, his mother, Viola, a sadistic alcoholic, supported the family with proceeds from whoring. His father, Anderson, also an alcoholic, lost both legs after being hit by a freight train. The household was complete with boyfriend and pimp Bernie and his sons.

In the cramped one-bedroom residence, Henry Lee Lucas and his siblings were often present when their mother was engaged in her trade. In fact, the children were often severely beaten when they turned away from their mother's acts.

According to Lucas, "First thing I can remember was when my mom was in bed with another man in the house, and she made me watch it. I just couldn't stand there and watch. I had to turn and walk out of the house, and after that she beat me 'cause I didn't watch it."

His hellish existence took a new sadistic turn one day when the young Lucas refused to do as he was told. Mother struck the five-year-old over the head with a log of wood. His scalp was split open, and he was knocked out for three days. Taken to a hospital with a story that it was a fall from a ladder, Henry Lucas did recover. However, the legacy of sadism was a lifetime of dizzy spells, headaches, and blackout bouts.

Only Viola and Bernie ate well. Everyone else had to fend for himself, leading to an early career of theft from nearby stores and farms. Unable to endure this life anymore, the father crept out into the snow, contracted pneumonia, and died.

School was another odyssey into hell. On his first day, in 1943, the

Depravity

mother dressed him up: dress; stringy hair in ringlets—to the expected ridicule of his classmates; no shoes. A sympathetic teacher cut his hair and bought him a shirt, pants, and shoes. An angered mother rushed to the school and berated the teacher for interference. Enraged, the mother came home and beat her son for accepting gifts.

Also, in his first school year, while playing in the woods near his house, his half-brother's pocket knife slipped and gashed Henry's eye. After several days of concealing the pain, Henry was beaten by his mother for the accident; however, she decided no treatment for the infection was needed. Fortunately, a school nurse treated and saved the eye—until an accident shortly after. A ruler thrown by a student hit Henry in the eye. His eye was removed and replaced by a glass eye.

The mother was delighted with his misfortune. You're a one-eyed snip now," she roared, "and no one wants you except me. You're mine, Henry, and you're going to spend the rest of your life doing as you're told."

If he found a pet, his mother would kill it. He once had a pet mule. "Do you like it, Henry?" she asked. When he responded, she went into the house, came out with a shotgun, and then shot the animal. And she proceeded to berate her son for the expense needed to remove the carcass. Such episodes obviously shaped Henry's inability to love or admit to love, and made for a perverted attitude toward other living beings, whether human or animal.

Henry Lucas's teen years were filled with episodes of perversity. He had sex with his half-brother. The mother's lover, now known as Uncle Bernie, introduced the brothers to bestiality. Bernie raped, tortured, killed, and then performed bestiality. The animals were dog and sheep.

Activities were not limited to bestiality. Henry began stealing animals, usually for food and money. "I started stealing," he later told police, "I guess, as soon as I was old enough to run fast, 'cause I didn't want to stay at home. I figured if I could steal, I could get away from home and stuff."

Sexual perversities were expanded to include necrophilia. His first murder—in what would be a long list—was committed when he was fifteen. The victim was a seventeen-year-old girl he picked up at a bus stop in Lynchburg, Virginia. When she rebuffed his rape attempt, he strangled her. He buried her in the woods near Harrisburg. That murder was unsolved until Lucas confessed some thirty years later, in 1983.

"I had no intention of killing her," he said at the confession. "I don't know whether I was just being afraid somebody was going to catch me or what. That killing was my first, my worst, and the hardest to get over … I would go out sometimes for days, and nearly every time I turned around I'd see the police behind me and watching. Everywhere I'd go I'd have to be watching the police and be afraid they were going to stop me and pick me up. But they never did bother with me."

Burglary was soon coupled with murder. His first break-in, at age fifteen, was at an appliance store in the Richmond area. A series of other burglaries followed. His crimes got him a two-year term in a reformatory. The fifteen-year-old served one year before being released because of "a good adjustment." However, after his release, he resumed his life of burglary and was sentenced to a four-year term at the Virginia State Penitentiary in Staunton.

After serving two years, he escaped while with a prison road gang. His new adventures involved his teaming up with an associate to steal many cars, stretching from Virginia to Michigan. He was rearrested after several months, in Clinton, Michigan. He served out his original sentence in a Chillicothe, Ohio, prison and returned to his half-sister, Opal, in Tecumseh, Michigan.

While at large, he met a girl named Stella. He dated her regularly after his release. They planned to marry. Upon visiting Henry and Opal, their mother learned of the engagement. She pleaded with Henry, "I am getting old and need you to care for me." Henry refused. The battle began. Stella realized that she did not need any of this and broke the engagement.

Henry left for Opal's apartment. The mother followed and the fighting continued. The mother took a broom and broke it across his skull. Henry then struck the mother across the neck with a knife.

He actually had not killed her with the initial attack, but he thought so. "All I remember," he said, "was slapping her alongside the neck, but after I did that I saw her fall and decided to grab her. But she fell to the floor and when I went back to pick her up, I realized she was dead. Then I noticed that I had my knife in my hand and she had been cut."

Henry got into his car and drove to Virginia. Opal found her mother in Henry's apartment, forty-eight hours later—still alive. Taken by ambulance to a hospital, she died a short time later. The cause was determined as a heart attack brought on by Henry's attack. He was picked up by police five days later in Toledo, Ohio, and returned to Michigan. He confessed to murdering his mother—in self-defense—and told the stunned police that he raped her corpse. His sentence was twenty to forty years for second-degree murder to the State Prison of Southern Michigan.

His prison stay was a nightmare that would not end. He complained of hearing voices in his head. He was tortured by these voices, one of which was his mother. "She wanted me to commit suicide for what I had done to her."

He wrote his sister, "I can't take this anymore. I am going to kill myself." That he didn't was not for lack of trying.

He cut open his stomach with a razor blade. Next, he tried slashing his wrists. Prison psychiatrists advised transfer to Ionia State Psychiatric Hospital. He underwent drug and shock therapy for four and a half years.

The diagnosis: Henry Lucas was a psychopath, sadist, and sex deviate. He was "grossly lacking in self-confidence, self-reliance, willpower, and general stamina." In addition, the doctors found evidence of a "general preoccupation with sexual impotence."

Lucas warned doctors that if he were released he would kill once more. Threats notwithstanding, Lucas was returned to prison. Amazingly, one prison psychologist told the parole board that Lucas was "making good progress." However, Lucas told police that his prison time drove him to the determination to kill as many people as possible.

He made profitable use of his time in prison. Lucas immersed himself in criminology: techniques police used in their investigations, studies of other criminals. "I learned every way there is in law enforcement. I learned every way there is in different crimes; I studied it. After I got out of that hospital, they put me in the records room. And every record that jumped through there, I would read it, study it, and see how what got who caught."

Michigan prisons were overcrowded, so Lucas was paroled in 1975. According to Max Call, in 1970 the cost of maintaining a prisoner in Michigan was eighteen thousand dollars a year; with thirty years remaining on his term, the state would have to spend some six hundred thousand dollars.

He told officials that he was still sick, was still hearing a voice from the dead, and he felt compelled to kill. No one listened.

Years later in a Texas prison, he told of that episode: "I knew I was going to do it. I even told 'em I was going to do it. I told the warden, the psychologist, everybody. When they come in and sent me out on parole, I said, 'I'm not ready to go; I'm not going.' They said, 'You're going if we have to throw you out.' They threw me out of the prison because it was too crowded. So I said, 'I'll leave you a present on the doorstep on the way out.' And I did it, the same day, down the road a bit. It wasn't too far away from it. But they never proved it."

Lucas claimed his first victim in Jackson, a few miles from the prison. In fact, he killed her and dumped the victim within walking distance of the prison.

He did not enjoy his freedom long, arrested for the attempted kidnapping of two teenage girls. Back he went to Jackson for four years and was paroled, again over his own objections.

Now, his serial criminal career was in full swing. His murders were committed throughout the Southwest and in Florida. Children were abducted. Young girls were raped. He killed whenever he was moved to these acts. "I was bitter at the world," he said. "There wasn't nothin' I liked. I was bitter as bitter could be."

The criminal career of Henry Lee Lucas, one of America's first studied serial killers, has interested criminologists, psychologists, and psychiatrists as fitting a certain pattern of violence. Dr. Joel Norris has analyzed Lucas as following a "sequence of ritualistic acts" that can be broken down into "seven key phases."

The phases are: aura phase, trolling phase, wooing phase, capture phase, murder phase, totem phase, and depression phase. The aura phase is two-part; "a world of normalcy, of social convention, in which laws are observed and rules observed ... "a world of compulsion, a world dominated by the replaying of the fantasy of violence in which there is no social convention or obedience to rules."

In the second phase, the killer acts compulsively, actively searching for victims. Lucas, observes Norris, trolled on the interstates that crisscrossed Texas. He found his prey in gas stations and alongside roads seeking a hitch.

Serial killers trap their victims in the wooing phase. Capture of the victim is brought about in varied ways in phase four. Before beginning the physical abuse, Lucas spoke to his victims—once completing the "capture."

All serial killers have a commonality, according to Norris, in that "the murder phase is a ritual reenactment of the disastrous experience of the killer's childhood." Of course, now the killer is in control. Lucas was abused and scarred by his mother. He now wreaked violence upon women, burning and cutting into the private parts of his victims.

This violence is carried into the totem phase, in which killers "try to preserve the intensity of the murder ... by attempting to preserve the body through a ritualistic dismemberment of the dead victim."

"Feelings of emptiness and hopelessness mark the depression phase. Lucas was depressed because he never achieved an emotional release from the murders. Those he killed were "slaughtered as a form of sacrifice to the killer's own past."

Now that Lucas had fully entered into the world of the serial killer, his "wandering" life took new directions. He moved to Pennsylvania with his niece and her husband. He worked on a mushroom farm, where he met Betty Crawford, the widow of his nephew. They married, and together with two young daughters from a previous marriage, they moved to Port Deposit, Maryland.

The family lived in a trailer park, with Henry eking out a living with a series of small jobs. Their short-lived marriage ended when Betty accused him of molesting her daughters. Actually, Lucas walked out of the marriage. The Crawford family totaled fifteen, and Lucas tired of supporting that many.

For the next two years, he was continually on the road: in West Virginia, in Louisiana, in Virginia, in Delaware. While in Hinton, West Virginia, he worked in the carpet store of Joe Crawford, a relative of his ex-wife. There he met Rhonda Knuckles, lived with her several months, and abandoned the relationship. He returned to Port Deposit. His sister, Almeda, and her husband offered him lodging and a job in his wrecking yard.

It was time to leave when Almeda accused her brother of molesting her granddaughter. He denied the charges, and borrowed their truck. The truck next turned up, wrecked, in Jacksonville, Florida.

Henry Lee Lucas had no money and nowhere to turn in this new setting. He found a mission, a soup kitchen that offered food and shelter. As he was waiting his turn, Lucas was approached by a twenty-nine-year-old man. Their chance encounter would put the murder career of Henry Lee Lucas on unprecedented levels of depravity, when matched with Ottis Toole.

Like Lucas, Toole was brought up by dysfunctional parents. Born in Jacksonville, Toole was the son of an alcoholic who abandoned the family when Ottis was a child. The mother was a religious fanatic. The sister dressed the brother in girl's clothes as a playmate. Toole's grandmother, a would-be Satanist, called Ottis "the devil's child" and at times took him to the cemetery for human body parts that could be used in "magic" charms.

As a youngster, Ottis fled his home, only to return every time. While Henry Lee Lucas was never labeled as an idiot, Ottis, with an IQ of 75, was evaluated as one. He dropped out of school while in the eighth grade.

Like Lucas, Toole suffered from seizures. He got a thrill from burning empty houses in Jacksonville. "I just hated to see them standing there," he offered as a rationale. While the flames grew, he masturbated.

His first murder, by his own confession, was at age fourteen. Toole targeted a traveling salesman, drove him into the woods, and engaged in sex. When he "got nervous" afterward, he ran the salesman down with his own car.

However, his first arrest was for loitering, at age seventeen, followed by a series of petty thefts. He was married briefly—three days—when his wife walked out, turned off by her husband's homosexuality.

By the time Toole and Lucas met, the former had compiled a record of murders in several states. He was not arrested for any of those crimes. However, he had served time in Kentucky for car theft.

The two hit it off quickly, as they reminisced about their criminal histories. Toole brought Lucas home to share food and sex. They looked forward to a partnership in crime.

Toole invited Lucas to move in with his family in the Jacksonville suburb of Springfield. The family soon included Novella, Toole's wife, twenty-four years younger than Ottis. Novella was shared with Lucas and other men. "A few nights after marriage," Novella said, "he told me he would get nervous a lot, especially when he couldn't get a man. He'd get angry, he said, and then he couldn't get excited with a woman."

When Novella and Toole separated, Lucas and Toole moved in with the latter's mother, also residing with Toole's sister Drusilla Powell and her children Frank and Frieda. The deadly duo worked with a Jacksonville roofing company. When Lucas quit his job, he brought wrecked vehicles and parts into the backyard and had his own scrap metals business.

With more time now, Lucas developed a relationship with the twelve-year-old Frieda, whom he called Becky. Meanwhile the two escalated their deadly activities. They left bloody trails through the Midwest—in Indiana, Illinois, Michigan, and Wisconsin; in Canada; in the South and Southwest—in Georgia, Louisiana, New Mexico, and Texas.

Who was deadlier? During his confession, Toole boasted of the incident on the I-35 through Texas as illustrative. A teenage couple, whose car had run out of gas, were walking to a local filling station. Toole left his car, shot the boy nine times in the head and dumped the body into a culvert. Not to be outdone by his pal, Lucas dragged the girl into the car and raped her repeatedly as Toole drove. Angered at the one-upmanship, Toole stopped the vehicle, dragged the girl into the highway, shot the girl six times, and rode back to Jacksonville.

In another episode—without attribution of who did what—one girl was discovered, dumped in a field. The nude corpse had been stabbed thirty-five times in the back, neck, chest, and arms. She had deep cuts along the inside of her arms, and from the middle of the chest to the pubic bone. Both nipples had been cut off.

A sampling of their outlook can be seen in a dialogue between the two taped by Texas Rangers:

> Toole: Remember that one time I said I wanted me some ribs? Did that make me a cannibal?
>
> Lucas: You wasn't a cannibal. It's the force of a devil, something forced on us that we can't change. There's no denying that we can't change. There's no denying what we became. We know what we are.
>
> Toole: Remember how I liked to pour some blood out of them.
>
> Lucas: Ottis, you and I have something people look on as an animal. There's no way of changing what we done ...

During their wanderings, Lucas, his "child bride," and Toole found themselves in Texas, and were approached by a stranger, a member of a Pentecostal religious cult, the Hand of Death. He first offered them a "job" of delivering stolen cars to various locations. When the duo refused, he made them an offer they couldn't refuse: ten thousand dollars for each contract killing.

They went to Florida to meet the head of the cult, Don Meteric, who gave them an instant "training session." He told Lucas and Lee, "We worship the devil."

They were taught the finer points of arson, kidnapping, child abduction, and all techniques of murder. They were also schooled in preparing human sacrifices and other rituals, including necrophilia. They roared through the South, seeking children for sacrificial ceremonies or for sale to wealthy Mexican families. Some of the older victims were abducted, drugged, and used in pornographic movies created and distributed by Hand of Death.

Cult leaders had used Lucas and Toole extensively. Lucas was told to return home, while Toole remained for a while. Lucas and Becky set out for California, attempting to settle down as Mr. and Mrs. In the past, Lucas's craving for sex had been satisfied with rape, so any normal family life would have been difficult if not impossible.

While on many of their hitchhikes, the couple were noticed by a local businessman, Jack Smart. An owner of an antique shop in rural California, Smart felt sorry for the couple and took them to dinner at his home, offering them lodging in exchange for Lucas's helping at the shop.

Lucas did not abandon his murder sprees, but he became somewhat settled, working hard at the antique store, and was called on for varied jobs in the area. With an improved reputation, the Lucases were asked by Mrs. Smart to go to Ringgold, Texas, and care for her ailing mother, Kate "Granny" Rich, and maintain the house. Unfortunately, the couple spent the money on their own needs and neglected both Granny and the house. The Lucases were fired and asked to leave.

Their next destination was Wichita Falls, and once more hitchhiking led to a pickup. This episode would initiate a series of incidents that would eventually end the career of Henry Lucas. "Hello, I'm Ruben Moore. I am minister at Stoneburg. We call it the House of Prayer. It's a very religious community. You're welcome to live at my ranch."

Actually, Moore was a roofer and his House was little more than transformed chicken coops, and headquarters consisted of rundown shacks. Nevertheless, Lucas and Becky had nothing better available, so they agreed to join Moore and attend Sunday church services.

Henry Lucas worked while Becky underwent a complete change. The experience was uplifting. Apart from doing the daily chores of a housewife, she was embracing Christian values. She even returned to offer care to Granny Rich; in fact, she spent more time with her than she did with Henry. Lucas hardly took notice. However, Becky asked that they return to Florida, go to authorities, and begin a new life. Lucas was somewhat appeased when she assured him that the crimes of Henry and Toole would not be divulged.

Reluctantly, he agreed to pack and hitchhike to Florida in the summer of 1982. All such wanderings had been difficult, but this adventure seemed worse. They could not find a lodging and could not get a hitch. They decided to spend the night in an open field. Heavily drunk, Lucas opened a tirade: how he really didn't want to leave the House of Prayer, how he made friends in the religious community, how he had a decent job. And he had decided to return to Stoneburg.

Becky responded emotionally: how she wanted to turn around her life, even in a reformatory. The argument got heated. Finally, Becky slapped Henry hard across the face.

That was the end for Becky and the beginning of the end for Henry Lee Lucas. Impulsively, he reached for the knife in the bedroll and hit her smack in the chest. "That was it," he later told police. "I just stabbed her with my knife. I just picked it up, brought it around, and hit her right in the chest with it. She sort of set there for a little bit and then dropped on over."

He also told police that he cried because he had loved Becky. But that did not seem to enter into what followed. "I took her bra and panties off and had sex with her. That's one of those things I guess that got to be part of my life—having sexual intercourse with the dead."

What should be done with the body? He removed her ring from her finger and then cut the body into pieces. The remains were stuffed into three pillowcase. Two were placed in a shallow grave. The pillowcase that contained her legs was dragged and buried in the brush.

For the first time in his criminal career, Henry Lee Lucas felt pangs of remorse. Undoubtedly, he did love Becky, although his expressions were not the norm. In the past he had been clever in concealing clues or suspicions that would point the accusatory finger at him. This had now broken down.

It was back to the House of Prayer. Where was Becky? People asked. "Oh, Becky ran off with a trucker and went back to Florida," was his usual response.

The word of Henry's return reached the greater Stoneburg community. Granny Rich reacted with the greatest excitement. Becky had been her favorite. He agreed to visit Granny and talk about Becky. The plan was then to take her to church services.

Before church, they drove into Oklahoma to buy beer. They drove, drank, spoke for hours. Unfortunately, they missed the services, so they started back to Ringgold, Texas. The conversation became irritating to Henry. Granny could not believe that Becky would run off. Once more. Henry Lee Lucas had his fill. He stopped the car, got out onto a deserted road, and plunged his knife into the widow. After she collapsed, he carved an inverted cross on her chest, had sex with the corpse, and dumped her into a culvert.

Why had he done this? Lucas doesn't remember except for the irritating questions. When Moore queried Lucas about Granny, he said that she was sick and could not attend church.

It was then time to return to the scene of the crime. Collecting several garbage bags, Lucas drove to the scene. He cut the remains into small pieces, put them in the bags, and returned to the ranch. Taking the bags into the House of Prayer kitchen, Lucas burned the body parts in the wood stove. He took Moore's car before sunrise and left, headed for California. Moore knew that Lucas was the last to see Kate Rich alive.

Granny's relatives worried when they could not contact her, so they drove to her home and contacted local sheriff William Conway, known in Montague County as "Hound Dog." He interviewed the relatives and learned that Lucas was the last to see Granny alive. They also told Conway that he had stolen money from Granny. Conway then contacted Moore at the House of Prayer, who corroborated the fact that Henry Lee Lucas had been with Granny before her death.

Conway ran a criminal records check on Lucas and learned of his history of rape and murder and outstanding warrants for parole violations. Hound Dog circulated an arrest order.

However, Lucas was no longer under Conway's jurisdiction or in Texas, He went to California to visit Granny Rich's daughter, hoping to find employment and lodging. But Granny's relatives thought Lucas might be headed there and tipped off police. Meanwhile, Conway had put a trace on the car Lucas had taken from Moore. The car was found, with dried blood on the front seat. The vehicle was impounded. California police went to Smart's antique shop and took Lucas into custody as a witness in the case.

Lucas told police that the blood was his own, having cut himself. Conway contacted Granny's relatives and learned that her blood type was A. The blood in the car was O, matching Lucas's blood type.

California police released Lucas. He then fled to New Mexico, Oklahoma, Missouri, Indiana, and Illinois. He arrived in Decatur, Illinois, applied for a job at a construction site, and applied for welfare benefits.

Hitchhiking once again, Lucas hitched a ride to Missouri and was dropped off at a truck stop. He noticed a woman traveling alone. He quickly approached her from behind and warned her, "Get in the car and be quiet." She drove south for the rest of the day. As the woman slept, he took over the driving.

What followed was the last murder of Henry Lee Lucas. "I was drivin'," he told police, "and I felt this chill come over me and I knew she was goin' to die." He drove off the highway onto a back road in Magnolia, Texas. He took out his knife and stabbed the woman in the neck. As she grabbed her neck, he stabbed her a second time. He then dragged the body from the car, cut the clothing off, and had sex with the corpse.

He stripped the body of valuables and IDs, dragged the corpse to a grove of pine trees, and left, without burying or even covering the body. He went back to the car and head south for Texas.

He abandoned the car in Fredericksburg. To distance himself even more from the murder scene, he hitched a ride north and dropped off in Bloomington, home of the University of Indiana. Too conspicuous in a college town, he headed back for Texas.

Lucas called Moore and said that he needed lodging. He told him that he had been searching for Becky but ran out of funds. Moore refused. Knowing that the police were looking for Lucas, Moore contacted Conway, who urged the religious leader to invite Lucas to Stoneburg.

Moore sent Lucas one hundred dollars for return to the House of Prayer. Conway learned that Lucas was wanted in Maryland for the theft of his brother-in-law's truck. When Lucas returned to Stoneburg, he was greeted by Moore and, a day later, by Conway. However, Maryland police told Conway that no way would they issue an extradition for such a petty crime as car theft.

Lucas met with Moore on June 4, 1983, and told the religious leader that he wanted "to clear his name" by finding Becky Powell and Granny Rich. But Lucas made one final mistake. He left his gun with Moore. When Lucas returned on June 11, he was arrested for illegally possessing a firearm. Four days later, in what he called a "religious conversion," he summoned a guard. "I've done some bad things."

The confessional and jailing periods could not be separated from the crimes and confessions of Ottis Toole. As discussed, they acted as a team. Ironically, Toole had been jailed a few days earlier in Florida.

In tracing the odyssey of Toole after his separation from Lucas in the beginning of 1982, the narrative shows no slackening in Toole's criminal activity. He felt betrayed by the permanent absence of Henry Lee and Becky. He went on his own wanderings, supposedly responsible for nine victims in six states.

It was his arson activities that finally brought him down. In May 1983, two houses were burned in his Jacksonville neighborhood. Two teenage accomplices turned in Toole. He was arrested in June and confessed to have set some forty fires through twenty years.

Both Lucas and Toole had been arrested, and the confessional process was under way. Lucas first confessed to the murder of Granny Rich, then Becky Powell, and over the next eighteen months, one hundred others, later three hundred, and finally six hundred. All this was apart from the murders carried out together with Toole.

He was explicit in detailing the locations and methods of murder: knives; a variety of guns—rifles, Magnums, 367s, 38s, 22s; their own automobiles; nylon rope; a roofer's axe; a framing hammer; table legs; vases; statues; items of clothing; vacuum cleaner cords; telephone cords.

The arrest and confessions of Lucas brought to the forefront the creation of the National Center for the Analysis of Violent Crime (NCAVC). While Lucas was wandering, NCVAC was established by police throughout America to set up a national crime computer. According to Colin Wilson and Damon Wilson in *The Killers Among Us*, the confessions of Lucas showed that the "wandering killer" was obviously a new type of menace. Suddenly, every newspaper in America was talking about serial killers.

But how many did he kill? Were the confessions truthful? A few weeks after confessing to Becky Powell's murder, he stunned a Texas court by pleading not guilty. Once more, he was crafty and cunning.

"The old Henry Lee Lucas, the Enemy of Society, was reappearing," wrote Colin and Damon Wilson. "He could no longer kill at random when he felt the urge, but he could still satisfy his craving for control over victims by playing with his captors like a cat with mice."

Yet law officials and journalists all did not fall for his plots. At times he confessed to two murders in the same day—impossible because the areas of the crime were too far apart.

On the other hand, his insistence on innocence did not convince the court. In October 1983 he was convicted for seventy-five years for the killing of Granny Rich. A month later he received life imprisonment for the murder of Becky Powell. What followed were another seventy-five-year sentence, four additional life sentences, an added sixty-six years, and, finally, the death sentence.

Law officials nationwide sought to find out from Lucas whom he had killed as a means of putting to rest a string of unsolved murders. In October 1983, officials in Ouachita Parish in Louisiana convened a conference to solve some sixty-nine cases in ten states.

In attendance were eighty investigators from twenty states. In addition to Louisiana, other states were Texas, Florida, Colorado, Alabama, Nevada, California, New Mexico, Michigan, Wisconsin, Maryland, Arizona, Utah, Oregon, South Dakota, Minnesota, Oklahoma, Kansas, Illinois, and Montana.

Many of Lucas's confessions took place in Williamson County, Texas. In the foreword to *Hand of Death*, county sheriff James "Jim" Boutwell spoke of the breakthroughs in the case. It revealed the "mobility" of crime in the United States:

"Local law enforcement agencies can no longer afford to be restricted by the old jurisdictional lines. The continuing investigation being conducted by the Henry Lucas Homicide Task Force is demonstrating the necessity of expanded police action ..."

The difficulty with assessing the truth of his confessions was that for every deceptive story, many were proven true. The murder of hitchhiker "Orange Socks" is very illuminating. The victim was so named because all she was wearing when found was one pair of dirty pumpkin-colored socks, each bunched around her ankle. The body was found in October 1979. After his arrest, he related how he and Toole had picked up a girl, seeming to correspond with Orange Socks. When she refused to have sex, he strangled her.

He confessed to the crime on three other occasions, but later he said that he had lied. And the circumstances proved this: Evidence—work records and a cashed check—pointed to his not being in Williamson County when the murder was committed.

The details surrounding the murder of Debra Sue Williamson in August 1975 also dented holes in claims that Lucas was America's greatest serial killer. When asked about the murder by a Lubbock official, he confessed to the crime. However, when the stepfather and mother, Bob and Joyce Lemons, read the confession and absorbed the details, they announced, "This man did not kill our daughter. No way."

The *Texas Monthly* of September 1984 asked in its headline: "True Confessions?" Joseph Nocera reported, "Lucas has claimed that he killed upwards of three hundred women across the country, all of them in gruesome fashion … In many of his confessions, he has recited the details of years-old murders with such uncanny accuracy that some law enforcement officials believe Lucas has a photographic memory for murder."

However, the Williamson case raises the strong possibility, according to Nocera and other journalists, that Lubbock police and other Texas police "are using Henry Lee Lucas's willingness to confess as a means of closing the books on long-unsolved murders."

On the other side, continues Nocera, it was to Lucas's advantage to feed police information. "And it's a good deal for Lucas too—as long as he keeps parceling out a confession here and a confession there, he gets to stay alive … About once a week, he is flown somewhere by the Texas Rangers to talk to local police officers about murders they haven't solved; he gets three square meals a day, including hamburger and malts when he's on the road; and in general he seems to enjoy

Depravity

being the center of so much attention. Recent photos of him show him relaxed, smiling, and with a bit of potbelly."

Adding to the truth versus hoax confessions was the role of Hugh Aynesworth, a reporter for the *Dallas Times*. In 1985 he wrote a series about the false confessions. But in 1983 he signed a contract to author Lucas's biography and followed with a Lucas interview in *Penthouse*. It has been suggested that the journalist's reversal was the killer's signed contract for his story with a Waco used-car dealer. Aynesworth lost his contract and the theory was that the journalist wanted to throttle any book that would not be his.

And then, there was the question: was the crime that of Lucas, of Lucas and Toole, or of Toole? Investigators lucked out in this matter. Lucas took credit for murders, omitting mention of Toole, and vice versa. In fact, Lucas fingered Toole for the murder of George Sonnenberg, who had died in a fire set in Jacksonville. Toole poured gasoline on the man's mattress and lit the fire.

Toole admitted to 25 murders in 11 states and joined with Lucas in 108 other homicides. The most sensational murder was that of Adam Walsh. Toole cleared his partner. However, the revelation came out because the duo was "singing."

According to Jacksonville Police Chief Samuel D. Martin, "Toole got upset with Lucas, who was involving him in murders he didn't think he should have talked about. So he got upset and decided he would implicate Lucas in some."

Adam and his mother were shopping at the Hollywood (Florida) Mall in July 1981. Adam, six, was left alone in a video-game display area of the Sears store while she went shopping for lamps. Adam was gone when she returned.

Toole had taken the youngster out to the turnpike and lured him into his car with promises of candy and toys. Adam's severed head was found in a Florida canal. The full details were "grisly."

Police launched a nationwide search, but it was the investigation of Lucas that led to the resolution of the abduction and murder and the enactment of the Missing Children Act. It required the Federal Bureau of Investigation to keep more detailed records on missing children, facilitating parental search for their children.

As for Toole, Assistant Chief Leroy Hessler said the hardened serial killer cried in his confession about the Walsh killing. "Of all he talked about, this was the only homicide that really bothered him." Added Hessler, "There are certain details only he could know. He did it. I've got details that no one else would know. He's got me convinced."

In a bizarre twist, the police changed their position several weeks later. Toole was "no longer a suspect" in the murder, they announced.

But the Walsh confession did lead to other confessions, said Police Chief Martin. "He gave details of murders he and Lucas committed. The details make Charles Manson sound like Tom Sawyer or Huck Finn."

At the time of the confession, Toole had been on death row in a Florida prison for the deaths of Sonnenberg and for the murder of nineteen-year-old Ada Johnson in Tallahassee. But on appeal, both were commuted to life imprisonment. He pleaded guilty in 1991 to an additional four slayings and was given four more life sentences.

The Walsh case remained open over the years, and, in fact, was being reviewed when Toole died of cirrhosis in 1996. The police were red-faced when all traces of DNA evidence disappeared from the files.

As a result of his son's murder, John Walsh became a leading voice for missing and exploited children and established the Adam Walsh Child Resource Center. He became the host of *America's Most Wanted*, a television program that began in 1988, to publicize and bring to justice fugitive crime suspects.

In December, 2008, newspaper headlines across the country announced that Florida police closed the case and concluded that Toole was the murderer. Said John Walsh, "We needed to know… and today we know. The not knowing has been torture. But that journey's over."

But is it really over? In the last week of December, a story in the *Miami Herald* by David Smiley said that doubts remain. Smiley writes,

Depravity

"The announcement drew instant questions from critics who say the evidence against Toole has been shaky, at best, from the start, and who note that police never charged him while he was alive."

Criminal profiler Pat Brown said, "I was appalled, absolutely appalled. There is no reason to close the case without sufficient evidence that one particular person has committed the crime."

In her book *Vampires of Crime*, Sondra London observed that psychiatrists had determined that Ottis Toole was schizophrenic, psychopathic, and retarded.

Sondra London had the following conversation with Toole:

"What do psychiatrists and doctors say about you, Ottis?"

"They can't figure theyself out, less figure me out. They got to figure theyself out 'fore they can figure me out."

London analyzed Toole from biological, psychological, sexual, social, and spiritual perspectives. Dr. Joel Norris, author of *Serial Killers: The Growing Menace*, was also an art therapist who encouraged Toole to draw.

In all his drawings, Toole produced disembodied heads, which Norris interpreted as a disjointure of mind and body. "The best way I can describe Ottis," said one of his defense attorneys, "is that he represents the lower end of the gene pool." His IQ is borderline retarded—between 54 and 75.

A homosexual, Toole was raped as a youngster. "Well, I was raped when I was a little kid," he said. "A real little kid, about six years old. I told my mother about it and she said he wouldn't do anything like that you know."

London identified Toole as a "member of the lowest social stratum of the poorest part of the country." London notes the Southern attitude against blacks, but more despicable is "poor white trash," which have always been considered the absolute dregs of society."

The cannibalism discussed above, writes London, "was a perverse sacrament first learned at the altar of the devil-worshipping cult he was inducted into" from birth.

Echoing the response of Toole, London concludes: "Before we understand the likes of Ottis Toole, it is truly necessary for us to examine ourselves and to face the unpleasant evidence of the growing epidemic of the breakdown of the social fabric into the impersonal violence that is everywhere we look."

While the book on Toole was closed with his death in 1996, the narrative of Lucas went through twists and turns for twenty years until his death from a heart attack in prison in 2001. Lucas was "toying" with authorities about the number of murders he had actually committed, alone or in combination with Toole, so no one can really determine the truth.

During the episode involving the Lemons, Vic Feazell, District Attorney of Waco, was investigating Lucas for three murders that he had confessed to—without witnesses, fingerprints, or any forensic evidence. Feazell confronted Lucas, who announced with pleasure, "I was wonderin' when somebody was goin' to get wise to this."

The press was incensed at Feazell's withdrawal of charges. The FBI investigated the DA, searched his house: Feazell was accused of all sorts of charges, was cleared, and came home with a record damage award of fifty-eight million dollars.

Colin and Damon Wilson are convinced that certainly the confessions of the murders of Becky Powell and Kate "Granny" Rich were truthful; many of the confessions of other killings on his own and in duo with Toole were truthful. Beyond that, the Wilsons have theorized this scenario:

"As the confessions brought notoriety and comfort, he became aware of the benefits of being a 'star,' and began to wonder now he could maintain his status without the inevitable penalty of the electric chair. The answer was to continue confessing to more murders, and to hope, that sooner or later, these confessions would be recognized as lies, and that this would throw doubt on the murders for which he had been convicted."

By 1998, Lucas had confessed to six hundred murders; many had been recanted. Lucas was serving five life sentences, in addition to two hundred ten years for the murder of Orange Socks and eight other murders in Texas. A death sentence set for that June was for the murder of Orange Socks. District Attorney Ken Anderson, who was prosecutor in that case, was convinced Lucas had killed anywhere from three to one hundred twenty people. "I don't think he knew exactly. It's difficult to imagine you can rely on anything he says, but the fact remains he is a serial killer even though we're are unable to pinpoint the exact number." Former Texas attorney general Jim Mattox gave the devil Lucas his due: "After you've dealt with the individual, you had to give him some credit for being able to engage in the kind of hoax he was engaged in."

Surprise and shock greeted Texas Governor George Bush's announcement that he was commuting the death sentence to life in prison. During Bush's six years as Governor, one hundred fifty-two were executed; Lucas was the only exception. Bush followed the recommendation of the Texas Board of Pardons and Parole because of evidence that Lucas was in Florida when Orange Socks was killed in Texas.

"As a supporter of the death penalty for those who commit horrible crimes," said the governor, " I feel a special obligation to make sure the State of Texas never executes a person for a crime they may not have committed. I take this action so that all Texas can continue to trust the integrity and fairness of our criminal justice system."

Jim Choate, husband of one of the victims, and other family members of other Lucas murder victims, met in Houston to criticize the decision. "Governor Bush," said Choate, "let him slip the noose and here we are, victims still hurting because justice has never been done ... I'd actually let them turn him over to Florida and let them fry him. They ought to beat the hell out of him for lying six hundred times."

Was Henry Lee Lucas America's most prolific serial killer? We may never know. But the Wilsons concluded he "achieved what he always wanted: a place in American history."

LEONARD LAKE AND CHARLES NG

Sex Slave Masters

Leonard Lake and Charles Ng are not unique as team killers because serial killer history had produced other team serial killers. The sixteen in this book include Martha Beck and Raymond Fernandez and Henry Lee Lucas and Ottis Toole. The Lake-Ng partnership differed from the others. The addition of Beck to Fernandez's operations gave a different dimension to his activities. In the Lucas-Toole jointure, the latter enhanced Lucas's well-advanced criminal career. In fact, Toole broke off the partnership after traveling together for less than two years.

On the other hand, Lake and Ng, both ex-Marines, were both morally bankrupt in their own right, but were not killers. However, when fused they flourished in the forefront of sadistic and depraved serial killers, whose trade was sex slaves.

Collectively and individually, Lake and Ng call attention to intriguing facets of serial killer history. The upbringing of Lake indeed contributed to his later degeneracy. However, Ng's parents, perhaps too strict, were middle class and gave their son a boarding school education.

Ng was born in Hong Kong. The Asiatic serial killer represents about 1 percent of all serial killers. While Ng was educated in England and Lake had less formal schooling, both were intelligent individuals, not an uncommon trait among serial killers.

The continuing saga of Ng through the courts has demonstrated the high costs of serial killer justice. The costs to date have been estimated at twenty million dollars to the public. No wonder one prosecuting attorney bitterly remarked about the case: "The justice system in America has gone haywire."

Leonard Lake was born in 1946 in San Francisco, child of an unhappy marriage. His mother was worried about the family tree: a history of mental illness and alcoholism. With funds running low and increasing debts, the father sent Leonard to live with his grandparents.

Unfortunately, the grandfather was an alcoholic himself and was a rigid disciplinarian, with a militaristic approach that stressed punishment. The young Lake told friends and relatives that he felt rejected and abandoned by his family.

Still, Leonard maintained contact with his parents, whose influence was negative. The father disciplined the son; the mother promoted a sense of pride in the human body, best realized through photographing nude girls, including sisters and cousins. The mother's encouragement advanced Lake's obsession with pornography.

While in his early teens, Lake intensified his photography of nude women. Norris notes that Lake "took pictures of pretty young girls all of his life and kept them in picture albums like a hunter keeps a trophy." He enjoyed these "successes," which he equated with domination over women.

Brother Donald was overprotected by the mother, experienced a head trauma, exhibited cruelty to animals, set fires, and sexually assaulted his sisters. To protect the sisters from Donald, Leonard extorted sexual favors.

In his treatment of serial killers, Norris examined "the serial killer profile." Norris examined twenty-one behavioral patterns. Lake's was compulsivity, developed as a youth. He was always clean and neat at home. He showered several times a day, and before starting any activity, he would thoroughly wash his hands. When he launched his career as serial murderer, he made victims shower before they were raped and murdered.

In addition, Norris speaks of Lake's "early signs of hypergraphia" [excessive writing; disorganized writing; writing without logical reason—often associated with epilepsy] and obsession with precise details in experiments with mice and rats. Early on, he became a self-trained geneticist, writes Norris:

"He traced the life cycle of mice from conception to death and kept detailed notes on the various stages of their development. He kept records of which pairs of mice bred from which litters, and was able to trace genetic features through many successive generations of offspring."

According to the 1984 *Journal of Mental Deficiency Research*, four types of hypergraphia have been found: excessive comprehensible writing; excessive legible but incomprehensible writing; repetition of the same symbol; and scribbling.

Writing in the November 17, 2001, issue of *New Scientist*, Alison Motluk cites the research of Dr. Eric Altschuler, a neuroscientist at the University of Califormia at San Diego. Motluk describes Altschuler's findings:

"People with the disease [temporal lobe epilepsy] experience partial seizures, often accompanied by a dreamy feeling that things are not quite as they should be. Patients are often misdiagnosed with psychiatric problems. Neurologically, Ezekiel [Prophet] displayed some obvious signs of epilepsy, such as frequent fainting spells... not being able to speak."

When nineteen, Lake joined the Marines during the Vietnam conflict and trained as a radar operator. He served a noncombatant tour in Da Nang. Medical records reveal hospitalization for "exhibiting incipient psychotic reactions. He was treated and returned to his unit to complete the tour of duty. However, after a few months he was evaluated as suffering from "unspecified medical problems" and returned to El Toro Marine Base in Orange County, California.

Having served for some seven years, Leonard Lake was discharged on medical grounds, earning the Vietnam Service Medal, a Vietnam Campaign Medal, and two other medals for good conduct.

Lake returned to San Jose. He entered the Oakland Veteran's Administration Hospital and was treated for "psychological problems." Upon release, he enrolled and took a few courses at San Jose State University. Those who knew Lake during the first years after return from Vietnam spoke of a concerned neighbor who taught youngsters in a local 4-H Club, who gave of his time as a volunteer firefighter in Philo, and who worked for a community group that offered free insulation to senior citizens who had no funds to maintain their home.

However, most neighbors have other memories of the late seventies. He married and became known to neighbors as a survivalist and weirdo sex freak who boasted of sex bondage exploits. His wife divorced him after learning that he was filming bondage scenes featuring handcuffs, leather straps, and shackles. In 1980 he was placed on one-year's probation on a grand theft charge of stealing weatherizing material from a construction site.

Lake married again, meeting his spouse at the Renaissance Fair in Marin County. Lake was operating a stall, hoping to attract visitors who would take a photo with a goat that he had disguised as a unicorn.

They married in 1981 and took up residence on a communal ranch in the foothills of Ukiah, California. It was ideally suited for swindling, whoring, and wife swapping. Lake allegedly grew marijuana on the ranch, called Alibi Run. He also collected automatic weapons.

The second Mrs. Lake was an appropriate partner. Supposedly, she had been fired as teacher's aide at Anderson Valley High School in Boonville because she allegedly taught children how to make explosives.

In 1982, federal agents stormed the ranch and arrested Lake for firearms violations. Freed on bail, Lake became Charley Gunner and retreated to a ranch in Wilseyville in the Sierra Nevada. The ranch had been purchased for the Lakes by their families for their future retirement. However, Lake had other designs: a center of depravity. On one level, it was a "survivalist enclosure" fortified with ammunition to thwart the "siege," with the approaching nuclear genocide.

But the heart of their activities was the torture chamber centered around "sex slaves." Victims were drawn to the ranch by classified ads that promised jobs, sale of video equipment, or sale of cars. He also became immersed in mythological figures Odin and Valhalla. He described himself as "co-creator of the unicorns." He worked for those who grafted the single horn onto the head of a goat that became part of the Barnum & Bailey Circus.

His second wife divorced him in 1983, tired of hiding and drifting to avoid police. However, Leonard Lake had found another partner. They met in 1983; details have not been verified. One version is that Charles Ng answered an ad that Lake had placed in a survivalist magazine. Another story is that Ng, while in military custody, had attempted escape from an armory. Ng was pointed out to Lake by a mutual acquaintance. Lake helped Ng hide from authorities.

Charles Ng was born in Hong Kong into a wealthy family. No evidence of parental abuse has ever been advanced. But Ng was expelled from school and tossed out of an exclusive boarding school in England after he was caught stealing from other students as well as from a department store. He returned to Hong Kong and obtained a student visa to study at Notre Dame College in Belmont, California. One semester was enough for Ng.

After an arrest for shoplifting, he enlisted in the Marines. After four years of duty, in 1981, he had been promoted to the rank of lance corporal. But he, along with two others, was arrested for stealing eleven thousand dollars' worth of automatic weapons from a marine arsenal in Hawaii.

He escaped from custody before trial and was listed as deserter when he teamed up with Lake. On the surface, the jointure seemed unlikely because Lake was a racist who did resent African Americans and Hispanics.

After Lake and Ng were arrested by federal agents for firearms violations, Lake jumped bail; however, as a Marine deserter, Ng was not granted bail, but he agreed to a plea bargain that reduced the fourteen-year-sentence to three. He was paroled after eighteen months at Leavenworth, the government unaware that he was not an American citizen; otherwise he would have been deported.

Meanwhile, Lake was strengthening his sexual operations in the bunker. The first murder, however, was unrelated to the sexual activities. His brother, Donald, never returned from a visit to the ranch in 1984. Leonard Lake had once told their mother, "The world would be better off without Don."

A sign was posted on a car outside the ranch: "If you love something, set it free. If it doesn't come back, hunt it down and kill it."

Lake was keeping a journal of activities on the ranch. The memoirs began, "Leonard Lake, a name not seen or used much these days in my second year as a fugitive. Most dull day-to-day routine—still with death in my pocket and fantasy my goal."

His beliefs were clear about women. They had victimized him, and in the era of a post-nuclear genocide, they would have to serve him. He sought sexually attractive women, sexually tortured them, and then killed them. Males were killed if they were companions of the women, or if they had cash or credit cards. Children, if accompanying the women, were also killed.

He wrote in his diary, "God meant women for cooking, cleaning house, and sex. And when they are not in use, they should be locked up."

The sordid deeds were on video. One example of directions to a victim: "While you're here you'll wash for us. That's your choice in a nutshell. It's not much of a choice unless you have a death wish. You'll probably think worse things in the next few weeks."

In June 1985, employees in a San Francisco lumberyard reported a seemingly routine shoplifting incident. Ng had walked out of the store with a $75 vise, put it in the trunk of the pair's Honda, and ran away before the police could nab him. Unsuccessfully, Lake tried to pacify the police by offering to pay for the vise.

Lake produced a driver's license that read "Robin Stapley." The car was registered in the name of Paul Cosner, a founding member of the San Diego chapter of the Guardian Angels, also missing after having visited the ranch. Along with the vise, police also found a .22-caliber pistol and booked Lake on theft and weapons charges. At the police station, Lake revealed nothing. The stocky, bearded suspect asked for a glass of water and paper and pencil.

He took out a cyanide pill, swallowed it with water, and wrote a note to his ex-wife Cricket Balazs:

"I love you. Please forgive me. I forgive you. Please tell Mama, Fern [sister], and Patty [sister] I'm sorry."

Lake then gave the police his true identity, slumped over, and died four days later without ever regaining consciousness. The police also learned that Robin Stapley had been missing for months, and Lake had taken the victim's identity.

Now the police set out to find out who Leonard Lake was, and in the process learn of the sordid activities at the ranch, and who Charles Ng was, what his role in the tortures was, and where he was now.

Why was Lake carrying the cyanide pill? According to Norris, "His dreams of success had eluded him. He admitted to himself that his boasts about heroic deeds in Vietnam were all delusions, and the increasing number of victims he was burying in the trench behind his bunker only added to his unhappiness.

"Lake had reached the final stage of the serial murderer syndrome; he realized that he had come to a dead end with nothing but his own misery to show for it. And he performed the final act of execution upon himself. He had prepared for it in advance by carrying the cyanide pill with him."

Police were not prepared for the revelations on the ranch. The diary was filled with the tortuous fantasies conceived by Lake. Caches of weapons were revealed. More shocking, indeed, were the videotapes showing women being abused and tortured by both Lake and Ng.

More gruesome was the finding of burnt fragments of many bones—forty-five pounds—and human teeth, partial remains of missing men, women, and children. One of the members of the body-search team was Terry Parker, a local coroner.

"When we started digging," he said, "we didn't have a clue what we were getting into, but more and more evidence kept turning up—a bone here, a shoe there, an entire body in a ditch. It got to the point where you were thinking, 'Am I walking on someone's remains now? There could be more under every rock. How much longer could this go on?'"

When the press learned of the search for bodies, everyone expected another media circus like that of the search for Dean Corll's victims in the seventies. However, that did not happen. The usually sensational press seemed "oddly subdued," said Colin Wilson and Damon Wilson. "It was as if the sheer horror of the details was too much even for the most news-hungry editor."

The grisly five-day totals were the bodies of seven men, three women, and two baby boys. All told, there were body parts of some twenty-six victims. Police suggested that up to twenty-five people, previously reported missing, might have been murdered in or around the compound. Identification was extremely difficult because most of the bodies had been cut up, burnt, and diffused around the site.

Hoping for positive identification, the district attorney's office released fifteen photographs to the news media. Twelve were identified, including Donald Lake, brother of Leonard Lake, and Charles Gunnar, his best pal from the Vietnam years.

A warrant was issued for the arrest of Charles Ng for twelve murders. Two video segments are illustrative of his ranch activities. In one, Ng is ripping off the shirt of Brenda O'Connor, one of the victims. He takes a knife, cuts off her brassiere, and warns her, "You can cry and stuff like all the rest of them, but it won't do you no good. We're pretty cold-hearted."

In a second tape, Ng in a reclining chair tells of plans at the ranch. "What I want is an off-the-shelf sex partner. I want to be able to use a woman any way I want. I want to be able to simply put her away."

California State Attorney General John Van de Kamp was convinced of Ng's significant involvement in the serial murders. The evidence was documented in Lake's diary and videotapes. However, Van de Kamp admitted, "Unless we can locate Ng and get him to talk, the chances are slim that we'll never know everything that went on out there. It has become a case so overwhelming, so enormous, and so gruesome that our computer system hasn't been able to keep up with it."

The FBI were successful in tracing Ng's movements after fleeing San Francisco. Cricket Balasz had driven him to the airport, and he boarded an American Airlines plane to Chicago. Upon arrival, he checked into the Chateau Hotel as Mike Kimoto. The next route took Ng to Detroit, where he met an unidentified friend, and then crossed the border into Canada.

Wanted posters went up throughout Canada. One informant told the FBI he had spotted a man fitting Ng's description in a bus station restroom in Chatham, Ontario. Another witness caught Ng in another restroom shaving off his sideburns and eyebrows. One call from Chicago told of driving a hitchhiker with Ng's description from Chicago to a motel in Chatham.

Canadian authorities concentrated on the Vancouver area of British Columbia. From there, Ng could drift to the Pacific Coast and then journey back to his native Hong Kong. Charles Ng had now eluded authorities for more than a month.

But his weakness did him in. He could not resist shoplifting. In early July 1985, he entered a Hudson Bay store in Calgary and left with groceries, unpaid, in a backpack. In fact, he was seen slipping a bottle of soda water under his coat.

Two security guards stopped and challenged him. One guard was shot in the hand, while the other guard, reinforced by Calgary police, overpowered Ng and brought him into custody, into the Calgary Metropolitan Police station. Ng was charged with robbery, attempted robbery, possession of a firearm, and attempted murder.

Immediately, the Calgary authorities placed Ng at the Calgary Remand Centre under a twenty-four-hour suicide watch. Law officials were convinced that Lake and Ng had agreed to commit hara-kiri rather than confess and sit in jail.

California officials flew to Canada to interview Ng. Faced with a mountain of evidence, Ng blamed all on his deceased buddy, although admitting to having disposed of one body. Canadian justice needed to be served first, said Calgary officials. Ng was found guilty of aggravated assault, robbery, and illegal use of firearms. This added up to four and a half years in prison.

California was not impressed. The murder charges against Ng called for death at San Quentin. But California and the U.S. Department of Justice were thwarted. The Canadian Minister of Justice, John Cosbie, declared that a 1976 extradition treaty with the U.S. precluded extradition. Having done away with capital punishment in 1976, Canada would not extradite any prisoner charged with a capital crime that called for the death penalty.

A six-year battle ensued before Ng would be extradited to California. George Deukjemian, the governor of California, wrote to Canadian Prime Minister Brian Mulroney asking for extradition. To allow Ng to stay in Canada, the governor argued, "could have the unfortunate consequence of making Canada a haven for death-penalty fugitives."

Relatives of the murdered were embittered by the Canadian position. "It's fine for your country to have no death penalty, if that's what you want," said Sharon Sellito, mother of Paul Cosner, a car salesman murdered at the ranch. "But why are you making it applicable across the border?"

While Canada had the moral obligation to deliver Ng to America, at least Canada could demand that fugitives not be killed, reasoned

Henry Schwartz, director of the capital punishment project of the American Civil Liberties Union.

Ng was represented by Calgary attorney Donald W. MacLeod. He insisted that many Californians were opposed to the death penalty. "There are a great many people opposed to the death penalty in the very state that seeks to prosecute Charles Ng to death," he said.

In 1988, the Alberta Court of Queens Bench ruled that Ng could be extradited without assurances that Ng would not be subject to the death penalty. The court ruled that it was "satisfied beyond a reasonable doubt" that Ng participated in "a general conspiracy that related to weapons, money, and sexual gratification." Ng appealed the ruling, which was scheduled for hearing by the Supreme Court of Canada.

Amnesty International opposed the death penalty, so it opposed extradition, which would violate the extradition treaty and the Canadian Charter of Rights and Freedoms, guaranteeing the right to life, liberty, and history "except in accordance with the principle of fundamental justice."

Beyond extraditing Ng, many Canadian officials wanted extradition laws revised. "If the Supreme Court of Canada decides we have a moral obligation to protect Mr. Ng from execution, we're going to have a flood of potential death row inmates escaping from your beautiful country and coming to Canada," said William Domm, a member of the Canadian Parliament sponsoring changes in the law.

In September 1991, the Canadian Supreme Court ruled that Canada could extradite Ng without assurances that he would not be subject to the death penalty. Ng was flown to McClellan Air Force base and transferred to Folsom Prison. That commenced the most drawn-out criminal proceedings in American criminal history.

Once back in California, another seven years would pass before the trial of Ng opened. Ng and his defense exploited all legal loopholes in the legal system to stall justice. Ng continued to dismiss attorneys, filing malpractice suits against them for incompetence (at one point he applied for the right to represent himself but withdrew the application).

The defense also challenged the competence and impartiality of judges, moved successfully for change of venue from Calaveras County, and demanded that prison conditions—notably bad food—be improved.

To support their motion for change of venue, the defense put forward an independent survey that revealed 95 percent of Calaveras County residents already considered Ng guilty of the ranch murders.

When the case was moved in 1995 to destitute Orange County, hundreds of hours over ten years had been devoted to the case. More than six hundred witnesses had been interviewed. Three rooms were needed for the case files.

According to William Kelley, public defender, the case had already cost more than six million dollars. The defense needed another two years.

"This will be one of the most expensive trials in California's history," said Carl Holmes, the county's deputy public defender. In short, the public defender's office insisted that it could not continue unless the state attorney general and county would cover all costs. They agreed.

During the pretrial proceedings, Ng was housed in a small cage between appearances. When a federal magistrate called the cage "barbarous," the cage was removed. Before the case opened, Ng had appeared before six judges. The cost had now soared to ten million dollars.

Talk shows featured incensed state attorneys. "This is just one of those situations where you have a defendant intent on using every mechanism for delay," said Alameda County District Attorney Tom Orloff. That interview followed Ng's complaint that his glasses "were the wrong prescription." In addition, prison practices had deprived him of his need to practice origami, the art of paper folding.

Judge John J. Ryan had enough. In August 1998, he verbally lashed out at Ng and accused him of "playing games within games within games." Ng had also seen enough. He cursed the judge and the legal system. While prosecutors saw the chastisement as further proof of Ng's manipulating the legal system, the defense was heartened because Ng's outburst highlighted his mental illness.

Depravity

The case opened in October 1998. Ng's defense was simple. Lake was the killer, not he. The trial itself lasted eight months.

After thirteen years of delay, the opening statements seemed anticlimactic. The state presented its case in fifty minutes; the defense took fifty-four minutes.

State prosecutor Sharlene Honnaka told the families and friends of the victims, the media, and the jury how Lake and Ng selected and abducted victims, bringing them to the Wilseyville compound for torture, rape, and murder.

The prosecutor selected choice chilling videos found at the site that showed both Lake and Ng had abused and tortured victims. In particular, there was footage of Kathleen Allen and Brenda O'Connor. In the latter video, Brenda begged Lake to tell her about her baby. Lake tells her, "Your baby is sound asleep like a rock." Both mother and baby were murdered.

Photographs and stolen property were submitted as evidence linking both Lake and Ng to the crimes. In addition, the state presented a long line of witnesses, many of whom recited the sordid nature and demented fantasies of Charles Ng.

For example, one acquaintance recalled a conversation with Ng: "You should hear the screams; sometimes I have to gag them because they scream so hard I can't hear myself."

The jury also heard of the Lake-Ng creed and a ghastly example. The creed was "if you love something, set it free. If it doesn't come back, hunt it down and kill it." Lake and Ng played a power game in which they freed some of their victims, and let them run into the woods, only to hunt them as if they were wild beasts.

What was excluded by Judge John J. Ryan were military records and Lake's diary because much of the entries were irrelevant to the case.

William Kelly was Ng's court-appointed attorney. The defense sought to place the killings at the door of Leonard Lake, the demented survivalist.

Ng, the master of delay, had the same script for the trial. Throughout the course of the proceedings, he had ten defense attorneys; some were dismissed, only to be retained once more. "I want to defend myself," Ng shocked the judge. Ng was granted an adjournment but soon asked for another attorney.

Understandably, the case was not going well for Ng. In an attempt to elicit sympathy for their son, Ng's parents came from Hong Kong to testify and plead for Charles Ng's life. Mr. Ng admitted that he was a severe disciplinarian who hoped to make his son a better citizen.

Charles Ng worsened his case by insisting, over counsel objections, to take the stand in his own defense. This gave prosecutors an opportunity on cross examination to show Ng in his cell, with incriminating cartoons behind him on the wall next to a favorite saying: "No kill, no thrill—no gun, no fun."

According to Kelly, when Ng took the stand, "It gave the tabloids one more juicy element to chew on … It reconfirmed Charles Ng's position at center stage, his status as a killer without remorse, who loved the limelight."

Added Kelly, "When our client decided against our wishes to take the witness stand, we felt tactically that wasn't a particularly wise choice on his part. I believed that sealed his fate."

The defense sought to counter the prosecution by calling Cricket Balasz, Lake's former wife, who would hopefully support Ng by saying the survivalist ranch and plans were basically her ex-husband's. However, the plan was for naught when Judge Ryan told counsel that Lake's ex had made prior statements implicating Ng in the murders.

The four-month trial having ended, the jury retired to consider a verdict. Within hours, on February 24, 1999, the jury convicted Ng on first-degree murder for six men, three women, and two baby boys. On June 30, 1999, Judge Ryan sentenced Ng to death.

When the proceedings closed, the cost to California was twenty million dollars. To date, Ng has not been executed, so that cost has risen because of appeals and maintaining Ng on death row. It has been estimated that the process could extend through 2009. Evaluating the case in terms of justice, one prosecuting attorney bitterly observed, "The justice system in America has gone haywire."

The twenty-year-plus saga from crime through justice still searches for answers to explain the motives of two ex-Marines, Vietnam veterans. According to Colin Wilson and Damon Wilson in *The Killers Among Us*, the experience in Vietnam was reflective of Lake's fantasies. He spoke of heroic deeds but had never seen combat. "On the other hand, it seems clear," write the Wilsons, "that his experiences in Vietnam caused some fundamental change that made him antisocial and capable of violence."

The upbringing of Leonard Lake has already been explored. Not much has been revealed of Ng's upbringing except he rebelled against stern discipline.

His Marine service did highlight a troubled person. He boasted that he had "assassinated" a Californian. He also was proud that he placed cyanide in mess hall shakers. However, none of these boasts was reality. According to defense attorney Kelly, "From the psychiatrist's point of view, most of Ng's stories came from an overworked imagination and bizarre braggadocio."

Both Lake and Ng were not model citizens when they left the service, but no one envisioned the deadly duo their alliance effected. In *Serial Killers*, Mark Seltzer called Lake "an obscene record keeper," with home videotapes and photographs. Having added Ng to his enterprise, Lake himself, "self-taught, self-made, self-caused," now could be more immersed in "mass technologies of reproduction."

It is not accurate to compare Lake and Ng to Lucas and Toole. Lucas had amassed brutal numbers before meeting Toole. But it is true that the serial killer chemistry of Lake and Ng reinforced each other's sado-sexual desires to torture and kill others. Put succinctly and perhaps simplistically, the duo exemplifies what psychologists call Gestalt: "the organized whole is greater than the sum of its parts."

Ng has not been as scrutinized psychologically as has Leonard Lake. And those who have examined Lake lament the fact that many family and acquaintances refused to acknowledge that he was mentally sick and accepted his status as an independent thinker living as a survivalist in a hostile world.

Norris clearly places the blame on those who knew him but did nothing:

> He had been living off stolen property, money sent to him by his ex-wife and his mother, and money he made from pushing drugs, selling stolen goods, and producing porno films. Never had Lake been confronted with his own shortcomings, even though he was painfully aware of them. His mother, a licensed nurse who worked in a mental ward, had simply looked the other way, believing that her son was incapable of violence. His ex-wife participated in his pornographic movie business and delayed in revealing that Lake had been systematically murdering the people he was doing business with. And his grandmother ... refused to release any documents that will incriminate Lake in any way. His sister, Fern, a registered nurse and the family member who was closest to Leonard, grieved because she too failed to intervene.
>
> Lake's life, therefore, was a series of missed opportunities for intervention, any of which might have short-circuited the career of a killer who claimed people from all walks of everyday life as his victims of chance ... Each of these victims, and numerous others who had crossed Lake's path years earlier, was a sacrifice to the refusal of those who knew of Lake's propensity toward violence to intervene in his life.

To many Leonard Lake will remain an enigma, a decorated Vietnam War veteran who performed some good deeds in his community. However, before he moved into his survivalist ranch, in the years before the murders, he was described by a neighbor as "the most unpleasant man I have ever known."

ANDREI CHIKATILO
Teacher, Grandfather, Sadistic Killer

When considering the dimensions of the serial killer narrative, one can readily accept the designation of the case of Andrei Romanovich Chikatilo as the "mother of all serial killer" episodes.

The multifaceted elements of the case include a study of the city of Rostov, the number and methods of the murders, the mindset of Communism toward serial killers, the torturous pursuit of the "forest strip killer," and the personality of the killer.

In a 1999 *Newsweek* article, Owen Matthews speaks of Rostov-on-Don as the "capital of serial crime: City of the Dead." Psychiatrist Aleksandr Bukhanovsky, an expert on mass murder, cannot explain the phenomenon. Writes Matthews, "For reasons neither science, religion, nor the occult can satisfactorily explain, the bustling riverport city has become a crucible for the rage of an extraordinary high number of vicious criminals—psychopathic serial killers and sadistic rapists most prominent among them."

From 1989–99, twenty-nine multiple murderers and rapists were apprehended in the area, making Rostov the "serial-killer capital of the world." From 1978–91, Andrei Chikatilo stalked and preyed on those found in the area along the marshes of the Don River and the dense woodlands around the town. The investigation of Chikatilo uncovered ninety-five murders and two hundred forty-five rapes that could not be traced solely to the Rostov Ripper.

The number of his victims has been set at fifty-three. As grisly as the figure denotes, Pedro Alonso Lopez confessed to murdering more than three hundred in the seventies and eighties in South America. However, Chikatilo's murders—in Russia, the Ukraine, and Uzbekistan—have been recounted in greater detail, filling twenty-two tall red volumes. His victims were boys, girls, and young women who were raped; mutilated—bitten, eviscerated, often cannibalized; and buried.

Interestingly, in reviewing Robert Cullen's 1993 book on Chikatilo, Julian Symons wrote in the *New York Times* that the case of the Rostov Ripper accentuates the change of designation from "mass murderer" to "serial killer."

"In the past, Mr. Chikatilo would have been called a mass murderer. Now the description has been softened to serial killer ... A serial sounds agreeable, something we watch on television, and killing is what we do to vermin. The new phrase marks a contemporary fascination with extreme physical violence, the fascination that has helped to make books and films like *Silence of the Lambs* immensely successful."

The twelve-year manhunt involved more than fifty special investigators and five hundred police officers from Rostov to Siberia who interrogated some twenty-five thousand suspects.

Immersed in the case were Mikhail Gorbachev and the Central Committee of the Communist Party; Victor V. Burakov, the chief of the section for serious sexual crimes in the Rostov criminal investigation bureau; and Issa V. Kostoyev, head of Russia's Department of Crimes of Special Importance.

Other serial killer manhunts have been exceedingly frustrating. Bela Kiss eluded capture. The Torso Killer was neither found nor identified. But in the Chikatilo case, there were so many killings, so many clues, and so many on the case. What was the problem?

The answer rests in a Soviet system that was disintegrating. For one thing, Soviet thought considered crime an inherent evil of capitalism but absent in Communism. The Communist disbelief in homicide was noted in Poland's lethargic attitude in the sixties to the murders committed by Lucian Staniak.

Concerning the crimes of Chikatilo, the system had a non-workable attitude about sex crimes, and a totalitarian crime mechanism bent on securing false confession, which in this case executed the wrong murderer who was posthumously cleared.

"In Russia, both under Communism and before it," observes Cullen, "the confession was the pivotal stage in any investigation. Russians are accustomed to the idea that a guilty man must confess; some Russians, even now, hold the mistaken belief that a defendant who does not confess cannot be convicted." The case brought these deficiencies into public view. In short, the Soviet tradition was followed: ideology supercedes public security. The attitude toward sex crimes was archaic.

"Most Russians knew little about homosexuality. Most Russians, in fact, knew little about sex in general. The official mores of the country were still, by and large, the mores of Stalinism. Like Mao and Hitler, Stalin saw sex solely as a means of creating new revolutionaries, new servants of the state."

In covering the trial for *USA Today*, Tony Mauro filed a report titled "Shedding Light on Russian Justice." The trial was a revelation of pre-glasnost secrecy. "Russian officials kept the existence of a repeat murderer secret from local residents for years," wrote Mauro, "and after another man was mistakenly executed for his crimes." The concern was seconded by Gwendolyn Whittaker, who kept an eye on human rights in the former Soviet Union for Amnesty International USA:

"One of our concerns about capital punishment in Russia has been the lack of public access to any information."

The Chikatilo case is notable in that cultural/ethnic influences are added to the influences of family/development. Chikatilo was born in 1936 in Yablochnove, a Ukrainian farm village. For Ukrainians, Stalinization meant forced resettlement and collectivization, accompanied by starvation and state-organized brutality. Some five hundred thousand Ukrainians were sent to the Gulag, never to return.

Approximately six million Ukrainians died in the ten-year period, which began in 1930. Woes increased with the Nazi invasion in 1941, ended in 1943.

Chikatilo recalled for psychiatrists, during his imprisonment, the visions of corpses and blood. One psychiatrist, Andrei Tkachenko, described the consequences: "It was one of the strongest experiences of his childhood. When he saw them [corpses and blood], he felt a mixture of fear and excitement, an excitement that in this type of person is almost sexual."

The Chikatilo family also included a younger daughter, Tatyana. The father was captured, and as a returning prisoner was sent to a prison camp—as a traitor to Communism—in the lower Volga. The young Andrei was told and retold many gruesome stories by his mother: a cousin had been kidnapped and cannibalized; an older son died during the famine and was eaten by famished neighbors.

According to Colin and Damon Wilson in *The Killers Among Us*, the story of the cousin "made a deep impression on Chikatilo. For years afterwards ... he would brood on the story and recreate his cousin's sufferings in his imagination. There can be no doubt that this strongly influenced his sexual development."

During imprisonment, doctors discovered other negative elements, starting with Chikatilo's birth. According to Dr. Tkachenko, Chikatilo was not a normal child, which was evidenced in his electroencephalograph, the recording of electrical activity in the brain:

"His electroencephalograph showed certain disturbances associated with the early period of brain development. It was probably the result of something that happened in the uterus during his mother's pregnancy. We found other symptoms characteristic of this. He had a slightly hydrocephalic skull. The pupils of his eyes were of different sizes. When he stuck his tongue out, it didn't come out straight, but to the right."

Worst of all was the direction this brain abnormality took, concludes Cullen: "For Chikatilo, unfortunately, this brain abnormality manifested

Depravity

itself in his genitalia. Until he was twelve years old, Tkachenko learned, he was unable to control his bladder. Later, the abnormality would manifest itself as a tendency toward premature ejaculation, often before Chikatilo achieved an erection."

When the father returned after the war, the ten-year-old Andrei had become a devoted Communist. The father's survival was not welcome; in fact, Andrei saw the survival as humiliation. As an escape, he turned to reading. His obsession with sadism was nourished by a novel *Molodaya Gvardiya* or *The Young Guard*, dealing with heroic young Russian partisans fighting the Germans. The scenes of torture—either prisoners tortured by the Germans or partisans torturing the Germans—made a deep impression on Chikatilo. According to Colin and Damon Wilson, "This positive, even heroic depiction of torture in isolated woodland made a deep impression on the child."

The school years were difficult for Chikatilo. He felt inferior because of his chubby breasts, bed-wetting, and nearsightedness. However, Chikatilo sought to overcome or compensate for his deficiencies. He became a strong teenager, earning the nickname Andrei the Great. He received good grades and was involved in many extracurricular activities, including chairman of student activities and editor of the school newspaper.

But he received a setback when rejected for admission to the law school at Moscow State University. He blamed the rejection on his father's war record. Rather than applying to another university or retaking the exam, Chikatilo had enough disappointments.

"I decided to find work somewhere," Chikatilo told Issa Kostoyev, who came into the case as the procurator from Moscow. "I took the train to Jursk, and I worked there for three months as a laborer." It was farewell to a career in law. He trained as a communications technician—a telephone repairman—in a vocational school. His career was interrupted by three years of army service with a KGB communications unit.

No doubt his greatest frustrations were with women. He could not establish any lasting relationship. Fear of impotency was responsible for failed sexual activities. Dr. Tkachenko related the results of his research on Chikatilo:

> He tried to have sex with a woman in 1960, just after he got out of the army. She said that when he tried to have sex with her, he couldn't manage it. And there were a few other attempts he made earlier that were unsuccessful. Either he didn't have an erection or he quickly ejaculated.
>
> The inability to get an erection was the result of his personality problems. He didn't believe in himself; he felt inadequate, and so on. But the premature ejaculation was the result of a physical condition. Because of the peculiarities of the organic functioning of his brain, he had what sexual pathologists called a lowered threshold of excitement. He could become excited without sexual stimuli or with asexual stimulation. He could ejaculate without an erection.

The tandem of sex and violence is graphically detailed in *The Killer Among Us*:

"It was during his national service that he first experienced orgasm with a girl, and that was because she suddenly decided that things were going too far and tried to break his hold on her. She had no chance against his abnormal strength, and he was surprised at the sexual passion her struggles aroused in him. He held her only for a few moments before releasing her unharmed, but he had already ejaculated into his trousers. Thinking about it afterwards, he realized that it was her fear and his power over her that had excited him so much. He had started to find sex and violence a stimulating concoction."

Following national service, Chikatilo left Rostov for Rodionov-Nesvetayevsky and worked as a telephone engineer. Looking to better himself, he enrolled in a correspondence degree course in Russian philology and literature from Rostov University.

His sister, now married, sought a wife for Andrei and found the

Depravity

match in Feodosia Odnacheva, daughter of a coal miner. As expected, the marriage was not consummated at first. Married in 1963, they had a girl and boy in 1963 and 1969, respectively. However, sexual relations were infrequent. But family life continued with no apparent problems.

The troubles began after Chikatilo, now thirty-five, entered the teaching profession. He was appointed deputy director of a vocational school and teacher of Russian language and literature in Novoshakbinsk. He failed as an administrator because he could not supervise other teachers; he failed as a teacher because he couldn't maintain discipline. He obviously was not suited for teaching but refused to listen to those who advised him to return to technical work. For the next seven years, the frustrations with teaching were diverted to sexual fantasies in the form of molesting young children.

His actions rose to more serious proportions in 1977 and involved a student, Tonya Gultseva. Chikatilo forced her to stay after classes for a remedial session. Chikatilo had his own lesson plan. "I noticed that her skirt had ridden up," he recalled years later for investigators, "and I could see her panties and bare legs. This excited me. I got a passionate desire to touch her breasts, her sex organs. She resisted, pushed me away, and cried out."

The girl fled, and told her parents, who informed school authorities. This was the first time that Chikatilo's sexual actions had been brought before Soviet authorities, and certainly the first time they could respond. Seeking to hush the matter, Chikatilo was allowed to resign. The police were not informed, so Chikatilo had a clean record. Similar incidents happened in succeeding positions: each time Chikatilo resigned, maintaining a spotless record.

He purchased a hut in Shakhty, several miles from his family's dwelling. His intention was to have a hideaway for sexual activities with pre-puberty children and destitute, homeless young women.

Chikatilo's first murder was on December 22, 1978. He was then forty-two, contrary to most other serial killers who began their sadistic journey in their teens or early twenties. He noticed Lena Zakotnova, nine, waiting at the train stop, waiting to go home. As she left with Chikatilo, she told a classmate that she was going with a "nice old man" who would give her "imported" chewing gum.

Having lured Lena to his shack, Chikatilo wasted no time. He threw her to the floor and tore off her clothes. When she started screaming, he choked her with his forearm, blindfolded her with his scarf, and tried to rape her. As in past perversions, he failed to achieve an erection. The frustrated Chikatilo pushed his semen into her with his fingers. Her blood produced excitement and an orgasm.

Realizing that Lena was still alive and fearing discovery, he stabbed her with a knife three times in the stomach. As she lay still, he wrapped her and her belongings and dropped her in the Grusheva River. The girl was still alive as she hit the river.

Chikatilo had been careless in his first murder: the victim's blood was on the doorstep, and his light had been left on all night. Because of the light and because of the continual entry into the hut with young girls, Chikatilo was a likely suspect. He was called in for questioning, but his alibi of being with his wife all evening was corroborated by Mrs. Chikatilo.

Police attention was focused, however, on Alexsandr Kravchenko, a local resident who had been previously arrested and served a prison sentence for the rape and murder of a seventeen-year-old girl.

This was the first instance of sloppy police and investigative work in this case. The girl's classmate, Svetlana Gurenkova, had identified the man with her friend as middle-aged, wearing glasses. Kravchenko was twenty-five and had never worn glasses. In fact, while Kravchenko was being interrogated, a circulating sketch caught the attention of a school principal where Chikatilo had taught. Afraid that they had made a mistake, the police warned the principal, "Do not tell anyone who you identified!" And the police later disregarded the all-night light and the blood splashes.

Kravchenko was their man, the police announced, and extracted a "confession." A quick trial brought a fifteen-year sentence in a labor camp. The citizenry of Shakhty roared their disapproval, forcing a new investigation and a death sentence. Kravchenko was shot by a firing squad in 1984, as Chikatilo was on the loose, having amassed a long list of victims.

At the time of this murder, he was still a teacher and not yet a serial killer. In early 1981 he left the teaching profession, this time because of budget cuts. He became a supply clerk for a Rostov-area industrial company. The job involved a good deal of travel and more time to hunt for human prey.

Six months out of the teaching profession, Chikatilo resumed his career as murderer. The victim, Larisa Tkachenko, seventeen, was awaiting a bus near the Rostov public library. Larisa had been irregularly attending boarding school and frequently dated young soldiers who offered food and drink and other favors. In short, she was more sexually experienced than Chikatilo's previous targets. While not her usual date, Chikatilo asked Larisa to accompany him to a local recreation area, and she agreed.

The walk took them near a wooded area. While expecting a sexual encounter, she did not expect his method: throwing her down and tearing at her pants. She fought back but was no match for the powerful attacker. He pounded her and shoved earth into her mouth to muffle her cries, and then choked her to death.

He then went into a rapture of sadosexuality. He bit off one of her nipples and ejaculated. Next, he ran around the corpse, delirious and ecstatic. In an allusion to his youthful favorite, *The Young Guard*, Chikatilo shouted, "I am a partisan!" When the joy subsided, he covered her corpse with branches and buried her clothing.

The murder of Larisa Tkachenko fueled the serial murder career. The murder of Lena Zakotnova was a bewildering experience, perhaps to be expected for his first murder. The murder of Larisa whetted his appetite for sex and murder. "Her murder," write Colin Wilson and

Damon Wilson, made him "aware of the basic nature of his desires. The murder ... made him aware that he was destined to go on killing."

This was a crucial moment that all serial killers experience, continue the Wilsons. "All serial killers seem to cross this mental rubicon. The initial horror and guilt gives way to an addiction to hunting that transcends all social and moral boundaries. They never seem to break the habit; once hooked, they continue until they are caught or die."

The third murder, in June 1982, targeted Lyuba Biryuk, from Zaplavskaya. A new modus operandi was fashioned. When he did not succeed in raping her, Chikatilo knifed the victim repeatedly, including the eyes. Lyuba was found two weeks later.

Six more victims were added in 1982, with a new twist: two victims were boys, ages nine and fifteen. Victims were from Rostov or in areas visited during business trips. The police and the Soviet criminal justice system were ill-prepared for the investigation. They quickly adapted the view that there were two separate killers.

The next murder was six months later, in June 1983. The victim was a fifteen-year-old Armenian girl, Laura Sarkisyan, whose body was not found until Chikatilo directed police to her grave years later. In July, he killed a thirteen-year-old girl near the train station. Three more victims were added during the summer: two women, ages fifteen and eighteen, and a boy, seven. The total of his butchery was now fourteen, almost all vagrants. Only about half of the bodies were found by police.

Not unexpectedly, the Russian media, bowing to government wishes, downplayed the news of the murders, usually in an obituary notice. But with the growing number of victims and people brought in for questioning, wild rumors began circulating: the murderers were cannibals; they were roving Rostov gang members; they were perverted medics. According to Cullen, one rumor identified the killers driving around in a luxury sedan, usually belonging to Party officials—the first letters on the license plate were DSC, Death to Soviet Children.

Panic gripped Rostov, so the central Moscow police launched an official investigation and Major Mikhail Fetisov, deputy Vladimir

Kolyesnikov, and their team arrived in Rostov. To accent the importance of the investigation, Fetisov chose as head of the team Victor Burakov, the most talented forensic specialist in the Moscow militia. Burakov's operation was known as DESC—the Division of Especially Serious Crimes. Because the bodies had been retrieved from the woodlands, the case became popularized as the Lesopolosa, or the Forest Strip, killings.

Serial killers existed only in the West, according to Soviet thought, so investigators would not use that term, nor would they refer to the perpetrator as a mass murderer. The criminal had to be abnormal. Therefore, the records of mental hospitals were searched, with a focus on those with histories of sex and violence.

As DESC probed, Chikatilo continued his murder spree. Two women and a male youth were killed before 1983 ended; 1984 was the most horrific year: fifteen women and children were killed between January and September. Most of the victims lived in the Rostov vicinity, while others were killed on his business visits, in Moscow and Tashkent.

Chikatilo persisted in victim hunting. Many potential victims—at train depots, bus stops, airports, public facilities—did not go for the bait: food, vodka, money, sex, and video games at his home for the younger set. And in his most brutal year, Chikatilo soiled his record when accused of allegedly stealing one automobile battery from the Shakhty enterprise he worked for. The police decided not to prosecute because of the petty nature of the crime. Because his company dropped charges, he agreed to leave for another position.

Enter Major Aleksandr Zanosovsky, one of those assigned to DESC, who set up his search at the Rostov bus station. One August evening he noticed a man striking up a conversation with a young woman. No action. Chikatilo then turned to another woman. Zanosovsky stepped in, showed his badge, and took Chikatilo to a waiting room. The documents were in order. "I enjoy talking with people. After all, I travel often on business," said Chikatilo. The major let Chikatilo go.

The next month, Zanosovsky spotted Chikatilo again and, joined by a plainclothesman, followed Chikatilo as he boarded a bus. On the two-hour chase, they watched Chikatilo switching buses and striking up conversations with women.

The last stop was at the center of Rostov. Chikatilo entered a restaurant, a cafe, sat in the public garden. He talked to many women. The major noticed Chikatilo making a pickup on the park bench and saw what he felt could be a charge of oral sex, of perversion in public. The Major and the plainclothesman followed Chikatilo onto a bus. The evening, close to dawn, ended at the Central Bazaar.

The major was convinced he had a genuine suspect. At the station, Chikatilo's suitcase was opened to reveal a jar of Vaseline and a kitchen knife about eight to ten inches long. Upon seeing the knife, the major exclaimed, "Ah, I caught the Lesopolosa killer."

Procurator Yuri Moiseyev interrogated Chikatilo, who insisted that as a frequent traveler he needed the knife to cut food, especially sausages. Then came the critical blood tests. This is where the investigation hit the wall. Semen samples found at the scene of nine murders revealed type AB. The forensic lab reported Chikatilo's blood as type A.

Dr. Svetlana Gurtovaya was the head of the biology lab of the Bureau of Forensic Medicine at Moscow's Ministry of Health. Her lab determined that the semen at the murder scenes was type AB. Unfortunately, the investigators grouped suspects only by blood types. Thus, Chikatilo slipped through.

Ironically, four years later, in 1988, Dr. Gurtovaya informed law enforcement agencies that blood and semen types could differ. Indeed, this was an unconventional approach, but it proved true concerning Chikatilo. Aside from forcing DESC to redo their investigative work, Chikatilo continued his killing. And even in 1988, no quick investigative mind thought of the Rostov Ripper.

As for 1984, Chikatilo was a Communist Party member with no blemishes. But the militia refused to accept the facts of the semen type. They were faced with the need to charge him or release him within ten days. Therefore, they checked the files and found the theft blotch, minor as it was. That gave the Party a reason to try him. He was found guilty in December 1984 of theft of state property. The year sentence of correctional labor was waived by the judge, since Chikatilo had spent three months in jail.

Chikatilo was back home; as for Zanosovsky, always convinced that Chikatilo was the man, he was reprimanded and demoted for being "overly zealous in the performance of his duties."

Wisely, Chikatilo did not immediately resume killing. He waited until August 1985, when he killed eighteen-year-old Natalya Pokhlistova during a Moscow business trip. Perhaps in an attempt to confound investigators, Chikatilo gave the murder a new wrinkle: the victim's mouth was stuffed with leaves and dirt.

He killed again in August, another eighteen-year-old girl, Irina Gulyayeva, in Shakhty, the same setting of his first murder, and the last murder for 1985. The victims now numbered thirty-four.

Chikatilo, now fifty, rested murder-wise for twenty-one months. The police investigation beefed up its operations, now led by Issa Kostoyev, director of Moscow's Department for Violent Crime. The investigators were reorganized into three units, focusing on Shakhty, Rostov, and Novoshakhtinsk. All those convicted of sexually motivated crimes or in custody were checked and rechecked. Those in the gay community were brought in and thoroughly interrogated.

All sites relating to sexual activity and interest were checked: nightclubs and pornographic video shops. Also checked were policemen dismissed for perverse actions. Because of the centrality of buses and trains in the murders, the investigation examined the records and work habits of transportation workers.

Army helicopters were brought in to patrol buses, railway lines, and forests adjoining the stations. All this was observed by Chikatilo, now employed in the locomotive factory in Novocherkask, in the three-area radius. How strange it was that Chikatilo, employed with the Department of Internal Affairs, aided the police in patrolling trains looking for the forest belt killer. Clearly, he would not kill in the range of the three areas.

And that is exactly how Chikatilo went back to killing. In May 1987, he killed a ten-year-old boy in Siberia; a twelve-year-old boy in the Ukraine in July; and a sixteen-year-old boy in September in Leningrad. The victims' list now stood at thirty-seven.

The total rose to forty in 1988: a thirty-year-old woman in Krasny-Sulin in April; a nine-year-old girl in May in the Ukraine; and a fifteen-year-old girl in the Ukraine in July.

The year of 1989 was awesome and savage: four murders, including a fifteen-year-old girl in his married daughter's house in Shakhty. His actions reached new levels of depravity: sawing of legs, biting out tongues, and the cutting out of the uterus, nipples, and penis.

Number-wise, Chikatilo was more active in 1990—nine murders; but he had become careless. His next-to-last victim, on October 17, 1990, was Vadim Tishchenko, sixteen, whose body was found in the heavily patrolled Rostov Leskhoz railway station. Ironically, the day of the murder, the area experienced a manpower shortage.

When the body was found three days later, police circulated photos of the victim. Chikatilo was observed by the woman who sold Vadim the rail ticket. Moreover, her daughter had seen Chikatilo several days before the murder trying to convince a young boy to get off the train with him.

Now the police were ready for the killer at previous murder locations. But Chikatilo eluded them three weeks later in mid-November. The final—and fifty-third—victim was Svetlana Korostik, twenty-two, who left for the woods with Chikatilo, near the Leskhoz station. After beating, stabbing, and mutilating her, Chikatilo removed and ate both her nipples and tongue. The body was covered with leaves and branches. As he returned to the station, he was spotted by a policeman of the investigating team, who noticed a sweating Chikatilo with blood on his cheek and ear, and a bandaged right-hand finger. He also washed his

Depravity

hands in a well. The policeman checked Chikatilo's papers and finding no problem allowed the murderer to board an oncoming train.

The policeman filed a report of the incident. It received little notice until the victim's body was found several days later. The name of Chikatilo rang bells among investigators. Upon checking, they found he was a previous suspect released because of non-matching semen/blood types. By chance, research findings of Japanese scientists came across the investigators' desks: the odds were overwhelming against it, but semen and blood types could be different for one individual.

Investigators agreed; Chikatilo was their man, but they needed to snare him in the act. They chose November 20, 1990. Chikatilo was trailed from work to his home. Returning home, he struck up conversation with young boys, who had little interest in his designs. As he headed toward his apartment, police jumped out from their hiding spots and announced he was under arrest.

"Why am I being arrested?" Chikatilo asked. The three arresting officers did not answer, nor did the suspect talk again on his ride to the regional headquarters of the Department of Internal Affairs in Rostov.

Ideally, the police wanted a quick confession, but it did not come easily. At first, he was resistant. "Why me?" he turned on his interrogators. On November 22, he wrote a letter to the Prosecutor General of Russia. It said in part:

"In perverted sexual manifestations, I feel a certain rage, out of control, and I can't control my actions.

"Because since childhood I could not show myself as a man and a complete person, this [perverted sexual activity] gave me not sexual but psychic and spiritual calmness for an extended period."

A letter the following day began with "In my difficult, depressed condition, I remember my life with all its suffering and humiliations." Still, the letter was not a confession. November 29 would be the end of the ten-day deadline period needed for a confession. After a meeting with psychiatrist Aleksandr Bukhanovsky, Chikatilo was ready to sign a confession on November 29:

"I have read and become familiar with the declaration of charges lodged against me on November 29. I fully acknowledge my guilt in the commission of the crimes listed. Now, deeply regretting what I have done, I wanted to truthfully tell about myself and my life and the circumstances leading me to these serious crimes."

Bukhanovsky arranged the meeting between Chikatilo and his wife. At first, she was disbelieving. They had been married for twenty-five years, and she always considered him a good provider, a faithful husband, and doting grandfather. No one, especially her husband, could be that monster he was portrayed as.

This disbelief vanished during their meeting and confessions. Chikatilo cried and she cursed him. The police were fully convinced of her unawareness of the crimes and gave the family new names and new homes far from Rostov.

For one week following, Chikatilo gave full details of thirty-four of the thirty-six murders he was charged with. He also offered details of murders he had not been charged with. When completed, the confessions detailed fifty-two murders.

Following the confessions, Chikatilo was taken to the scenes of the murders. Investigators marveled at his recall of sites, times, dates, methodology, and names of victims. On one trip, he recalled the murder of a Latvian girl, twenty, in 1984. The total of confessed murders was fifty-three.

Teacher, father, grandfather—all this mattered little in the spring of 1992. Andrei Chikatilo was now the man in the iron cage. Chikatilo was led into court on April 14, 1992, and locked inside a cage built for his security, surrounded by armed guards. It was designed to prevent an onslaught by friends and relatives of the victims.

The post-glasnost media filled the court along with those wishing to see the man the press had called "the Maniac."

The cage was a wonderful concept. At Chikatilo's appearance, one woman jumped up, shouting, "Sadist! Murderer! What have you done?" She ran to the cage before being stopped.

Depravity

Judge Leonid Abkuzhanov opened the case with a two-day reading of the accusations against Chikatilo. When permitted to address the court, the defendant proceeded with a rambling, idiotic monologue. Throughout the trial, Chikatilo continually displayed maniacal behavior. He took off his clothes and waved his penis and shouted, "Look at this useless thing. What do you think I could do with that?" On another occasion, he announced his pregnancy and charged brutal guards with hitting him in the stomach to "harm his baby." On another occasion, he took off his clothes, waving the shirt over his head, screaming: "Under this banner I battled the Assyrian Mafia."

At one point, the judge ordered Chikatilo removed and continued the proceedings without his presence.

All this seemed a contrived plan for an insanity defense although the defense attorney, Marat Khabibulin, maintained in his closing that there was no material evidence linking Chikatilo to the murders.

As the judge adjourned the case before sentencing, a brother of one of the victims threw an iron bar at the prisoner that just missed his head. On October 15, 1992, Chikatilo was convicted of fifty-two murders and was sentenced to death. In announcing the verdict, the judge said plaintively, "The Soviet Union also must share this guilt because for years it would not acknowledge that such crimes could happen here."

Chikatilo's last words shouted to the court were: "Why me? Fraud! I'm not going to listen to your lies."

Why was Chikatilo not judged as insane? Psychiatrists from Moscow's Serbsky Institute flew to the trial and repeated their findings that Chikatilo was fit to stand trial. All his trial outbursts were contrived.

Above all, Chikatilo, like other serial killers, had to be cunning and wise; otherwise, he could not succeed. We have accentuated this point throughout the book. In the case of Chikatilo, he studiously selected his victims. He was clever enough to cease killings after his 1984 arrest. When the police focused on three areas, he killed in other centers.

"He always displayed well thought-out, controlled behavior that he could change in response to circumstances," said an examining psychiatrist. "I think Chikatilo could have refrained from killing if he had forced himself to. Or if the danger was real and strong that he would be caught. That's why he was able to stop for a while after his 1984 arrest."

On the other hand, as argued by Cullen, all this would mean little in the American justice system. Cullen cites Robert Ressler, who has divided serial killers into the disorganized—those careless in the carrying out of their murders, and the organized—those careful and precise in their actions. Chikatilo was organized, and judged sane. Yet, reasons argue, so was Jeffrey Dahmer, and he was judged insane.

Also, consider the words of Victor Burakov, one of the heroes of the investigation: "I believe he is really sick. He seems to be in the same extreme condition, extreme agitation, in which he would commit his crimes. He needs release now, but if released now, I'm sure he would commit a crime."

An appeal for clemency was rejected by President Boris Yeltsin. Japanese psychiatrists offered Russia an undisclosed sum for study of Chikatilo's brain when dead. However, that was of no value as Chikatilo was executed with a shot to the back of his head on February 15, 1992.

Only one "joyous" note was sounded that day. Alexander Kravchenko, executed for the murder of Chikatilo's first victim, received a posthumous pardon.

The singularity of this case—often called the "trial of the century" for the world and particularly Russia, is reflected in the words of Judge Abkuzhanov, at the end of a day three months into the trial: "You see, I'm wrung out, and this was not an easy day. There's never been such a day in Russian jurisprudence. I'm forty-one. I've been a judge fifteen years and I get all the worst crimes, but the worst I've had to date is a man who killed four girls."

The case of Andrei Chikatilo also answers the question of why serial killers have universal appeal. In his *New York Times* review of three Chikatilo books, Julian Symons wonders about the interest. One answer refers to Stanza XXVI of W. H. Auden's "O Who Can Ever Gaze His Fill."

> The greater the love, the more false to its object,
> Not to be born is the best for man;
> After the kiss comes the impulse to throttle,
> Break the embraces, dance while you can.

ADDENDUM

Chikatilo stood in danger of losing his title as Russia's most prolific serial killer. In June 2006, Alexander Pichushkin was caught and accused of murdering forty-nine, but he admitted to killing another eleven. This would have eclipsed Chikatilo's mark of fifty-three. He has been labeled the "chessboard murderer" by the Soviet press because his goal was to place a coin on all sixty-four squares of a chessboard, one for each murder.

Reminiscent of another Russian serial killer, Vasili Komaroff, he lured victims to secluded parts of Moscow, filled them with vodka, and then bashed their heads with a hammer. Other victims were strangled, tossed off balconies, or drowned in sewage pits.

Before his trial in October 2007, Pichushkin, a shelf stocker in a grocery store, tried to confess to sixty-three murders. But Chikatilo's notoriety was safe. He was convicted of murdering forty-nine and trying to kill three others. He had evaded authorities for years but was nabbed after murdering his final victim, a fellow employee at the grocery store.

And, unlike Chikatilo, Pichushkin was not sentenced to death by the Moscow City Court. He was sentenced to life because Russia has put a moratorium on the death penalty.

DEAN ARTHUR CORLL
Texas Candy Killer

In a computer-assisted study of rampage and serial killers, the *New York Times* examined one hundred murderers over the past fifty years. The South and Southwest were represented with thirty-three killings. The study did not detail where the killers were born or raised. California was the most prevalent state, with one-fifth of the killings. Still, Texas, with seven, and Georgia, with six, were among the leaders. D. K. Rossmo, in his 1995 doctoral dissertation at Simon Fraser University, lists the five leaders: California, Florida, New York, Texas, Illinois, and Georgia.

Representative of the Southern serial killer was Dean Corll. Born in Indiana, Corll grew up in Houston, Texas, where he developed his notoriety as a serial killer. His career as serial killer brought a new focus to the phenomenon of serial killer. America, as well as other countries, had its share of serial killers through the twentieth century and earlier. But the numbers were becoming more frequent, starting in the seventies, and the crimes were becoming more sadistic.

Exemplifying the depravity of the serial killer was Dean Corll, who was, according to Colin Wilson and Damon Wilson (*The Killers Among Us*), "the first serial killer to create this feeling that human depravity had reached new heights." He is considered the first major mass murderer in modern American culture. The homosexual nature of his crimes attracted great attention and concern from many quarters, most notably the Vatican.

In his biography of Corll, *The Man with the Candy*, Jack Olsen profiles Houston as the metropolis of crime. In 1957, with the highest per capita rate in the United States, Houston earned the title "The Murder City." In a 1971 book *Houston: The Once and Future City*, George Fuermann offered this verse:

> In Houston we feel no aversion
> When others are casting aspersion
> We never mind much
> The murders and such—
> We take them as week-end diversion.

The reasons are complex, although the *Houston Post* attributes the statistics to indifference: "The public is silent. There is no outcry against murder. And silence gives consent."

Dean Corll was born on Christmas Eve 1939, but that did not herald a tranquil family life. His parents fought continually, divorced, remarried, and then separated. Young Corll was punished severely, for little reason. Said his mother, "The boys [Dean and his brother] did things that I thought were real cute and funny, but he'd think it was something to be punished about. One day, Dean stepped in the toilet, and then he got in the sink and turned the water on. I thought that was a real accomplishment, but when I told Mr. Corll about it, he said, 'Well, he ought to be whipped for that.'"

If one looked for disturbing signs in Dean Corll's childhood, it was that he seldom played with other children, including his brother, Stanley. "Dean never cared," said his mother, "if anybody played with him or not. From the time he was little, he never went anyplace to see anybody else."

After his mother separated for a second time, she married a salesman, Jake West, and the family moved to Vidor, Texas. Dean had a non-distinguished high school stay. "He didn't fail," said his mother, "but he was no Truman Capote ... I never wanted a genius and thank God I never had one."

His high school years were also restricted because he contracted rheumatic fever and then developed a heart problem.

His mother was looking to earn added money by baking pies. A pecan salesman stopped by one day and suggested that Mrs. West became a candy maker. One day the family drove to a candy plant and acquired a praline recipe for fifty dollars.

Dean Corll jumped into the family business with great enthusiasm. "I remember when the machines came in," recalled a high school classmate, "and putting 'em in the garage for separating and cracking different size pecans, baking 'em, cleaning 'em, all by machine, and Dean kept those machines running, wrapped the candy in boxes, and delivered 'em. That's one reason he didn't have a lot of social life. He was busy all the time."

Nevertheless, he was a well-liked high schooler. "Good ol' Dean," as he was known, played trombone in the band.

The candy career was interrupted when his grandfather died and the mother sent Dean off to be with the grandmother in Indiana. The family business moved to the Heights section of Houston. The nineteen-year-old Corll remained a year later to help with the family business. He was now paid for his services. When the Wests were divorced, Mom was president of the Corll Candy Company; Dean was vice president.

The Army called; he was drafted in 1962 and honorably discharged ten months later. Olsen cites a close friend of Corll, who theorized that Dean's later troubles had their roots in the service: "He told me, that's where it started, when you know, the first time ever—he turned to a fag, really. I guess that's the only way I can say it. And ever since then I guess it just got worse and worse and worse."

Dean became a favorite of children and young men in the neighborhood, dispensing candy. However, the factory workers, but not his mother, noticed strange behavior. Writes Olsen, "Young Corll acted giddy around young men and boys. 'He was giddy,' one of them recalled. 'If a guy'd walk by, maybe Dean'd reach out and pinch him. He always had boys around him, and it seemed odd … It began to be obvious what he was. I don't know how his mother could not have known. Everybody around the candy factory knew it; we just kept quiet about it 'cause he was such a nice decent person.'"

The never-ending marital problems of Dean Corll's mother brought on a fifth divorce and a decision to get out of Houston. She moved to Dallas and the candy company crumbled and closed.

At age twenty-nine, for the first time in his life he was on his own. He entered an electrical training program, and then accepted a position as a relay tester at Houston Lighting and Power. He moved from place to place, seemingly aimless. He was alone, only a few minutes from the Heights—not quite a slum, but a Houston neighborhood where life was a struggle, so people had little time to concern themselves with crime. Such was the description of Olsen, who elaborated, citing an unnamed journalist, that people in the Heights were "too busy coping with what they can feel with their hands. They don't extrapolate, they don't philosophize. Life is tough enough."

People began to notice a change in Corll. His trademark of humor and good spirit had been replaced by hypersensitivity and gloom.

Now his companions were not his peers but teenagers, most notably David Owen Brooks and Wayne Henley. In general, Corll wanted to be with those his junior. "He wanted to pretend that he was just another kid like us," said an acquaintance. Although many wondered why Corll, now thirty, was spending time with teens, the Candy Man—so designated for passing out candy to youngsters years before—was still respectable and well-dressed and held a steady job.

Still, friends noticed a clear change in his personality. His company indeed was more selective. Olsen quotes a friend, "But then I'd see Dean and he'd be in a real bad mood toward me. He'd just want certain people around him, and that's all."

His mother felt his job at the electric company was related to his changed mood. "He never did like it. It didn't keep him busy."

Depravity

On the other hand, fellow workers saw nothing to be concerned with. One said, "He was a fairly stable-minded person ... I knew him just to work with. Pretty nice fella. I never saw him get into fights, never saw him mad. I like him. He was just one of the fellas you worked with."

At that time, Corll had stopped passing out candy. Now the offer was homosexual sex for five and ten dollars. The list of takers was long. Because he changed residence often, detection was difficult. Corll arranged pot and glue-sniffing parties. The profusion of takers was due to the teenage drug culture in Houston's Heights.

"In the claustrophobic, run-down environment," wrote Colin and Damon Wilson, "all the kids were bored and discontented. They felt they were stuck for life. The mere suggestion of a party was enough to make their eyes light up. They all smoked pot—when they could afford it."

The fare was Nembutal, Seconal, Phenobarbital, Quaaludes, even aspirin, which was added to beer or Coca-Cola. While these activities might have been the norm in the Heights, and the Corll demand of sex was no problem, the road to tragedies began with demands for more painful, sadistic sex.

The path to murder was systemized once Corll enlisted the services of David Owen Brooks and Elmer Wayne Henley. While Eric Hickey features the trio among his team killers, Corll was the murderer—except for one victim. Brooks and Henley were the procurers.

Corll first met Brooks in 1969. The fourteen-year-old, like Corll, was the product of a broken home. Corll was attracted to the teen's personality. "Nobody can figure me out," Brooks boasted. The Candy Man had so captured Brooks that the latter dropped out of high school so that he could spend more time with Corll. At the start, Corll paid Brooks ten dollars to commit oral sodomy. Brooks supplemented his funds by stealing, shoplifting, and burglarizing.

According to Brooks's confession to the police, at first he was unaware of Corll's sadism. One day, without calling, Brooks dropped in to Corll's apartment. He found a naked Corll and two naked boys strapped to a board. Corll permitted the boys to leave and offered Brooks money in exchange for a promise of silence.

Wayne Henley was a friend of Brooks, also the product of a broken home. Brooks introduced Henley to Corll. A heterosexual, Henley had only one motive for the association—money. On occasion, Corll paid two hundred dollars each to Brooks and Henley for procuring boys. Now that the three were joined, both the sadism and murder advanced in Houston.

Victims ranged from age nine to college age. After the guests drank, sniffed, and became unconscious, Corll tied or handcuffed them to specially built wooden boards and committed sodomy. They were kept on boards for several days as Corll performed various sexual acts. Some of the bodies showed removed genitals and teeth marks on the genitals. At times Corll chewed the victim's penis or attacked the youth with a seventeen-inch double-headed dildo.

Testimony at the trials of Brooks and Henley revealed some of the procedures: "pulling out their pubic hairs one by one, shoving glass rods up their penis, and shoving a bullet-like instrument in the victim's rectum." On one occasion, Corll shot a bullet up the nose of a victim and then shot him once more in the head. Corll "seemed to enjoy causing pain," testified Brooks.

The first murder victim, in the fall of 1970, was Jeffrey Allen Konen, a twenty-one-year-old student at the University of Texas, who was hitching a ride to his home in Houston. The decomposed bound body was found in 1973.

The list of Corll's victims grew. Victims were shot two at a time. James Glass, fourteen, and Danny Yates, fifteen, in December 1970; two brothers were killed at one time: Donald and Jerry Waldrop, seventeen and thirteen, respectively.

The obvious question was, with the proliferation of teen victims and parental outcries, why did it take until 1973 for the resolution of the case?

The simplistic answer was that the Houston police, like those in

Depravity

other cities, considered the missing teens as runaways, not victims. No evidence of foul play had been presented. Moreover, Houston was a doomed metropolis, and there were not enough police to deal with crime. And runaways from the rundown Heights were quite likely.

In May 1971, David Hilligiest, thirteen, and his friend, Gregory Malley Winkle, sixteen, went to the neighborhood swimming pool. They did not come home. Frantically, the Hilligiests phoned the police, who sought to assure them:

"Times had changed. Boys were running away from the best of homes nowadays and he said he would have to list David in his runaway classification. No, there would be no official search for the child, but if he were spotted during school hours, he would be stopped and questioned. That was all the law allowed. A runaway was not a criminal."

The evening of his disappearance, the Winkles got a call from Gregory. He was in Freeport, sixty miles from Houston, with some boys with whom he swam. Neither David nor Gregory was seen again.

And there were other stories. In August 1971, Reuben Watson, seventeen, was given movie money and intended to return that evening. He never returned. Neither did Frank Aguiree, in March 1972, return from his shift at the restaurant. At that time four friends had disappeared from the Heights. Again, the police told the families the teens were runaways: investigation closed.

In May 1972, Johnny Delome, sixteen, disappeared, along with his friend Billy Baulch, seventeen. The Baulches received a letter, three days after the disappearance, from Madisonville, seventy miles from Houston:

"Dear Mom and Dad. I am sorry to do this. But Johnny and I found a better job working for a trucker loading and unloading from Houston to Washington, and we'll be back in three to four weeks. After a week I will send money to help you and Mom out. Love, Billy."

The Baulches were far from relieved. The note did not look like Billy's handwriting and Mr. Baulch, himself a truck driver, was convinced that there was no such job that Billy was doing. The Delomes also received a letter from Johnny, but because the spelling was perfect, they could not believe that Johnny had no "help" in composing the letter. They went to the police—the usual lack of help—so the Baulches acted on their own, looked for all clues, and examined past events in Houston.

They remembered that David Brooks had given Billy some dope and also recalled the host Dean Corll. On one occasion, Mrs. Baulch asked her son, "Billy, what do you do when go to Dean's home?"

The response was without any concern or suspicion: "We play the stereo and watch TV, and Dean shows us things. Once he showed us his handcuffs. We were there with a couple of other boys, David Brooks and somebody else, and they got to playing around with the handcuffs and put them on one of the boys, and then Dean couldn't find the key. He like never found the key to take them off."

As Mr. Baulch recalled the conversation, he was displeased and worried. "It's not normal," he said, for a man that old to be playing games with little boys. The Baulches found the Candy Man, who was very courteous but said that he had not seen Billy or Johnny and had no idea where they might be.

The killings went on from 1970–73; no one had any idea of the dimensions of the Houston tragedies. It all came to an end, starting August 8, 1973. That morning, the Pasadena Police Department received a tearful call from Wayne Henley. "I jes't killed a man …"

The police rushed to Lamar Street and found an agitated Henley; his girlfriend, Rhonda Williams; and friend Tim Kerley. This was the story Henley told police:

The three had arrived early that morning for a glue-sniffing party. Corll was furious that Henley had brought a girl—without his approval. "You spoiled everything!" roared the host. Henley managed to placate Corll as the host drank beer while the guests busied themselves by hallucinating on acrylic paint fumes from a paper bag.

The three visitors fell into unconsciousness on the floor. Henley woke up to see Corll handcuffing his wrists and binding his ankles.

Depravity

Torture and painful death were imminent, Henley feared. Tim and Rhonda were bound with rope and their lips sealed with masking tape. Tim was stripped.

Henley was dragged into the kitchen, with Corll's revolver jammed into his stomach. "I'm going to kill you all. I'll teach you a lesson. But first I'm gonna have my fun."

Henley begged for his life and tried to sweet talk Corll. He promised to help Corll torture and kill Rhonda and Tim. Corll would attack Tim; Henley would rape Rhonda. Then the two would kill both. Corll released Henley.

Corll stripped and handcuffed Tim to his torture board; Corll strapped Rhonda on the board, but was unable to rape her. An aroused Tim fought off Corll; Henley asked Corll to allow him to remove the girl from the gory scene. Corll ignored Henley.

Henley took the gun Corll left on the nightstand. He pointed the gun at Corll. An enraged Corll taunted Henley: "Kill me, Wayne. Kill me! You won't do it." Henley fired until Corll collapsed, dead, on the floor. Tim and Rhonda were released.

Police asked Henley why he killed Corll after such long service to him. "He made one mistake," said Henley. "This morning he told me I wouldn't be the first one he'd killed. He said he'd already killed a lot of boys and buried them in the boat shed."

At police headquarters, Henley continued the narrative. Corll was a homosexual and pedophile, whose victims Henley procured. The requirement was that prospective victims be young and handsome. It was amazing that Henley procured his longtime childhood friends. The detectives were not immediately convinced. This was probably, they reasoned, a typical teenage drug group. Certainly, the murdered man was not a criminal.

A disbelieving father and stepmother insisted, "Dean has never been a homosexual. He has never been a violent person. He had also loved kids and for years, gave them candy. Those who accuse him have taken advantage of his generosity and hospitality. Then, when drugged, they killed him in his own home."

With all the machinery of sexual torture in Corll's home, the police could not dismiss Henley's story. "Take us to the boat shed," the police told Henley.

No one in Houston was prepared for what followed. The destination was Silver Bell Street, site of Southwest Boat Storage. Stall Number 11 was Dean Corll's. The scene is described in *Mass Murder in Houston* by John Gurwell:

"The stall had no windows, and the officers moved slowly as they accustomed their eyes to the gloom of the deep interior. Two faded carpets covered the earthen floor, stretching from the entrance back twelve feet. One was green, the other blue. Inside the doors on the left stood a huge, empty appliance carton. A half-stripped car body, covered by a sheet of canvas, sat in the right area of the stall … behind the barrel in the corner was a plastic bag and inside this was an empty lime bag."

In the oppressive August heat of Houston, prison convicts or "trusties" dug until they reached a layer of lime. After digging a few inches, they saw a plastic sheet, with the naked body of a boy about thirteen.

The scene was described by Colin and Damon Wilson: "Suddenly, the shed was filled with a sickening stench; the detectives held their noses. The next carefully excavated shovelful revealed a face looking up at them. The younger trusty dropped his spade and rushed outside, making retching noises."

Next came a skeleton of a second victim. To the right of the first grave were two additional teens. One had been shot, one strangled.

The boat shed area became jammed as the news media, from Houston, from across America, and across the globe, learned of the discoveries. By midnight, eight bodies had been found. After the first day, the worried parents had realized their worst fears. The owner of the facility, Mrs. Mayme Meynier, was stupefied. "He seemed like such a nice person, the nicest person you'd ever met," she told police. "He rented the shed for nearly three years and came by several times a week. I do admit that I was surprised when he recently told me that the shed was almost filled and wanted to rent more space. I do admit that I was surprised that he needed more space. Surely, he had plenty."

Houston police were horrified. As Olsen writes, "They had all seen death, but none had encountered the wholesale transfiguration of rollicking boys into reeking sacks of carrion."

While the digging went on, Henley sat in the police car. As the first body was carried out, he groaned, visibly shaken. "It was all my fault."

"Why?" asked the detective.

"Because I introduced him to them boys." He then told the detective how he had procured boys for Corll.

What was David Brooks doing while the bodies were brought out? He went to the police in Houston, insisting that he had no role in the killings. His "confession" involved admission of procuring while blaming Henley for joining with Corll in the murders. When the detectives told Henley that Brooks had visited the police, Henley decided to open up and admit to his role in the tortures and murders.

The police decided that the morning would be ideal to invite Brooks and bring Henley in to face each other. Henley stared at Brooks when he entered the station. "David, I told everything. You better do the same thing."

Brooks tried to avoid the inevitable. "I don't know what you're talking about."

Henley would not be denied. "Yes, you do. And if you don't tell everything, I'm gonna change my confession and say you was responsible for all of it." Brooks was arrested later that day.

Henley was still valuable for the police, for he had told them that he could lead them to additional bodies at Lake Sam Rayburn and on High Island Beach, near Galveston.

The trip to Lake Sam Rayburn was more than one hundred miles, offering detectives a chance to understand Henley. "You seem like a decent kid," queried a detective. "How could you do such bad things?"

The answer was stunning. "If you had a daddy that shot at you, you might do some things too."

Henley led police to the sites of four bodies; two more bodies were found on the shores. Meanwhile, at the boat shed, digging was continuing. By the day's end, seventeen bodies had been found. The total went to nineteen, with bones of two added corpses. On the third day, with both Brooks and Henley present, eight more bodies were found on Lake Sam Rayburn and High Island. Both Brooks and Henley had given police a list of victims they recalled. The total was twenty-nine, so two missing teens were unaccounted for.

The twenty-seven murders had given Corll top notoriety, exceeding the record of American serial killers, twenty-five, "achieved" by California migrant Juan Corona in 1971. Interestingly, Corona follows Corll in serial killer reference works. H. H. Holmes confessed to twenty-seven crimes at the beginning of the century, but before his death he recanted many of the crimes; this was also true of Henry Lee Lucas.

What about the two unaccounted bodies, or others not on the list? Olsen felt that there might have been more bodies in the area surrounding the former family candy company. Hickey and others felt that the Houston police lost interest, with the new serial killer record. "Some observers believe," writes Hickey, "police stopped searching for bodies once they had surpassed the existing number of homicide victims found in a single case at that time."

Understandably, the murders dominated talk and thought in Houston for a long time. While the Corll killings were going on, a prostitution ring was operating in Dallas, but no link was established. But across Texas, mothers wondered how such activities went on so long without detection. Said one Houston mother, "We're always worried about our little girls. Suddenly, we find out it was our boys we should have been cautioning all along."

Houston had a large gay community. They were worried about

the hostility they might endure. Appearing before Houston's city council, the head of the gay community asked for understanding. "That the person believed responsible was an alleged homosexual is only incidental," he said. "It could just as easily have been the bodies of young girls that were unearthed."

The case also caught the attention of Pope Paul VI and was discussed in the Vatican daily *L'Osservatore Romano*. "We are in the domain of sadism and demonism," lamented the editorial. "This is beyond the borderline of crime because it is beyond the borderline of reason. What wicked force can produce such a degradation … One kills to the point of such cruel and inhuman aberration because one is no longer a man, but an evil force. The two evil monsters—sex and drugs—have generated a new and different behavior—monstrous and demonic."

However, the number-one target for the incensed Houston citizens was its police force. Where had the police been for three years? The police gave the standard explanation: simple runaway. Olsen presents a number of responses from police officials and detectives, shifting the focus to delinquent teens and absentee parents:

"These kids, most of them knew what they were getting into. They were little whores out for quick money." Said another, "Those kids were what you would call little turds, most of 'em. Several had police records. Several had nutty parents."

This case was over, observed a detective as the number twenty-seven reached headquarters. Current cases were what counted: "I got live cases to work on, where the murderer's at large right now, and could kill again. Why should I [expletive] with this Corll thing?"

The most agonizing times were experienced by parents of the victims. Olsen records their thoughts, among them Fred and Dorothy Hilligiest. They had always thought David would return. The mother could not blame anyone. It was the "age we live in."

"I'm not angry with anybody," she said, "and never have been. I put myself in Miz Henley's place because I've had six children myself, and I know that she's bearing a bigger cross than I am. Her son's life is ruin't.

I don't blame Miz Henley, and I don't blame anybody else. I think that for too long we've all been blaming each other, when it's the times we live in that's to blame."

As for the future, she sought to console her youngest son, Stanley: "Well, just say a prayer. God'll give you strength. I know. Put yourself in Wayne's [Henley] two little brothers' place. Look at what their brother has done. And your brother, he's not suffering. Sometimes these things have to happen to help other people. Out of every evil comes some good. Time will heal for us. We'll never forget David, and we'll have good memories of him."

Wayne Henley had shot Dean Corll in 1973, so now justice waited for Henley and David Brooks. The Texas Legislature had enacted new guidelines for capital punishment. The guidelines called for capital punishment only when murder was committed during arson, burglary, kidnapping, rape, and robbery. Neither Henley nor Brooks was likely to receive capital punishment. In 1974 Henley was sentenced to six consecutive ninety-nine-year terms for murder in the deaths of six boys. The following year, Brooks was sentenced to life for the death of one boy. Brooks's conviction was overturned on appeal in 1978 because of pretrial publicity, but he was retried in Corpus Christi, convicted, and sentenced, as before, in 1979. Incredibly, Henley became eligible for parole in 1983, but all his requests have been denied.

Houston has no Son of Sam Law, which precludes criminals from profiting from their notoriety. This includes books and paintings. According to Marilyn Bardsley, in her biography of Corll for Crime Library, Houston has been angered that Henley offers paintings and other personal items on eBay. Henley spends his prison time painting flowers and other tranquil subjects and scenes.

Dean Corll was killed and emerged as America's greatest serial killer. Yet, having served in the American armed forces, he was eligible for burial with military honors. An American flag covered his coffin, as he was buried in Houston's Grand View Memorial Park Cemetery.

Corll's murder without confession deprived students of a special opportunity to understand the mind and mental workings of America's greatest serial killer. In one photograph, Corll is shown with a toy Snoopy dog; in another, he is shown holding a teddy bear. Olsen sees the Candy Man as a boy who never grew up.

In their *Encyclopedia*, Colin Wilson and Daniel Seaman saw parallels with Marcel Proust. They write, "His personality seems to have something in common with that of another oversensitive homosexual, Marcel Proust. And in case the comparison seems unflattering to the novelist, it is worth bearing in mind that Proust had a distinctly sadistic streak, and enjoyed watching rats being tortured to death."

Dean Corll is examined in a monograph on "Homosexual Serial Murder Investigation" by Vernon J. Gebirth, former commander, Bronx Homicide, New York Police Department. For those like Corll, "The most frequent motivation was sadomasochistic sexual acts followed by male pedophilia."

Gebirth's conclusion fits the story of Dean Corll:

> There was a style and pattern to their killings which involved domination, control, humiliation, and sadistic sexual violence. The murders were committed without the least sense of guilt or shame, and the killers displayed a total lack of remorse ....
>
> The circumstances and dynamics involved in the homosexual murder investigations require detectives to be able to effectively communicate with the homosexual community. They must be able to break through various subcultures in a non-threatening and non-judgmental manner in order to open up critical lines of communication in pursuit of the necessary information relating to the murder investigation.

For his mother, Mary West, Dean Corll always remained a good person. She reminisced about her son, recorded by Olsen: "The police, the TV reporters, the psychiatrists are trying so hard to convince the whole world that Dean Corll was homosexual, sadistic ... Dean Corll was good, not a goody-goody that hides behind a title, a church, or a philosophy. He was basically good. He never spread rumors, he made up no lies. He did not choose his friends; his friends chose him."

To her, Dean was as her clairvoyant saw him: "I see Dean. He's completely clear. He's robed in white. He has an aura of white around him."

Postscript: On June 26, 2003, the U.S. Supreme Court ruled that a Texas sodomy law was unconstitutional, after a challenge by two Houston homosexuals, Tyrone Garner and John J. Lawrence. In his dissent, Justice Scalia noted the thinking of the majority: "The Texas statute undoubtedly seeks to further the belief of its citizens that certain forms of sexual behavior are 'immoral and unacceptable' … Bowers [Supreme Court decision of 1986—Bowers v. Hardwick] held that this was a legitimate state interest. The Court today reaches the opposite conclusion."

SECTION V—

STEREOTYPES:

INTELLIGENCE, RACE

MARCEL PETIOT

Doctor of Holocaust Atrocities

Stalin, Hitler, Hussein: is there a more awful, awesome trio of murderers in the twentieth century? Still, not one of the three is included in a listing of mass murderers or serial killers in the twentieth century. It is clear why they have been omitted from serial killer designation. Serial killers have been studied from emotional and psychological perspectives. One could agree with Colin and Damon Wilson that "serial murder is a disease." And mass murderers in our culture exclude political ideologists and genocidists.

In this vein, Adolf Eichmann, Martin Bormann, et. al.—those who were responsible for carrying out the Holocaust, the annihilation of millions, are not found in reference works of mass murderers. True, they did not personally kill, as did serial killers. But even those who did, for example, those who turned on the gas at Auschwitz, are still part of the political ideology of Holocaust and genocide.

But Marcel Petiot carried out his killings in the milieu of the Holocaust. In fact, his setting for the murders was akin to a concentration camp. Still, he killed for profit, not for the glory of Nazism. True, the Frenchman told his countrymen that he killed pro-Nazi collaborators. Why not? The Nazis were occupiers. For Dr. Petiot, one applies the line, "Patriotism is the last refuge of a scoundrel" (Boswell's *Life of Dr. Johnson*).

In his 2000 study of serial killers, Elliott Leyton links Petiot to other middle-class serial killers: "middle-class functionaries—doctors, teachers, professors, civil servants [who] preyed on members of the lower orders, especially prostitutes, and housemaids." In particular, he joins Petiot with Scottish Dr. William Palmer and Dr. Thomas Cream, whose murders were committed in the late nineteenth century. Petiot achieved notoriety in the twentieth century. Moreover, Leyton describes Cream as one of the "enforcers of the new moral order" who terrorized London prostitutes. And Palmer was an "enterprising" murderer, who began a career of petty crime at an early age, ran a private abortion service, and later turned to murder to support his activities in racing and gambling.

Like other serial killers, a troubled beginning for Marcel Petiot led to a disastrous adulthood. He was born in 1897, one hundred miles south of Paris at Auxerre. His parents were civil servants, both clerks. Since their employer required them to be constantly on the move, the parents decided to send the youngster to live with his spinster aunt.

An older Marcel was convinced that his parents simply did not want him around. Many years later, in prison, he wrote in his notes that he had been conceived by accident.

Early on he displayed a sadistic side. He loved being cruel to his classmates and to animals. He impaled insects on pins and needles and bound the legs of flying insects so that he could be a spectator to their struggles for freedom. The greatest joy was watching them die. On one occasion, he blinded the eyes of birds by putting a needle into their eyes.

At age nine, he moved from insects and birds to torturing cats and dogs. He once dropped a puppy and kitten into a boiling kettle and sat by and relished their deaths. As a student, he graduated into advanced torture activities. He tore apart cats and dogs, fascinated by their interiors. While an undisciplined student who stole from classmates, he was brilliant, five years advanced over other students in writing and reading skills.

In *The Great Liquidator*, John Grombach relates a visit that a teenage Marcel made to his parents. Overhearing his mother tell the father that she had received erotic letters addressed to her, which she opened, Marcel decided that it would be exciting to read such mail. So he crafted a fishing pole, string, and weight that could be thrust into any mailbox and fish out the envelopes.

He was reading all Auxerre mail. All this came to an end when gendarmes came to the aunt's house. The punishment was a scolding by his father and expulsion from school. His lack of more severe punishment could be traced to a psychiatric report, which described the teen as "an abnormal youth suffering from personal and hereditary problems which limit to a large degree his responsibility for his acts." To which a judge added, "The accused appears to be mentally ill." However, that was not the end of his education. He studied on his own because he was moved by a desperate need to succeed. That meant being rich, powerful, important, and respected. He did exceedingly well on his high school entrance tests and was able to convince his parents to send him to a school in Paris and later Dijon. Marcel set out to become a doctor because that seemed a desirable profession to attain money, power, importance, and respect.

Before he settled himself into his studies, he sought sexual encounters. He became an avid reader of books about sexual deviants (e.g., Don Juan, Casanova, Mademoiselle de Maupin). After experiences with a prostitute and cabaret girl, he threw himself into his books. Marcel Petiot was determined to prove his father wrong.

As Grombach writes, "He knew that his father expected nothing from him—or rather expected that he would be useless all his life, given to mischief and 'dirty pictures,' and to torturing small animals. Marcel was determined he would rub his father's nose in the fact that the son he had disowned was a superior person."

World War I arrived, and despite being seized by the patriotic fervor of Frenchmen, he continued his studies and graduated at age eighteen. His army service was an added example of his distaste for discipline.

While fighting in the Aisne district, he was gassed and hit by grenade fragments. The wounds healed, but he suffered continual headaches, sleeplessness, loss of weight and appetite, dizziness, and memory loss. He was sent to clinics and rest homes. His mental status did not stand in his way of stealing blankets and morphine and selling it at black market prices to drug addicts. He was judged not guilty because of insanity, based on a doctor's diagnosis: Petiot suffered from "mental disequilibrium, neurasthenia, depression, melancholia, obsessions, and phobias."

But his military service did not end. Neither did his problems. Returning to the front in 1918, he suffered a nervous breakdown and literally shot himself in the foot. It is debatable whether he faked his mental state or the episodes were real. But his behavior and complaints of dizziness led to psychiatric treatment at Rennes. The diagnoses were amnesia, sleepwalking, depression, and suicidal wishes. The result was discharge with 40 percent disability pension. A 1920 review ruled 100 percent pension with suggested referral to an asylum.

Petiot was pleased with the pension but was unhappy because a 100 percent disability rating would be a bar to a medical career. Two years later, in 1922, his rating was changed to 50 percent disabled as an epileptic with "fits of depression" but sans suicidal impulses. In 1923, the diagnosis was "dementia praecox."

Meanwhile, as Petiot's ratings were reviewed and changed, he intensified his medical studies, benefiting from veteran status. He was graduated from the University of Paris in an incredible eight months. He earned a Doctor of Medicine degree with a grade of "superior" on his thesis from one professor who elaborated, "Normally, 'superior' is the mark I would give to God; 'excellent' is the mark I would give myself; and I would leave 'good' or less for the remainder of my students."

French Army records have shown, writes Grombach, that "Petiot very definitely showed every sign and symptom of being mentally deranged if not insane." Reviewing the record, Grombach asks in wonderment, "Why this extraordinary record did not prevent Petiot from practicing medicine and why it was not used in any effort to defend him in his final trial as a lunatic not responsible for murdering

… is one of the many mysteries—if not the major mystery—of the Petiot case."

Be that as it may, Dr. Marcel Petiot was now a practicing physician, demented and dangerous.

Petiot chose Villeneuve-sur-Yonne, a picturesque town on the Yonne River. His competition was two elderly physicians. Petiot sent out flyers advertising himself as a doctor who "treats patients with the most modern methods but without exploiting them." He did well, for he attracted patients who had been treated unsuccessfully by the other doctors or those hypochondriacs the other doctors did not want to bother with. In the words of Grombach, "He was drawn by nature to the disaffected, the rebellious, and the exploited."

He also helped himself by secretly enrolling the patients for state medical assistance, for which he received double payment—from patient and government. His treatment with addictive narcotics worried local pharmacists. He told a complaining pharmacist, "What difference does it make to you, anyway? Isn't it better to do away with this kid who's not doing anything in this world but pestering its mother?"

Apart from questionable medical practices, Petiot was involved in clearly illegal activities. He was a petty thief who pilfered money or possessions from patients, both live and dead. He even stole from his brother when visiting his home. He stole gas from the gas station. After accusing the local electric company of false bills, he stole electricity, bypassing the meter by attaching wires to the electric cable.

For after-hours entertainment, he fixed his attention on Louise Laveau, daughter of an elderly patient. The relationship became so intense that Petiot could not live without her, so he persuaded her to move in with him. Petiot had no thought of marriage. However, the relationship hit many bumps. Abortion was a major area of his practice; in fact, Petiot felt that overpopulation was the world's number-one problem. But Louise was a devout Catholic who was horrified at his practice. And she was horrified that she was "forced" into using contraceptives in their relationship.

Notwithstanding his flourishing practice, Petiot was stingy in giving her funds to manage the household. The relationship cooled, and Louise suspected that he had romantically selected one of his patients. She threatened to expose his irresponsible prescriptions, his petty thefts, and his widespread abortion practice.

Dr. Petiot was now ready to launch his career as murderer. An avid reader of true crime, he researched the careers of murderers Dr. Harvey Crippen and contemporary Frenchman Henri Désiré Landru. First, he displayed a public stance of concern toward Louise, so there would be no touch of suspicion.

One night he prescribed a drug for her minor complaint. He administered the drug by hypodermic, and she was dead quickly. Next, he had to remove the body. He eviscerated the organs and placed them in the kitchen stove. Next, he removed the head, put it in a canvas bag, and burned it in the stove the following day. Then, he dumped the body on an abandoned farm and scattered the ashes of the head in the cemetery.

When police asked about Louise, he calmly told them that they had an argument and she left. When the headless body was found, the police saw no link and thought it was a runaway.

Politics would be his next activity. What motivated him? An atheist, Petiot was an attractive potential candidate to the unions, the Socialists, and the Communists. With money not a problem, he listened to their pleadings, and he always communicated well with the poor and the working class. Petiot chose the Communists, not because he favored their philosophy but because it offered the best avenue for election:

"The Communist Party appeals to me for it is a new party based on the have-nots who believe they should have and is, therefore, overwhelming in desire and numbers, although just as unsound as any other form of dictatorship. It won't actually work, for it removes incentive and allegedly divides everything equally, no matter what share each person may deserve."

In 1927, Petiot was elected, running as a Socialist with Communist support. He won a seat on the municipal council, and then was named deputy mayor. The mayor was Paul Mayaud, who had challenged Petiot's prescription. Unfortunately, Mayaud died right after the election, but it was fortunate for Petiot, who not only became mayor but also medical examiner, which offered the doctor a chance to investigate his own actions. But give the devil his due: Petiot was a strong mayor who brought what the town needed—physical improvements.

Politician and physician, Petiot decided to settle down and marry Georgette Lablais, daughter of a prosperous businessman. They had a son a year later. He was a rising star. In fact, people—especially Petiot himself—liked to picture Marcel Petiot as Georges Clemenceau, the Tiger, the doctor-statesman who became Premier of France. But Petiot had too much baggage. However, Petiot overcame all local opposition. And he did cure the sick, regardless of money he pocketed. He was accused and sentenced for stealing cans of oil. But the conviction was reversed.

What stopped Petiot's rise, among other things, was continued petty thievery, including taking from homes of friends and from the dead while attending as medical examiner; he also helped himself to top choices of real estate through unrestricted access to city hall records.

Georgette was an excellent, devoted wife. However, that was a minus for Petiot. His sex life was lackluster because his wife was drained from her activities as mother and housekeeper.

He needed a mistress—and found one: Henriette Debauve, manager of a dairy cooperative, who was some ten years older than the doctor. She laughingly warned Petiot, with the words of a local priest, "Remember, a fire burns fastest in an old chimney."

But Petiot delighted with the flame. His only concern was keeping the affair secret; the only one who might have known was a bistro owner. All was fine until he was overcome with the lust for money—this was big money. One evening, for some reason, she had on hand two hundred eighty thousand francs, then about fifteen thousand dollars—not her money.

"Why don't we stage a fake robbery?" he urged his love. She was taken aback at the idea, and flatly refused. He pushed her to seize the money. She was angered and reached for a hammer to hit him, but he grabbed the hammer and pounded her to death. It was for good reason that Petiot was called the "Second Landru." He burnt down the house.

Now Petiot had to avoid being caught. Naturally, the medical examiner Petiot "investigated" and signed a death certificate, agreeing that she was murdered. Still, he saw no problems. However, rumors were rampant that Mayor Petiot was having an affair with Henriette and money was missing from the house. More important, Petiot was seen the murder night near the Debauve home. The bistro owner announced his readiness to testify.

Petiot was more a fox than a tiger. One day, he met the bistro owner and invited him for a drink. When the latter complained of rheumatism, Petiot suggested a "new treatment." Immediately, Petiot brought the dangerous potential witness to his office and injected him with a fatal air bubble. Petiot examined the body and signed the death certificate: "By accident … from heart shock or some unknown side effect resulting from a hypodermic injection."

Despite spirited opposition, Petiot won reelection. However, his enemies were relentless. And once more, thievery did him in and stuck. He was accused of stealing gas containers. He was sentenced to fifteen days and a two hundred franc fine. The prison sentence was removed; the fine halved. However, the sentence cost Petiot his council seat and mayoralty.

Petiot decided it was time to move on. For the non-politician, Petiot was beloved: he cured; he brought children into the world; he improved the physical face of the town. So when the Petiots left Villeneuve-sur-Yonne, "there was real mourning in town," records Grombach. "And there were political supporters who would remember him always as a valiant fighter for the underdog, a resourceful, witty, and indefatigable campaigner and a man who knew how to play wonder tricks on his enemies. None could ever believe that he was a mass murderer for his own gain. All, without exception, agreed that he must have been a misguided patriot, believed he was killing for his country and perhaps for its cure—a Communist France."

Paris beckoned. In fact, as soon as opponents became more vocal and numerous, Petiot began to look elsewhere. He chose the Opera section, a neighborhood throbbing with tourists and businessmen—definitely the right spot for a practicing physician. He advertised his credentials with outrageous claims of cures for anything and anybody. While the medical association complained, his medical practice was immensely successful.

However, Petiot was not free from trouble. Mrs. Petiot's dressmaker visited Petiot—now known as Henri Valery—for an abscess of the mouth. She was unconscious when Petiot drove her home. Raymonde Hanss never regained consciousness. Traces of morphine were found in her body. Fingers were pointed at Petiot, but he escaped prosecution for lack of solid evidence.

He also had to counter criticism for prescribing dope for drug addicts and for advocating and practicing birth control and abortions. "I feel certain," Petiot predicted, "that the Catholic Church and all civilized countries will legalize birth control and abortions, as have all Communist nations."

In 1935, Petiot was appointed state medical officer for the ninth arrondissement of Paris, with the power of signing death certificates. That was a green light for more trouble: Petiot pronounced the death of a wealthy lawyer and proceeded to steal nearly seventy-five thousand francs from the deceased's home; he was caught shoplifting and assaulted a policeman.

The plea of insanity resulted in the assault charge being dropped. Instead, he was committed to a private sanitorium and released in 1937. For the next few years, he changed direction. His crimes were merely tax fraud.

The day-to-day life of Petiot—and all other Frenchmen—changed with the start of World War II in 1939. New opportunities were available for Petiot, who developed links with the French Gestapo and the collaborationist Vichy government.

With the coming of the Germans, the real estate market collapsed, as people sought to carry away cash by selling their holdings. Petiot found a house at 21 Rue Le Sueur that would house the antiques that he had amassed or be a postwar clinic or serve whatever purpose he desired. It was quite a desirable and expensive house, which then cost four hundred thousand francs, or the equivalent of eighty thousand dollars.

It had a sewerage system, emptying into the famous Paris sewers. Other features were a secret courtyard and inner rooms. It also had a windowless, sound-proof triangular room with only one door. With the installation of peepholes, Petiot told the contractor that he was now ready to treat the mentally impaired.

Rue Le Sueur would become for Petiot what Holmes Castle was for murder-for-profit serial killer H. H. Holmes. Did Petiot plan this? Grombach offers these thoughts: "Whether the possession of the house prompted the plan for establishing the liquidation business, or whether the purchase was part of the plan, one cannot be sure. It seems from what Petiot said later that the ideas blossomed together, one fitting neatly into the other."

Certainly, Petiot's wartime activities fit well with the deeds of murder and plunder. Beyond that, Grombach reveals a fascinating aspect of the Petiot story.

In his Introduction to *The Great Liquidator*, Grombach notes that Petiot had espionage involvements and had "reported contacts with Soviet Secret Intelligence, the German Gestapo, the German Abwehr, and British Intelligence." Petiot gave U.S. secret agents "valuable information."

Grombach, from 1942–47, was the director of the Secret Intelligence Branch of the U.S. War Department general staff. He cites one report in which Petiot alerted U.S. agents that the Germans were seeking

Depravity

to win the atom bomb race. "With the help of these reports," writes Grombach, "the FBI converted German spies into controlled agents. They were fed wrong information—as can be proven by documentary evidence—that delayed the Nazi atom bomb. This may well prove that a strange Paris informer [Marcel Petiot] may have contributed to our winning World War II."

Having made contacts with the intelligence network, he knew that the Third Reich had targeted its enemies, mainly Jews, for their lives and for their resources. He reasoned that Jews—and he knew many—would spend their fortunes—whether money, jewelry, furs, or other resources—to escape from Nazi-occupied France. But, he continued, Jews were doomed, so why not be greedy, take their money, and do not deliver them to a haven. Why should the Nazis be the plunderers? He had as much a "right" to the plunder as they had.

Joachim Guschinow was not the first victim of this plan, but his story has received a great deal of attention. Client and neighbor Guschinow was ideal for Petiot's devilish plans. He was a partner in a highly lucrative fur business. The Nazis had forbidden the Jewish merchant to engage in business, so his non Jewish associate ran the enterprise.

Petiot told Guschinow in the summer of 1941 that he could help him escape to Argentina. Guschinow resisted until Petiot told him that his arrest was imminent. Petiot readied his mini death camp. At stake was two million francs, some forty thousand dollars. To avoid problems, Petiot told Guschinow that he must not communicate with his wife—of course, for her sake, Petiot told the victim. Eventually, Petiot reassured him, they would be reunited in Argentina.

The results of the planning were realized on January 2, 1942. Guschinow came to Petiot's charnel house, with pictures for his passport, all IDs removed from his person, packed suitcases, and, most important, valued resources carefully hidden.

When the victim entered the charnel house, Petiot cheerily greeted his client. He brought out a blank passport, took the pictures from

Guschinow, and placed them in the passport book. He went through a series of questions: about the hidden valuables, about Guschinow's identity, about all other preparations made.

"You cannot enter Argentina without a smallpox vaccination and being inoculated against typhoid," Petiot advised the victim. The latter quickly followed instructions and rolled up his sleeves. As he had done on other occasions, Petiot drove the fatal shot into the arm—the large bubble of air causing an embolism of the heart. No vaccination followed, and Guschinow waited in an adjoining room.

Guschinow began to choke, realizing he had been done in. He pleaded with Petiot. "Save me! I have much more money. We can divide it all!" Within twenty minutes, he was dead.

Petiot threw the body onto a table, eviscerated it, severed the head, and removed the hands. These would later go into a furnace, akin to the atrocities in the death camps. All entrails were flushed down the drain. Then the money and jewels were removed from the lining of his jacket. The corpse was dumped in the river near St. Louen. No links led to Dr. Petiot.

As a follow-up, Petiot posted Mrs. Guschinow on developments: her husband had reached Casablanca, later Buenos Aires, and then had opened a promising business. Later, in his death operation, Petiot convinced victims to write personal letters to their spouses testifying to their escape and calling on them to trust the good doctor.

Petiot lined up "customers" through scouts, Edmond Pintard and Raoul Fourrier, who were paid commissions. As far as they knew, Petiot was simply—for a fee—helping Jews escape the Nazi net. One family that did not come by way of the scouts, in the summer of 1942, was the Kurt Kneller family. They were revealed to Petiot through a German Swiss who had close contact with the Germans. The word was that Kneller had left Germany with great sums of money. In addition, Mr. Kneller had become a Petiot patient.

Petiot offered them a "special price" of one hundred twenty-five thousand francs for Mr. Kneller, his wife, and their seven-year-old son

Depravity

for escape to South America. Mr. Kneller was the first to visit 21 Rue Le Sueur; a day later, wife and son followed. None left the charnel house alive. The initial price of one hundred twenty-five thousand francs swelled to nine hundred fifty thousand francs for the entire family. To avoid any suspicions, Petiot and Mrs. Kneller—after being drugged—had written letters and postcards to Mme. Roart, the Knellers's neighbor. The correspondence said that they had quickly left the country.

Other clients, found by scouts, were those who had come to France by way of Austria, Poland, and the Netherlands. Not all clients were Jewish. Among early victims were Parisian pimps who had ventured into armed robbery disguised as Gestapo agents. Dr. Marcel Petiot was known to clients as Dr. Eugene. Then there were clients who were members of the French Resistance. The numbers have not been fixed, although the number of Jewish refugees was close to thirty.

The Nazis searched for Jews. They were stunned that they were missing. In 1943, Gestapo agent Robert Jodkum reported "a great deal of talk in public about an organization which arranges clandestine crossings of the Spanish border by means of falsified passports." A rich French Jew, Yvan Dreyfus sought to bribe the Gestapo, in particular Jodkum, to save him from death. Aside from payments, Dreyfus was blackmailed into investigating the organization that was saving "enemies of the Third Reich." Despite the best of plans, Dreyfus fell into the trap of the charnel house and disappeared in May 1943.

But the Gestapo persevered and enlisted secret agent Charles Betetta. The agent set himself up as a client for escape. He met at the shop of scout Raoul Fourrier, but Petiot was not there. Gestapo agents swarmed to the scene and arrested Fourrier and Edmond Pintard. Once in headquarters, they admitted working for Dr. Eugene but insisted they did not know his identity. Tortures improved their memories. But the address given was 66 Rue Caumartin. Petiot was arrested in late May 1943 there, so the charnel house and his network, called Fly-Tox, remained undisclosed.

Petiot and his scouts were confined and tortured. But they had no role in the Resistance and had no names for the Gestapo. Why were they released in January 1944? "And the reports read," said Grombach, "that Petiot had not only helped spirit Jews away, but even terrorists, enemy airmen, and German deserters. It would not have been in the least out of character, or even a departure from normal procedure, for the Gestapo to execute Petiot out of hand and not even notify the family of his fate."

The answer would seem to be that Mme. Petiot and Marcel's brother, Maurice, reached out to their vast network of friends and acquaintances with links to the Nazis. Also, there was probably an "arrangement" that included vast sums of money and a confession from Petiot about the charnel house. And, in the end, both the Nazis and Petiot were ridding the world of Jews.

Petiot decided to be more careful when he returned to the death factory. Neighbors hardly took notice of the goings in and out of the charnel house. Perhaps they were amazed at the activities in June 1943. The concierge of 23 rue Le Sueur counted forty-nine bags and suits being loaded onto a vehicle. But that was the end of the matter.

Maurice Petiot had from the start brought quicklime in bulk to the house. He treated the body parts in the quicklime before shoving them into his hellish furnace. However, Maurice and his family did not want to have involvement anymore, so the supplies of quicklime no longer came.

However, on March 11, 1944, neighbors became concerned when a stinking smoke poured from the chimney on 21 Rue Le Sueur. It was noxious smoke coming from an oven. Firemen entered the charnel house while police headed for his practice at Rue Caumartin. The horrified firemen found dismembered corpses on the floor. Heads, limbs, and torsos were scattered throughout the house.

Forensic experts determined there were twenty-seven human bodies. Calmly, Petiot told the police, "They were all Nazi collaborators, betrayers of France." The police were not fully convinced. Petiot fled for the countryside, while senior police officials came to the charnel house. They

Depravity

found a storehouse of plunder as well as Petiot's carefully kept records. The records noted that sixty-three had entered 21 Rue Le Sueur.

Having disappeared, Petiot perhaps would not have been caught as the Germans retreated and the Allies retook France. But the arrogant Petiot thought he could outfox and outtalk anybody. He joined the forces of the Free French Army. He wrote to the newspaper *Resistance*, signed Captain Henri Valery. "I am innocent," he wrote. While he was under arrest, he said, the Nazis had tried to frame him by dumping bodies near the furnace.

After liberation, the French sought to restore some law and order, and the case of Petiot was high on the agenda. Now, to find Petiot. It was easier than imagined. In November 1944, General Charles de Gaulle led the troops in a victory parade down the Champs Elysees. Lo and behold, there was Dr. Marcel Petiot, with a beard and fake medals on his chest. He was quickly recognized and arrested.

He was interrogated for sixteen months and continued to insist that he had only killed Germans and their collaborators. But no one would support his story, especially leaders of Resistance groups. No one would certify his tales of bombing missions or assassination of Nazis. He was charged with murdering and plundering twenty-seven victims. It was estimated that he had murdered them for two hundred million francs in cash, gold, and jewels.

A calm, defiant Petiot spent his time in prison 'productively.' He completed a three-hundred-page manuscript, *Le Hasard Vaincu* (*Beating Chance*), that detailed the ways of succeeding at gambling. Published at his own expense, he announced signed copies would be given to those attending his trial, scheduled for March 18, 1946, at Palis de Justice.

Proceedings were heard before a panel of three judges and seven-man jury. Rene Floriot defended Petiot, although the accused was very active in his own defense. Prosecutors were joined by twelve civil lawyers enlisted by the relatives of Petiot's victims.

The packed courtroom was silenced, shocked from the start as they viewed the wall of forty-seven suitcases stacked behind the dock. They contained clothing and valuables stolen by Petiot from his victims, including twenty-nine suits, seventy-nine dresses, and five fur coats.

If nothing else, Dr, Petiot was entertaining. He was witty and sarcastic as he verbally jousted with justices, prosecutors, and witnesses. He attacked one attorney as a "double agent" and "defender of Jews." He described one victim as being "easy to spot as a collaborator, with a head like a pimp—you know, like a police inspector." Supposedly a victim, Guschinow, was alive. "You can't find him because South America is a big place." Victim Yvan Dreyfus was a "traitor four times over." Many, he claimed, had survived the Fly-Tox journey. "You can't find them because they have changed names frequently."

When Chief Judge Michel Leser scolded the accused of doodling in court, Petiot responded, "I am listening, but it doesn't really interest me very much."

After the second day of the trial, reporters overheard Judge Leser and two jurors discussing Petiot in private, calling him "a demon" and "an appalling murderer." Attorney Floriot called for a mistrial. The appellate court refused, but did replace the two jurors.

There could be no doubt of the decision on the fifth day of the trial when the court met at 21 Rue Le Sueur. They walked through human bones and all other grisly fixtures at the charnel house. Petiot was taken along, as neighbors jeered. But he had not lost his macabre humor.

"Peculiar homecoming, don't you think?" quipped Petiot.

A powerful force on the minds of the jurors was the testimony of psychiatrists, which closed down any insanity plea. The judge's notes included: "The psychiatrists unanimously find that he is sane and, therefore, responsible for his acts."

To the end, Petiot maintained his stance. Nineteen of the twenty-seven victims were "Germans and collaborators." How about the other forty-four, Petiot was queried. "I don't have to justify myself for murders I'm not accused of committing!"

Petiot's attorney won a standing ovation from the audience when he described Petiot as a hero of the Resistance. The jury, however, needed

Depravity

little convincing. On April 6, 1946, the jury took three hours—ninety seconds for each of the one hundred thirty-five criminal charges—to convict Petiot on all but nine counts. He was guilty of twenty-six of the twenty-seven murders.

The court was not silent when the verdict was announced, so he turned to his attorney to learn the decision. He screamed, "I will be avenged!"

The conviction was appealed for two reasons: a mistrial should have been granted after the judge and two jurors publicly declared their belief in Petiot's guilt; and Marguerite Braunberger and her maid had perjured themselves because Marguerite's husband, Dr. Braunberger, was alive and well in South America. The appeal was rejected and death by guillotine was set for May 24 but postponed when the guillotine malfunctioned.

Petiot did not want to meet with the prison chaplain but acceded to his wife's wishes. "I am not a religious man," he said, "and my conscience is clean."

One of the witnesses at the guillotine was Dr. Albert Paul, the state coroner. He noted the calm of Marcel Petiot, who "moved with ease as though he were walking into his office for a routine appointment … In my forty years, I have never before saw a condemned man with so much scorn and confidence in death."

As he was prepared for guillotining, he was asked if he had last words. Petiot responded, "None. I am a traveler who is taking his baggage with him."

After his hands were bound, neck shaved, and collar cut from the shirt, Petiot was strapped to the guillotine's sliding table. He deadpanned to the observers, "Gentlemen, I ask you not to look. This will not be very pretty."

And pretty it was not. But witnesses insist that Marcel Petiot was smiling as the head made its way into the basket.

The death of Marcel Petiot closed the murderous career of the man also known as Captain Henri Valery, Tarzan, The Second Landru, and the New Blackbeard. However, many questions were still open for answers, and many issues were barely touched.

The French medical association has never given a satisfactory explanation how it allowed a mentally disturbed practitioner to retain his license, especially after reported criminal activity.

Petiot plundered a minimum of five hundred thousand dollars from his Jewish victims. No money or valuables have been recovered. Of less concern to the average Frenchman or world citizen is that more than four hundred thousand dollars was assessed to the estate of Petiot for the costs of the court case. At is peak after World War II, the estate held fifty-one real estate holdings, yet only 12 percent has been collected.

It has been estimated that apart from the real estate, the Petiot estate had cash, gold, jewelry, and furs worth fourteen million dollars. Where has it been hidden—in a Swiss bank, in a foreign country, with the French Communist Party? No one has come up with the answer.

The family remained wealthy. Marcel Petiot's son, Gerhardt, and cousin Daniel Petiot became wealthy South American businessmen. No one has suggested that all the wealth is traced to the crimes of Dr. Petiot. Indeed, Mrs. Petiot came from a wealthy family.

Still, what about the victims? Answers Grombach, "While justice would seem to require that this fortune … should be divided somehow among the unwilling contributors to Petiot's fortune, there is no way in which this could be accomplished. To sort out rightful money from sinful money has never seemed practicable, and French justice, in the Petiot case, has long since been appeased."

The sensational story of serial killer Marcel Petiot interested world readers, as did other mass murderers. But the story of Marcel Petiot should have resonated more inside France after the war. The Holocaust, as noted, fed victims into Petiot's furnace. They thought he could lead them to freedom from Nazi-occupied France.

And it was a France being ruled by a collaborationist Vichy government. Many of the Vichy officials remained in important posts after the war and escaped prosecution. Only in recent years has the government been open about the Holocaust in France and prosecuted Vichy officials.

According to Grombach, "The French Government did not seem particularly proud of the Petiot trial ... or it may be that it was sensitive about the degree to which many respectable figures were revealed as partial collaborators as, indeed, were all who tried to hold an official job during the Occupation. Or who were loyal to the Vichy Government."

Not surprisingly, the government of De Gaulle sequestered the trial records. Writers like Grombach were rebuffed and found other ways to obtain full records of the trial without getting hands on official records.

Grombach notes that the books of the Petiot case published in France were suppressed or had miniscule press runs. The police closed one shop that printed the book. One book was scheduled for publication, but both the authors and publishers canceled the agreement.

One book made the bookstores, but all copies were bought by a "strange, unidentified woman." Another book was published in Belgium. All copies quickly disappeared. The bookstores speak of a "mysterious lady" gathering up all copies.

While the government exhibited paranoia in its treatment, French cinema was treated in the early nineties to *Docteur Petiot*, directed by Christian de Chalonge and starring Michel Serrault. The film has been properly commended for opening wide discussion of the Holocaust and the role of French collaboration.

In *Encyclopedia of Serial Killers*, Brian Lane and Wilfred Gregg raise the issue of "true crime as public entertainment." In one scene, Petiot himself is in a theater watching a film "with evident disapprobation because the character is not evil enough."

Grombach leaves the reader with much to ponder about the story of Marcel Petiot; "The lessons from this book ... that our major and most dangerous enemy today in dealing with aggressors, criminals, rioters, student agitators, radicals, and drones alike is permissiveness under the guise of liberalism ..."

CLEVELAND TORSO KILLER
Mad Butcher of Kingsbury Run

The fact that he was never caught does not achieve uniqueness for the Mad Butcher of Kingsbury Run, also known as the Phantom of Kingsbury Run, the Horrible Headhunter, the Cleveland Butcher, and the Torso Murderer. Jack the Ripper of London is the most notorious example of those never apprehended. However, many of Torso's victims were so dismembered that they have never been identified.

Certainly, the Torso Killer was not America's first modern serial killer. For example, Carl Panzram left a bloodied record in the 1920s. However, the Torso Killer case was perhaps the most intensive and massive homicide investigation in history, and his besting of Cleveland's director of public safety, the celebrated Elliot Ness, was one of the great crime "battles." Ness and his Untouchables conquered the gangsters, but he could not triumph over the Torso Killer.

Still, students of serial killer studies have sought to link Jack the Ripper and the Torso Killer. Jack the Ripper was the Victorian England sexual psychopath, while the Torso Killer was America's first important recognizable sexual psychopath. And like the Ripper, the Torso Killer was methodical in his gruesome modus operandi. The Ripper slashed and eviscerated. He did not behead his victims, but he sliced their throats right down to the spinal column. The Torso Murderer dismembered and beheaded his victims.

In his book on the Torso Killer, Steven Nickel is convinced that the Butcher was a sexual psychopath but does not fit "neatly into any recognizable profile of the sexual psychopath." The Torso Killer can certainly be called a necrophile, one with an abnormal attraction to corpses. Edward Gein in Wisconsin of the 1940s and Edmund Emil Kemper in California of the 1970s also can be identified as necrophiles.

The unidentified Torso Killer also displayed an intelligence common among serial killers. The fact that he bested Ness is enough said. Moreover, his dismemberment of the bodies points to his being well versed in anatomy if not proving surgical skills.

But with our not knowing anything personally about the killer, the case of the Torso Killer is studied from the perspectives of the chosen victims, the method of murder, and his skills in eluding Ness and Cleveland's police department.

The crimes occurred from 1935–39 in the Kingsbury Run section, an ancient creek bed that slices through the center of Cleveland. During the Depression, it was a gloomy, haunted area, a nexus of railroads, whose citizens were hoboes and vagabonds.

Marilyn Bardsley offers this description of Kingsbury Run:

"An open sore, festering with refuse and decay. Yet, among the old tires and empty wine bottles exists a small city of nomadic men, swept into the ravine by the wave of Depression that surged across the country in the 1930s. Their squat cardboard and tin shacks dot the ominous landscape. Small campfires penetrate the darkness, illuminating the rugged and desperate ugliness of the Run. The men lay sleeping, their heads against the cool earth, oblivious to the haunting wail of passing freight trains."

The first victims were found on September 23, 1935. No blood was found on the ground or the bodies. The bodies were headless and the genitals were removed. The police report follows.

"After an extensive research, the heads of both men were found … buried in separate places, one about twenty feet away from one of the bodies, and the other head was buried about seventy-five feet away from the other body. Both men's penises had been severed from their bodies and were found near one of the heads."

One victim has never been identified. The second victim was identified by his family as Edward A. Anrassy, an orderly in a psychiatric ward at Cleveland City Hospital. His record was unsavory: arrest on a concealed weapons charge; involvement with a married woman; dealings in pornographic literature; reports of homosexuality. Police theories of motivation included revenge organized by gangsters or revenge for Andrassy's sexual misconduct.

"The most chilling discovery," wrote Colin Wilson and Damon Wilson, "was that Andrassy had been killed by decapitation ... The killer had apparently cut off his head with a knife. The skill with which the operation had been performed suggested a butcher—possibly a surgeon."

Not surprisingly, the Cleveland *Plain Dealer* called the killings "the most bizarre double murder" in the city's history.

Victim three was found in January 1936, not far from Kingsbury Run. One resident told a neighbor that she had found a basket with "hams." However, the neighbor quickly realized that they were parts of a human arm. Also found was a burlap bag with the lower half of a female torso. Two weeks later, the left arm and lower legs were found in a vacant lot. The head was never found. Fingerprints helped the police identify the victim as Florence Polillo, a local forty-one-year-old prostitute.

Elliot Ness had come to Cleveland to rid the city of gangsters. Now, he found himself in a more difficult, frustrating battle with a Torso Killer. He was convinced that the murderer was a sadistic killer. But the Butcher left no clues behind, so all Ness could do was wait for the next victim and hope the murderer would give himself away.

Two added killings unnerved Cleveland during 1936—and still no clues. The head of a young man was found under a bridge in Kingsbury Run on June 22. The body of the decapitated man was found about a quarter of a mile away. Because of the six tattoos, the victim became known as the Tattooed Man.

As the police pondered over motives for the four killings—jealousy, revenge, sexual perversity—victim five was found on July 22. A decapitated male body was found in a gully; nearby was the head. According to the coroner's report, "The body was in an advanced state of decomposition with the skin and flesh denuded in large areas. Rodents, maggots, and the process of decomposition had removed portions of the internal viscera. The head had been separated from the body at the junction of the second and third cervical vertebrae, the end of which bones showed no evidence of fracture."

The final Torso killing of '36 was found on September 10 in Kingsbury Run. The body of a man had been sliced in two and emasculated. The head had been decapitated between the third and fourth vertebrae, the trunk bisected. The remains were near a hobo camp. The city hired a professional diver to search for the head, arms, and genitalia of the final victim of '36. Nothing was found.

The local press caught the frenzy in Cleveland. The hysterical questions of one newspaper: "Is there somewhere in the country a madman whose strange god is the guillotine? Or has some fantastic chemistry of the civilized man converted him into a human butcher? Does he imagine himself a legal executioner of the French Revolution or a religious zealot saving the human race with an ax?"

The murders were surreal enough to warrant national and even international attention. The spotlight was even more on Cleveland because the killings competed with the city's hosting the Republican Convention, the Great Lakes Expo, and the American Legion Convention. The press of Nazi Germany and Fascist Italy delighted in the perversity and failings of Western democracy.

Ness needed to be involved. And he accepted the challenge. Twenty-five detectives from Cleveland's Homicide Unit were assigned full-time to the investigation. "Like everyone else," Ness told the press,

"I want to see this psycho caught. I'm going to do all I can to aid in the investigation."

The police laboratory was the setting for a meeting attended by Ness, the police chief, inspector, county prosecutor, county pathologist, and ballistics specialist, among others. The group of thirty-four reached seven conclusions: one individual was responsible for all Torso killings; the killer lived near Kingsbury Run; the killer could be described as "demented and psychopathic," but certainly not "recognizably insane;" while the killer had not proven he was medically trained, he clearly had surgical skills and was well versed in human anatomy; it could be his home, but the murders or butchery were performed in a private workshop or laboratory; the killer was a large and "exceptionally strong" individual; and the killer preyed on "perfect victims," those of the "lower classes," the drunks, drifters, and prostitutes who accessed Kingsbury Run.

All were pleased with the meeting and formulation of conclusions at the "Torso Clinic." But without clues, capture was near impossible. Investigators looked to similar cases in other cities. The case of a nude, headless corpse in the train yards near New Castle, Pennsylvania, might offer insights. While there were striking similarities to the Torso case, the New Castle slaying showed no definite link to the Torso murders.

Although no solution had been found as 1936 closed, Clevelanders at least were less terrified as several months went by without more Torso murders. But all that was shattered when another victim was found in February 1937. The body of a young woman was washed ashore at Lake Euclid. Like other victims, she was headless, with arms amputated and torso bisected. The lower trunk was found in another part of the city, but the head, arms, and legs were never found, and she has never been identified.

The newly appointed coroner Samuel Gerber studied six of the seven victims, not analyzing the results of an earlier Euclid Beach murder because too few details were known. Apart from identifying the murderer as right-handed, the murderer was most likely a doctor, according to the coroner. Other possibilities in order of likelihood were medical students, male nurses, orderlies, butchers, hunters, and veterinary surgeons.

In any event, observed the coroner, the murderer was "highly intelligent in recognizing the anatomical landmarks as they approached, or else, as is more likely, a person … with some knowledge of anatomy." Most likely, the Torso Murderer was a physician "who performs the crime in the fury of a long drinking bout or derangement following the use of drugs."

With all this, Gerber's conclusion said that too little is known to solve the case at this point. "In conclusion," he said, "it must be admitted that though many isolated facts are known, and a few conservative inferences are drawn here, there is yet much to be desired before the final solution is realized."

And there would be more victims. The skeleton found beneath the Lorain-Carnegie Bridge was that of Rose Wallace, forty, who might have been killed the previous year. She had been missing and was identified through dental records. The similarities were striking between this victim and another victim, Flo Polillo. Both were found a few blocks apart; the burlap bags with their remains were quite similar.

But still no clues for the identity of the Torso Killer. One month later, the murderer added one more. The dismembered parts of a man's body were fished out of the river. The victim was decapitated; the head was never found. The victim was mutilated to a greater extent than other victims had been. The first part taken out of the Cuyahoga was the lower half of a torso. Floating nearby were two halves of the left leg. Next, a burlap bag was pulled out of the water, with the upper part of the torso. The right thigh was later found squeezed in among bridge pilings. Some two hundred fifty yards from the bridge, a Coast Guard boat found the upper left arm. The next finding, on July 6, was the lower half of a lung.

The next day, searchers found both forearms with the hands attached. Several days later, the upper right arm and lower right leg were found. The coroner and his staff began the gruesome task of assembling the remains. All was complete—except for the head.

"The killer leaves his signature every time," said a frustrated coroner. "Yet this time the murderer had performed his work in a more extreme and erratic manner. The cuts were crude and erratic. Hopefully, this may indicate that the murderer is not as attentive to details as before. Maybe his knife is no longer sharp and the blood lust will stop."

August 16, 1938, was the date of a Torso murder discovery, the last official victim. People scavenging for scrap iron at a lakeside dump fell upon a female torso. Head, arms, and legs were missing, as in past murders. But the trunk was intact. The head was found only a few feet away. While cut into nine pieces, a complete body was available for analysis and hopefully clues to identify the killer.

But no clues were found. However, Ness himself swung into action as he had not done in the case. If the murderer was selecting victims from the hobo population, why not raid "shantytown," near Kingsbury Run, reasoned Ness. He ordered the razing of hoboville and arrested hundreds of vagrants. But all this led to nothing—except a scorching editorial condemning Ness in the August 19 *Plain Dealer*:

> Safety Director Elliot Ness's personally supervised raid upon the packing box homes underneath the Eagle Street ramp may contribute something toward the capture of the torso killer. We doubt it ...
>
> Director Ness himself did not believe that any of the transients arrested in this raid and two similar ones was the butcher who has slain and dismembered thirteen persons ...
>
> That such shantytowns exist is a sorrowful reflection upon the state of society. The throwing into jail of men broken by experience and the hunting of their wretched places of habitation will not solve the economic problem. Nor is it likely to lead to the solution of the most macabre mystery in Cleveland's history.

True, the Torso Murders ceased in Cleveland, but no killer was found. And the final victim was never identified. What followed—with no relation to the razing at Kingsbury Run—was a letter signed "X" from Los Angeles to Cleveland Chief of Police George J. Matowitz:

> You can rest easy now, as I have come to sunny California for the winter. I felt bad operating on those people, but science must advance. I shall astound the medical profession, a man with only a D.C.
>
> What did their lives mean in comparison to hundreds of sick and disease-twisted bodies? Just laboratory guinea pigs found on any public street. No one missed them when I failed. My last case was successful. I know the feeling of Pasteur, Thoreau, and other pioneers.
>
> Right now I have a volunteer who will absolutely prove my theory. They call me mad and a butcher, but the truth will out.
>
> I have failed but once here. The body has not been found and never will be, but the head minus the features, is buried on Century Boulevard, between Western and Crenshaw. I feel it my duty to dispose of the bodies as I do. It is God's will not to let them suffer.

The Los Angeles police searched and found nothing. So the hunt went back to Cleveland. Thirteen murders were certainly committed by the Torso between 1934–38. Other dismemberment victims turned up, outside of Cleveland. On June 30, 1939, the skeletal remains of a woman were found in a dump in Youngstown, Ohio. Like Torso victims, the woman was carefully dismembered. Detective Peter Merylo, assigned to the Torso case, traveled to Youngstown. After three weeks, Merylo found no killer and no proof that the murderer was the Torso Killer.

Next, there were the discoveries on May 3, 1940, in abandoned boxcars outside Pittsburgh. Three males were found decapitated. The only "complete" identifiable victim was James Nicholson, a thirty-year-old homosexual and former Wisconsin convict. The murderer had

Depravity

carved the word "NAZI" on the victim's chest. Authorities all agreed that it was the work of Cleveland's Butcher, in part because it very closely resembled his other killings. "Nicholson's photograph," writes Nickel, "revealed a narrow, boyishly handsome face with sleepy eyes that some found hauntingly reminiscent of Andrassy and the tattooed man." But once again the discovery brought no results.

Nevertheless, Cleveland police have declared that 1938 is the official close of the Kingsbury Run murders. According to Marilyn Bardsley, "Cleveland police officials examined the forensic evidence of these other murders outside Cleveland, but there was never anything of substance to prove that the Cleveland serial killer was responsible for murders anywhere else."

While the murders ended, Ness and others searched before and after for the Torso Killer. While the lack of clues has been stated above, that did not mean that no serious suspects existed.

Detectives Peter Merylo and Martin Zalewski were convinced in the summer of 1939 that the Torso Killer was Frank Dolzeal, a fifty-two-year-old bricklayer, who had lived with one victim, Flo Polillo, and had been acquainted with other victims Edward Andrassy and Rose Wallace. After he was arrested, the detectives felt convinced he was the right killer when they found dried blood in the cracks of his bathroom floor. They also found knives with dried bloodstains in his apartment. The detectives were additionally convinced they were right when Dolzeal confessed he had killed and dismembered Flo Polillo.

Cleveland citizenry felt relieved, writes Nickel. "Clevelanders studied the photos of Dolzeal with his crazed stare and read the story of his confession. There seemed little doubt that the psychopath who had terrorized the city was finally behind bars."

Unfortunately, the case came apart quickly. Upon close examination, the confession was seen as an inexplicable combination of precise details and incoherent ramblings. Some parts were absurd; for example, his insistence that he carried the head some three miles in frigid weather from his apartment to the lakefront and then crawled across the ice to throw the body into the open water. One might conclude that detectives had told him what to say.

How about murders other than that of Polillo? No one had asked him about the other murders. Coroner Gerber felt that it was all or nothing. "If Dolzeal is not the Torso slayer," he said, "then he had no hand in the killing of Mrs. Polillo."

Dolzeal was given a lie detector test. His murder of Polillo was consistent with the polygraph results, but the testimony of the disposal of the head was "inconclusive," according to the lie detector.

No one will know more. Before going to trial, he was found in his cell, hanged from a hood, less than six inches from the floor. Perhaps more shocking was the autopsy finding that he had suffered six fractured ribs close to two months before his death. The accused had claimed that he had been beaten by county officers eager for his confession.

So, Dolzeal was not the Torso Killer. Everyone was waiting—and hoping—that Elliot Ness would come through and locate the murderer. He felt he had found the killer—but only spoke of the supposed Torso Killer in 1947. Ness never revealed the real name of the suspect.

The approach of Ness was as follows: the killer was a homeowner who brought the victims home for dismemberment. He was probably comfortable economically to transport the victims in his car. He had to be either medically trained or well conversant in anatomy because the mutilations were so precise. Because some of the victims were big and strong, the murderer had to at least match that strength.

Ness dispatched three of his top agents—Virginia Allen, Barney Davis, and Jim Manski—to search the high echelons of Cleveland society. Ness was satisfied that the suspect was the right one. He was big, athletic, from an upper-class family. His record showed psychiatric problems. And Gaylord Sundheim had studied medicine.

Ness ordered Sundheim brought in for questioning in an informal setting, in a hotel room, more a lunch than an interrogation. He was a "giant of a man," Ness later told the press. Sundheim toyed with Ness,

Depravity

at times mocking Ness, neither denying or admitting to involvement in the murders.

"Take a lie detector test," Ness pressed Sundheim. The suspect agreed and emerged as untruthful.

Ness knew he had his man and confronted Sundheim. "I think you killed these people."

Sundheim was unimpressed and sneered at the "untouchable" hero. "Think? Prove it!"

Sundheim had outfoxed the master detective. Ness had no proof. However, he called on the Cleveland police force to open a full investigation of the suspect and watch Sundheim around the clock. But Sundheim frustrated Ness and his men.

Hardly had the order been issued by Ness when Sundheim had himself committed to a state mental institution. The game was at an end. Sundheim was now an untouchable. Ness had to prove him guilty. And if he did, Sundheim could claim insanity. Sundheim could not be criminally prosecuted. For Ness, Sundheim would be out of the reach of the law, hence untouchable.

Sundheim continued to mock Ness, who claimed that the asylum inmate had written him a series of sneering letters signed "Your paranoid nemesis." After two years, the letters ended. The supposed Torso Murderer had died in the asylum.

Nickel raises many questions about Ness's solution and identity of the murderer. The story is totally "unverifiable" and "presents too many unanswered questions and too many generalities for it to be considered seriously."

Nickel continues: "Was it merely a story concocted by Ness to show the world that he had, after all, solved the case? ... And what of the later murders at New Castle, Youngstown, and Pittsburgh that appeared to many to be the work of the same maniac? According to Ness, Sundheim was in the asylum long before those crimes were committed."

However, Colin Wilson and Damon Wilson say that Sundheim was "probably" the murderer ... "not certainly."

Because the modus operandi of the Torso Killer suggested a medic, the police checked all doctors, physicians, medical students, and male nurses. In particular, the police focused on those who were suspected of homosexual activity, or who had an involvement with drugs, liquor, or illicit sex.

Receiving a great deal of attention was Dr. Frank A. Sweeney, tall, large, and strong. He was raised in Kingsbury Run and had his office in the area. His history was a troubled one, including alcohol, and he was rumored to be bisexual.

The police lost interest in Sweeney because when victims were found, he was frequently out of town at a veteran's hospital in Sandusky, Ohio. No one would admit to it, but critics of the investigation insisted that the real reason was for not bringing in the medic that Dr. Sweeney was a cousin of Ohio Congressman Martin L. Sweeney.

The records of the Cleveland police included suspects not as seriously pursued as Sweeney was but fascinating in their own right. For example, detectives considered the Kentucky Butcher, who was in town during the time of the Torso murders. He was later sentenced in Kentucky for murdering, dismembering, and decapitating his victim. Once dead, the victim was then ground for sale to an uninformed sausage manufacturer.

While he had no suspects in mind, Coroner Sam Gerber remained on the case, even for years after the murders ended. His goal was not primarily to help the police but to define the Torso Killer from sociological and psychological perspectives. His conclusions were rooted on two facets: the remains of twelve definite victims and the psychological profiles of contemporary serial killers.

In one of his last reports, Gerber sought to answer this question: "What type of person is the Torso Murderer?" The report focuses on "the examination of the localities in which the bodies have been discovered and of the known surroundings and social history of the two victims that were identified."

Gerber offers these conclusions:

Depravity

These victims come from the lowest strata of society originally or may have sprung from an upper strata of society and because of incidents in their lives sank to association with the lowest strata.

Therefore, the murderer must be a person that associates with this strata of life. In all probability, he was at one time or another associated with people in the upper strata of life but through unfortunate incidents either sank to association with persons in the lowest strata of life or has himself become a member. He may have been a doctor or medical student sometime in the past, butcher, osteopath, chiropractor, orderly, nurse, or hunter in order to be able to accomplish the dissection with such perfect finesse.

The murderer undoubtedly gained the confidence and probably the friendship of these victims before killing them. The type of person most likely to commit murder falls into these groups: (1) The truly insane group, under which the paranoid may be classed, will commit murder as the result of his delusions of persecution…. The schizophrenic kills entirely without motive and without passion. (2) The constitutional psychopath is the borderline type of insanity where individuals are not able to comprehend the difference between right and wrong and the desire to kill is accompanied by an abnormal sex urge, such as some form of perversion. (3) The feeble-minded individuals… usually commit murder to obtain some object, trinket, money or something else that they may desire at the time of the killing.

From the anatomical examination of the twelve so-called 'Torso Murder Victims' the murderer may possibly be a schizophrene, considering the cold-blooded method of killing and then the dissection of the body and the apparent simple disposition of the remains. In some of the earlier cases, there were some genital mutilations of the individual, and it is conceivable that the murderer may belong to the borderline group of insanity, the constitutional psychopath.

The career of Cleveland's Torso Killer ended by almost all accounts in 1939. Later murders by similar means have received attention but not acceptance from serious students of serial killers. According to Colin and Damon Wilson, "No serial killer has ever been known to leave an eight-year gap between murders."

The Wilsons referred to the 1947 murder of model Elizabeth Short in Los Angeles, known as the Black Dahlia killing. Because the killer carved the initials BD into the victim's inner thigh, detectives thought that it represented the victim's nickname, Black Dahlia.

The killer tortured the victim before cutting the body in half at the waist. Cleveland police considered the case but rejected the link between the Los Angeles murder and the Torso killings, for lack of definite proof. As for the letter written to the Cleveland police chief, it was mailed from Los Angeles, as discussed above, but Cleveland police did not consider the letter or its contents authentic.

The Black Dahlia murder represented an eight-year gap; the 1950 discovery was an eleven-year gap. A man's decomposed leg was found in a field near the Pennsylvania Railroad tracks along Cleveland's lakefront. The torso, arms, and the other leg of the victim were found two hundred feet away. Four days later, police found the head.

Indeed, the similarities to the Torso Murders were remarkable. In fact, Coroner Gerber observed that the "Kingsbury technique" had been used in "disarticulating the corpse, skillfully beheading the victim in the midcervical region, and amputating the limbs at the hip and shoulder joints." However, the coroner would not accept the murder as the work of the Torso Killer. "After all," said Gerber, "it's been eleven years."

Eleven years, then sixty-one years. Obviously, the discovery in the summer of 2000 could not have been the work of the Torso Killer. Two Cleveland youths discovered a dismembered body in a vacant lot. Like the murders of the thirties, the body was dumped near Kingsbury Run and the police had no leads. The victim was never identified and the murderer never apprehended.

Cleveland and the nation still remain fascinated by the Torso killings.

Depravity

According to David C. Holcombe, director of the Cleveland Police Museum, "Next to the Sam Shepherd case, the Torso Murders are the most famous crimes in Cleveland history. And they are among the most famous unsolved murder cases in the nation."

Named for Francois Vidocq, a nineteenth-century Frenchman considered as one of history's first detectives, the Vidocq Society meets several times a year to try to solve "vexing murder cases that may trouble a member." In the spring of 1991, they met in Philadelphia, and the Torso Murderer was at the top of the agenda. Members advanced questions and theories:

"Did anyone flunk out of medical school?"

"Seven out of twelve of the heads were not found. Were they kept as trophies?"

"The fact that the bodies were drained—did anyone consider an undertaker?"

The Cleveland Police Museum Web site proudly proclaims, "To this day, the Kingsbury Run Murders remain one of the most sensational and intriguing unsolved crimes in the nation's history."

Of course, the Torso Killer is one of many killers never apprehended. And there are many killers who were never identified. But the joining of the legendary Jack the Ripper and the Torso Killer—as discussed above—has enhanced the story of Cleveland's serial killer.

And certainly the aura of Cleveland's unsolved murders has incorporated an important and sad chapter that has deflated the achievements of American hero Elliot Ness. Writes Nickel, "Ness has become one of the most celebrated figures among twentieth-century American lawmen ... Readers will find a demythiczed Elliot Ness ... a man who helped create his own larger-than-life image and then struggled to live up to it."

As soon as the city panicked when the killings mounted, a very concerned Cleveland Mayor Burton pleaded with Ness to become involved. "I want to see this psycho caught," Ness assured Burton. "I'm going to do all I can to aid in the investigation."

Marilyn Bardsley asks the question of the case's appeal and then offers an answer similar to Nickel's:

"Why does this story have such lasting appeal some sixty years after the fact? Like Jack the Ripper, the crimes are officially unsolved, which allows the audience to conjure up all kinds of frightening images. The murders were so daring and so cleverly conceived that the killer had to be a brilliant psychopath who matched his wits with the legendary Elliot Ness, crime fighter extraordinaire."

CARLTON GARY

The Stocking Strangler

In the spring of 2000, the *New York Times* ran a four-part series on American serial killers, designated as "rampage killers." In his opening article, Ford Fessenden offered a seemingly innocuous observation: "Most are white men, but a surprising number are women, Asians, and blacks."

A quick review of serial killer literature would conclude that indeed most serial killers are white males. In his 1997 book *Serial Murderers and Their Victims*, Eric W. Hickey writes that 73 percent of male killers were white, 22 percent were African American, 3 percent were Hispanic, 1 percent were Asian, and 1 percent were other racial or ethnic groups. In his 1992 book *Serial Slaughter*, Michael Newton places the figure of African Americans at 16 percent.

Hickey, a criminal psychology professor at California State University–Fresno, added, "It's a stereotype that … most serial killers are white. You ask most experts, and they can't name a black serial killer. We have Asians and we have Hispanics that were serial killers. We need to get away from all the myths."

The myths came to the fore with a furor in the fall of 2002 when John Allen Muhammad and his alleged accomplice, John Lee Malvo, were suspects in the sniper killings in the Washington DC area. If convicted, they would be America's most notorious black serial killers.

According to an article by Cynthia Tucker in the *Atlanta Journal-*

Constitution, the number of black serial killers was 13 percent of the total. The convictions, wrote Tucker, would forever change the conventional wisdom that serial murder is a "white man's sickness." True, black serial killers have not been absent, notes Tucker, but in the past, "white criminologists were willing to profile black men out of the category of serial killer, it seemed only fair since they are unfairly profiled into most other criminal categories. While racism has faded considerably over the last century, the stereotype of the black man as violent criminal remains a stubborn feature of the American cultural and political life."

When a white Claus von Bulow was suspected of killing his wife, that did not besmirch the white man, but, laments Tucker, O. J. Simpson as murder suspect "became representative of his race."

Turning to Atlanta, Tucker pointed to African American Wayne Williams, who in the eighties was convicted of two murders and blamed for twenty-two others. If so, was Tucker concerned about the African American image? Answered Tucker, the victims were poor and black ... "not the sort of crimes that keep middle-class Americans awake at night."

In an article in the *Los Angeles Times*, Earl Ofari Hutchinson reasoned that since most black serial killers victimized other blacks, police were not persistent in apprehending the murderer, so killers go unnoticed for long periods:

"Because black-on-black crime is so entrenched, it is far too often considered routine, and police are more often lax toward the violence than if the victims were white. This makes it easier for black serial murders to go undetected for longer."

The most incensed observer of the snipings was Carol Chehade, author of *Big Little White Lies: Our Attempt To White-Out America*, who wrote "Colorizing Crime" for blackelectorate.com. Ironically, she points out that white America portrays the serial killer as "white and brilliant." White America looks at African Americans as not having the smarts to be serial killers.

"The majority of profiles," she writes, "paint the barbaric world of serial killers as being not only white, but also white and brilliant, thus alluding that blacks aren't smart enough to carry out organized murder. Even savage behavior is affixed with ... racially favorable tilt when the overwhelming actors of that behavior are white."

After 9/11, Chehade was worried that the suspects also carried the burden of being Muslim. "Once again," continues the writer, "we Americans have radicalized an event where the culprits are known to be African Americans. Not only are these serial killers black, but they also claim the religion of Islam. A religion that is working overtime these days to defend itself ... We are living in a political culture where followers of Islam are carefully walking a tightrope on mercurial public opinion, while African Americans are still trying to make sure their own tightrope is not once again turned into a noose ... To say this could not have happened at a worse time is an understatement."

The most scholarly treatment of the African American serial killers is that of Philip Jenkins, for the 2003 *American Journal of Criminal Justice*. He advances the phenomenon that serial murder studies have basically overlooked African Americans and serial homicide. Conceding the difficulty of accurate figures, Jenkins looked at serial crime between 1971 and 1990 and found a 14 percent figure for African American killers.

According to Jenkins, police and law enforcement agencies do not press for evidence of serial murders when the victims are African Americans. He attributes this to "overt racism." Police attitudes, continues Jenkins, also designate many crimes of African Americans as "urban homicide ... the result of gang or drug-related conflict" rather than serial murder.

It is ironic, observes Jenkins, that for centuries African Americans have been stereotyped by linkage to crime and violence, and in serial killings the stereotyping omits their importance. "Racial attitudes here are profoundly linked to social stereotypes: it is not so much that blacks as such attract lower police priorities, but that poor people living in certain high-crime neighborhoods appear to inspire less concern when they die or vanish."

In his conclusion, Jenkins voices concern about the harmful effects of this seemingly "favorable stereotype:"

> The very failure to draw attention to Black serial killers might in itself arise from a form of bias within the media and law enforcement.
>
> African Americans make up a sizable proportion of serial killers and this has practical consequences for the fate of those Blacks and other minorities who are most likely to fall victim to this type of predator. Underestimating minority involvement in serial homicide can thus lead to neglecting the protection of minority individuals and communities who stand in greater peril of victimization.

Surprisingly, Cynthia Tucker did not speak of an earlier black serial killer, a fellow Georgian, Carlton Gary, whose crimes were committed in the seventies. But Hickey profiles Carlton Gary as an exemplification of his belief that "racial boundaries are not sacred."

Jenkins does take note of Gary, but wonders why he is relatively disregarded while white serial killers receive much more attention (e.g. Jeffrey Dahmer, Ted Bundy, Arthur Shawcross, and Larry Eyler). Searching for a reason, Jenkins notes, "Gary's crimes were also significant in that they were viewed in the community as racially motivated assaults on White people."

The stereotype of serial killer as white and brilliant was challenged by Carlton Gary as African American and brilliant. Born in Columbus, Georgia, in 1952, he was recognized early as near genius. However, whatever potential existed wasted away in a deprived childhood. He had little contact with his parents.

"I don't have any parents," a young Gary reportedly said. As far as a meaningful relationship, that was true. He saw his father only once, as a twelve-year-old. His father was a construction worker who died in

Depravity

an accident. His mother was continually on the move, settling in with the men she met.

At times, young Carlton moved in with her; when staying with her, he was abused by her and her men. At other times, he remained with his great-aunt, Alma Williams, or with his father's sister, Lillian Nesbit. He rummaged the streets and garbage cans in his battle with malnutrition. He survived on his wits. He ingratiated himself with women and any other adults who might help him.

Eight years old, Carlton stunned his uncle, William David, by appearing at the Fort Lee Army post in Virginia. The MP put the youth on the phone: "Unk, it's Gary. Come get me." The uncle always wondered how his nephew got to the army post by himself.

Uncle David enrolled his nephew in school. These were not fun days. On one occasion he suffered a head injury, left unconscious in the playground. Later medical and psychological interviews revealed minimal brain dysfunction. The absence of normal family life, aggravated by developmental disabilities and physical irregularities—webbing of skin between his fingers and an elongated middle toe—contributed to signs foreboding trouble to come.

He dropped out of school before his fourteenth birthday. Throughout his teens, he was a chronic drug user. Speaking of the young Carlton, Homer McGilvray, then a detective in Gainesville, Florida, said that it seemed the name of Carlton Gary turned up every time a crime was committed in the area. "He's always been a crook," said McGilvray. When first arrested, at age sixteen for arson, Gary had a resume of fifteen different residences.

Before his eighteenth birthday, he had been charged with auto burglary, assault, and arson. Without home and parents willing to take legal responsibility, he shuttled between his aunts in Columbus and his mother in Fort Myers, Florida. Gary assumed that he might have a fixed residence in Fort Myers with his mother. But one day he came home only to discover that Mom and her new boyfriend had moved out.

Gary was first arrested in 1969, along with five others, four of whom were teenagers. They were charged with arson in the attack on Gene's Grocery Store, in the Negro district of Gainesville. After a short term, Gary was charged with another burglary, was sentenced, and escaped from custody. Recently married, Gary fled to Connecticut and sent for his wife, and they settled in Old Saybrook, New London, Hartford, and Bridgeport. Gary held several jobs, including janitor. In Bridgeport, he assaulted a policeman, so he ran to Albany.

After arriving in New York, he played drums in a band, and started raising two children. But within a year, in 1970, he abandoned his family; however, his former wife had mixed praise for him: "gentle, kind, and dangerous."

In the spring of 1970, Gary, under the alias Carl Michaels, launched a series of rape-murders against elderly women. One was strangled in her hotel room in Albany. That July, another woman was strangled in a nearby residence. He was arrested for the latter murder when he admitted being at the murder site. But he squirmed his way out with a plea bargain by admitting that he was at the murder scene, but only took part in the burglary. Testimony of the murder was given against his accomplice John Lee Williams, who was placed in Dunnemora prison. But the verdict was reversed when Gary withdrew his story.

In his 1988 book *Serial Killers*, Dr. Norris presented Gary's confession, which did not include murder, to the Albany police.

> There was a cigarette stand and an elevator where John [John Lee Williams] was standing. Then this white dude came down and asked us what we wanted. I told this white dude that we were looking for a Mrs. Polite, as we were looking for a dishwasher's job that was advertised in the newspaper. This white dude said it was too late to find anybody in the housekeeping department. The white dude went back to the desk and John and I got on the elevator. John worked the self-service elevator. I didn't pay attention to what floor we got off, but John pushed the button. The elevator stopped. John and I got off, and we walked down the hallway, with John leading the way.

While walking down the hallway, John put on his rubber gloves. He told me not to worry about my fingerprints, as I had no record, and they couldn't be traced. We came to the hotel room door. I noticed that when John or Pop came to this door, he had some kind of material jammed in the door lock.

John went in first. I followed him. John turned to me and said, 'Check out the bathroom.' I looked around. I could see John in the other room, and he was holding a flashlight and going through the papers.

Outside of the bathroom there was a door. I opened the door and it was a closet. I looked in the room where this closet was, and John was holding a flashlight and he was looking through the dresser drawers. I noticed the bed was all messed up. I heard some people coming down the hall. I got scared.

Now after the sounds stopped, I seen John with the flashlight go over toward a drawer and I seen John direct the flashlight to the door at the bottom of which was a low, big trunk. John asked me to help him move this trunk. When the flashlight that John was holding shined on the trunk I noticed the head of a human being up against the trunk.

The head of this human being was stretched out on the floor. There was a lot of papers thrown over the rest of the body to which this head was attached. I could tell this was the body of a woman, a white woman, I seen John reach down and grab this human head by the hair and throw it to one side. I did not step over the body, but John asked me to help him put this trunk on the bed.

I reached down and with my hands I picked up the trunk, and with John helping me we put the trunk on the messed-up bed. John started to work on the lock of the trunk. There were some pots and pans and some household stuff in the trunk. Some of the stuff in the trunk was wrapped up in papers. We searched through the stuff in the trunk. I picked up John or Pop's new boots, and I walked out of the hotel room. I walked around the hallway and down to the elevator. John was still in the room. I walked out of the Wellington Hotel and up to the corner of State and Eagle Streets and he joined me. We walked down Eagle Street to the Gulf gas station at eagle and Howard Streets in Albany, New York.

Williams was released. The conclusion was that Gary acted alone.

His method was: robbing the old women, raping them, and clubbing them to death or strangling them with a stocking or scarf.

Gary escaped prosecution for sixteen years. But Gary did not escape problems with the law. He was convicted in 1973 for a series of burglaries, receiving stolen property, and possession of drugs.

He was sentenced to a term at the Correctional Institution at Janesville, New York, in Onondaga County. Gary escaped in the summer of 1977. The real tragedy, laments Norris, was that nobody was listening to the prisoner. Speaking of the later murders in Georgia, Norris writes, "The real tragedy is that these murders need never have taken place had someone in Syracuse or Onondaga taken Carlton Gary seriously when he warned that he was embarking on a path of episodic crime fifteen years earlier. He asked for help from a parole officer, even then. His pleas were ignored."

Back home in Georgia, he made good on his warnings. The first victim was sixty-year-old widow Mary Ferne Jackson in Columbus. This began a series of murders in Columbia's Wynnton district. The victim was found with a nylon stocking around her neck, giving rise to Carlton Gary as the "Stocking Strangler." Sexual assault was a possibility.

The murder on September 18, 1977, followed nine days later, a few blocks from the initial killing. The victim was Jean Dimenstein, seventy-one and single. Clear proof of sexual assault was established.

Some three weeks later, the Stocking Strangler Struck once more. The victim was Florence Scheible, an eighty-nine-year-old widow, and there was sexual assault. Gary didn't wait long for victim four—four days later. A widow, Martha Thurmond, sixty-nine, was strangled and sexually attacked.

The next three victims were all widows: Kathleen Woodruff, seventy-four; Mildred D. Borum, seventy-eight; and Janet T. Coler, sixty-one. The crimes were committed in December 1977, February 1978, and April 1978. No signs of sexual attack were present in the first victim, while the sexual factor was only a possibility for the others.

In the Woodruff attack, Gary hastened to leave the scene, so he changed the M.O. and strangled manually sans stocking. And in the earlier Borum attack, Ruth Schwob, seventy-four, fought off Gary, so Gary moved down two blocks to claim Borum as victim.

By March 1978, the police determined that the Stocking Strangler was black and his victims were white. In good part, Gary escaped prosecution because he was "competing" for the serial killer limelight with William Hance.

Also operating in Georgia, Hance was incensed that the Stocking Strangler, the murderer of white women, was at large. Calling himself Chairman of the Forces of Evil, he wrote to the Georgia newspapers: "If you do not stop this murderer of white women, I will kill a black woman every thirty days." He also wanted a ransom of ten thousand dollars. The letters were written on Army stationery. The writer was later identified as Pvt. William Hance of Fort Benning. The irony: Hance was black.

Hance kept his word; three murders were traced to him. He was arrested in April. Gary stopped the murders and now turned to robberies, primarily restaurants in Columbia, Georgia, and South Carolina. He also occupied himself with narcotics dealings. Carlton Gary had a new nickname: the Steakhouse Bandit, who went into action right before closing time.

And it was for robberies that Gary was arrested in 1981 in Gaffney, South Carolina. He was sentenced to twenty-one years at Goodman Correctional Institute in Columbia. Once again, Gary escaped, in 1983. He headed to Florida to see his wife.

He was arrested at a motel in Albany, Georgia, on May 3, 1984. The tracks led to Gary through Carlton's uncle Jim Gary. The Columbia Police Department traced a handgun stolen from a victim's home to Michigan and back to Phoenix City, Alabama, to Uncle Jim. The pistol was purchased from nephew Carlton.

A police captain who spoke to Carlton Gary, then thirty-three, called the suspect "an extremely brilliant young man." He was indicted for three of the seven murders and held without bond on nine counts of murder, rape, and burglary, and on a separate case of burglary.

How strong was the case against Carlton Gary? He was only charged with the murders of Florence Scheible, Martha Thurmond, and Kathleen Woodruff. The basis was fingerprints at the murders. While not charged with the killings of Ferne Jackson and Jean Dimenstein, these deaths showed a "pattern of related crime." And while cleared of Nellie Farmer's death, Gary was involved, even if only accomplice, in "a lifetime of similar criminal activity."

And Gary did confess being at the crime scene of the three murders. Moreover, he went with the Columbia police to the residences of the victims and gave details: how he gained access and what the victims were doing when they were surprised by the attacks.

However, he never confessed to the actual killing. The real murderer, Gary insisted, was Michael Crittendon. He detailed how Crittendon committed the murders, then raped and clobbered the women. But the prosecution used these details to place Gary at the scenes. Beyond that, results of semen tests were added proof that Gary could have been the rapist.

Laboratory tests revealed "negroid" pubic hairs found on the victims. While not clear proof that Carlton Gary was the murderer, the hairs certainly did not exclude him from suspicion.

And the prosecution brought in their star witness. Gertrude Miller testified and identified Carlton Gary as the man who beat, raped, and choked her with a nylon stocking in 1977—four days before the first of the stocking stranglings.

Depravity

The court proceedings were notable, according to Norris, because Gary displayed his compulsive personality. Like other serial killers, notes Norris, Gary was a compulsive showerer. As evidence was presented, Gary interrupted because of "self-criticism he had about the way he was dressed or the way he thought his physical appearance seemed to onlookers."

In the closing arguments, Muscogee County District Attorney William J. Smith addressed Gary, "You've got to watch your friends, Mr. Gary. They rape folks, they rob folks, and you are invariably with them." In calling for the death penalty, Smith added, "The proof in this case was overwhelming and that's the way it ought to be before you make that ... awesome decision to take someone's life. It ought to be overwhelming. Just any degree of proof shouldn't be sufficient."

A jury of twelve—nine men and three women—found Carlton Gary guilty, in August 1986, and sentenced him to death in the electric chair. Carlton Gary still lives.

Over the past few years, an aggressive defense has sought to raise questions about Gary's guilt. In the fall of 2000, his attorneys asked a federal court judge in Macon to approve new tests of Gary's semen. Said a member of his defense, "We think that there is no reason not to do a semen test and every reason to do one. That's not something without risks to Mr. Gary and could easily prove that the wrong person was convicted."

A forensic biologist who testified on Gary's behalf said that he was convinced that the FBI expert who testified against Gary in 1986 based his findings on unreliable testing methods to link to Gary the semen evidence found at three murder sites.

Georgia's senior attorney general insisted that the guilty verdict should stand because the tests related to rape, not murder or burglary.

The 1986 tests were completed before DNA testing was available in the early nineties. DNA tests are not possible because the semen evidence was destroyed before Gary's trial.

In June 2001, a test of a semen sample cast doubt on Gary's

conviction. However, the test in the California laboratory was effected through a journalist—not attorneys or the courts. So who was to say that the sample came from Gary? Moreover, the defense pointed to the research of a British journalist, David Rose, who suggested that Gary might be cleared by more scientifically advanced comparisons of his semen with notes of tests conducted on semen found on the bodies of one of the women.

In a previous order, Judge Hugh Lawson had ruled against further tests: "The court fails to see what would be gained for authorizing the testing of semen almost fifteen years after his trial and twenty-four years after the testing of the stains."

So the case goes on as Carlton Gary remains in prison.

In his conclusion to his book *Serial Killers*, Norris calls on public health and criminal justice institutions and individuals to be more responsible when they come face to face with a potential serial killer. Norris links Henry Lee Lucas and Carlton Gary as failures of the system:

"Sex offenders who claim that they are subject to hallucinatory experiences or delusions of violence should be taken seriously and given some form of treatment. Had prison psychologists listened to Lucas or Gary, for example, they might have short-circuited their careers before they began their serial murder careers."

Norris's insightful study includes a presentation of Gary. Written in 1988, Norris's projection of the case still holds true, twenty years later:

> The book on Carlton Gary is far from being closed. Throughout the course of the appeals process, and until his condition is diagnosed, the lawyers will seek to have the death sentence overturned on the ground that a proper defense was prevented from being presented.
>
> If in the process of these appeals, deep brain EEG's and CAT scans reveal organic abnormalities and skin and hair tests reveal high levels of mood-altering toxins, it will come as no surprise. The combination of physiological, psychological, and social

abnormalities set against the pattern of his criminal behavior will reveal that he was an individual who was in control of his behavior during the cycles of the Wynnton murders, and the missing puzzle pieces of Carlton Gary's life will come together.

Twenty years later, the above comments on the Gary defense have been magnified in the spotlight through the continued effort of crusading British journalist David Rose. In 2007, he published a book on the Gary case following eight years of research. The book is titled *Violation: Race and Serial Murder In the Deep South* (HarperCollins). Rose writes that he has often been asked "innumerable times" whether Gary is innocent. "It is the wrong question to ask," insists Rose. The question is not to prove Gary's innocence, but to present reasonable doubt about Gary's guilt.

Rose notes that he first met Gary at the Georgia Diagnostic and Classification Center, the euphemistic name for Death Row. In addition to details on the semen evidence that might clear Gary, in an article in the *Daily Mail* of London, Clive Stafford Smith detailed the efforts of Rose:

"Denied the right to compare it to the DNA evidence from the victims, Rose then relied on less sophisticated testing to provide strong evidence that Gary could not be the rapist.

"One of the women had been bitten by her assailant. Gary's lawyer had tried to get his hands on the plaster cast made of the bite mark, only to be told that it had been destroyed. Rose tracked down the dentist and discovered the truth: the cast still existed, but the trial prosecutor, a hunting buddy, had told the dentist not to let the lawyer see it."

Smith is legal director of reprieve in a Great Britain charity that provides frontline investigation and legal representation worldwide to prisoners denied justice. Smith is convinced that the Gary case is tied to Columbus's "intricate history of racism." The federal judge in the case is a prominent member of a Columbus family. Gary may be saved, concludes Smith, "if Columbus can face up to its history and overcome its prejudices."

In *The Observer*, Gary Wood reviewed *Violation*, and stressed the expertise of Rose, who "expertly unlocks the prosecution's line ... He has hard evidence to refute it—the criminal histories of Gary's supposed co-conspirators, new forensic tests to show his semen doesn't match that found at the crime scenes; a cast of the killer's distinctive and different teeth from a bite mark on the last victim's breast; footprints several sizes smaller than Gary's feet; matching fingerprints the police claimed were found at the crime scene were never, as was the procedure, photographed in situ."

When David Rose appeared on "The Charlie Rose Show" the TV host also sounded the racist theme:

"I'm from the South. The South has changed a lot. It doesn't mean there's not a lot of racism in the South, in the North, the East, the West. Everywhere. We still have vestiges of racism in significant degrees in this country ... my point is to help us understand why all these people don't seem to respond to what is clear to you ... a convincing case for a retrial."

David Rose told Charlie Rose that it goes beyond racism. David Rose pointed the finger at incompetence and conspiracy:

There's a lot of incompetence in Columbus ... they had a suspect who confessed to the first two murders, and they thought this was all over, and then there were more murders, and then they thought they had the right guy. And it turned out, he was also going to confess murdering President Kennedy ... But when you have a miscarriage of justice, it starts with a genuine belief in guilt. In a high-profile case, when there is tremendous pressure on the police to solve it ... it's even more likely than in a regular murder case where ... the pressure isn't so high.

"When that suspect is identified, everyone is tremendously relieved. Thank God we have this guy. Let's use everything we have to put this in overdrive. When you have somebody who's innocent, as the investigation goes on, because that person is innocent, inevitably you're going to come across exculpatory evidence, evidence that doesn't fit your theory. When you have somebody who's definitely guilty, you're not likely to come across exculpatory evidence, because by definition it isn't going to exist.

"If you then pursue that case with the same vigor, you're going to have to hide that exculpatory evidence, which is why in miscarriages of justice like this one, you see the pattern of exculpatory evidence being hidden. Now at a certain point, this crosses over from a genuine mistaken belief to a conspiracy, which has drawn in a great deal of people.

"Chance is it [Gary case] has become a conspiracy. They have a lot to hide, and potentially a lot to lose. I mean, they could be looking at federal indictments."

SECTION VI—SERIAL KILLERS FOR THE 21ST CENTURY—POWER OVER LIFE AND DEATH

ARNFINN NESSET
Scandinavia's Most Prolific Murderer

Norway had not experienced such a trial since the proceedings against Quisling, in 1945, who betrayed his country to the Nazis and gave his name to political treason. This was not a political trial that opened on October 18, 1982. Arnfinn Nesset, forty-six, the former manager of a rural nursing home, went on trial for poisoning twenty-five of his patients with curacit, a muscle relaxant used by South American Indians to tip their poison arrows. When dispensed in large doses, it paralyzes the respiratory system and causes painful death by suffocation.

The case was the longest—five months—in Norway's history, with one hundred fifty witnesses taking the stand.

When Nesset began serving his twenty-one-year sentence—the maximum under Norwegian law—his case generated interest because of the question of health care. Scottish researchers have found thirteen health workers who have murdered at least one hundred seventy patients in the past twenty years.

"Murder is the last thing people think about when there are unexpected deaths because it is so unbelievable," said Dr. Cameron Stark, who heads the project.

No health care serial killer has attracted as much attention in recent years as Dr. Harold Shipman, who was convicted in 2000 of killing fifteen of his patients. An official inquiry in 2002 set the total at two hundred fifteen. The practitioner of Hyde, England, injected patients in his care with deadly doses of the painkiller diamorphine.

One can go much further back, to Dr. William Palmer of Rugely, Staffordshire, England. Palmer was known as the Prince of Poisoners, who killed sixteen of his friends, relatives, and acquaintances with strychnine one hundred fifty years ago. Dr. Herbert Kinnell, a retired psychiatrist in Berkshire, published a review of medical murderers in the *British Medical Journal*. He advances the view that doctors have committed these crimes with the help of their medical training. "There are enough instances of multiple murders," he said, "to make at least a prima facie case that the profession attracts some people with a pathological interest in the power over life and death."

Health care murderers, notably serial killers, have been especially skillful in covering their misdeeds, as noted in studies including Michael Newton's *Serial Slaughter*.

Arnfinn Nesset also appeared on a list of those illicit users of biological agents, as part of a working paper on bioterrorism and biocrimes prepared in 1998 by the Center for Counterproliferation Research at the National Defense University. The users included "Dark Harvest," who spread anthrax-contaminated soil to send a political message, and the Bulgarian Secret Police, who attempted to assassinate a dissident with ricin.

This was Norway's most sensational murder case; Nesset stood accused as Scandinavia's greatest serial killer. The case was heard in the District High Court in Trondheim, one hundred miles north of Oslo and twenty-five miles north of the Orkdal Valley Nursing Home, which he managed.

The case had come to public attention at the March 1982 remand proceedings. Nesset admitted to the murder of an older patient in 1980, but the police termed it a "qualified admission." In other words, Nesset admitted administering a lethal injection of curacit but "denied guilt under the murder indictment." The Orkdal Court of Examining and Summary Jurisdiction sentenced Nesset to Tunga Regional Prison without correspondence or visitation, but his attorney promised to challenge the order.

Although it was established that Nesset knowingly administered a lethal injection containing curacit, purchased well in advance with forged prescriptions, the home manager was charged with willful rather than premeditated murder.

As a prelude to the trial, the hearing was a media circus. The large numbers of media people were locked out of the hearing room, forced to stand in the hallway. Two beefy police officers guarded the doors of the makeshift courtroom in Orkdal; the police did all in their power to protect Nesset against the photographers' obtrusive and merciless flashes. Foreign newspapers wired Orkdal for additional information.

To frustrate the media, Deputy Chief of Police Arne Karoliussen and assistant Judge Gunnar Ravlo misled the media by entering the wrong courtroom while the police sneaked Nesset into the actual courtroom.

Little information was released from the proceedings. However, the police stressed that while only one death had been investigated, they still had to investigate all of the approximately one hundred to one hundred fifty deaths at the nursing home since Nesset obtained curacit in 1977. More than fifty people had been questioned in the case, and more would be brought in.

A total of twelve officers were assigned to the case: from the Norwegian Headquarters of the Criminal Police, from the Ut-Trodclag Police Headquarters in Trondheim, and from the Orkdal Sheriff's Station.

The investigation focused on gathering evidence against Nesset. A decision was put off about exhuming the dead bodies for poison testing.

The defendant selected Morton Gunnes as his counsel, but Gunnes himself suggested a permanent counsel with more experience in criminal law.

Reflecting the unusual nature of the case, two prosecutors and two defense attorneys were chosen to handle the case. On March 11, 1982, five months and one hundred fifty witnesses later, Nesset was found guilty of killing twenty-two patients. The full indictment was read for fifteen minutes, and it took three days for the jury to issue its decision. The chairwoman of the jury, Marit Svara Kenriksen, explained that the panel found Nesset had killed twelve women and ten men and attempted to kill one woman.

He was also found guilty of five charges of forgery and embezzlement of patients' money. The money, thirteen thousand kroner (about twenty-six hundred dollars), was for the Salvation Army and missionary activities, according to Nesset.

Nesset was sentenced to the maximum penalty of twenty-one years in prison and up to ten years of preventive detention.

One of those reporting on the trial for *Aftenposten*, an Oslo daily, was Dag Pedersen, who recalled the proceedings from his office in the summer of 2000.

> The security was very tight. The press was told not to go beyond a yellow strip. The court was packed with press, including fifty photographers.
>
> Judge Karl Solberg presided over a three-judge bench. As this was considered an unusual case in Norway, two prosecutors and two defense attorneys handled the case. And, as is true in criminal cases, the accused was entitled to have the best defense attorney available.
>
> It was a long trial and not an easy trial for the prosecution. Nesset himself looked more like a victim than a murderer. And when you got down to it, there was little hard evidence against him.

As the trial opened, the prosecution was armed with a thorough police investigation of sixty-two deaths at the three nursing homes where Nesset worked from 1962 until his arrest in the spring of 1981. After that inquiry, Nesset admitted responsibility for twenty-seven deaths, all by curacit. In fact, he went beyond that. At one point, he proclaimed, "I've killed so many I can't remember them all." However, the prosecution felt that they could only prove twenty-five of these deaths, all at Orkdal.

When Nesset entered the packed courtroom, flashbulbs began popping. Clearly, the time in custody had adversely affected him. He was pale and had lost weight.

However, Nesset reversed himself at the proceedings. The court was completely silent when Judge Solberg asked the accused, "Do you admit to having committed one, more than one, or all of the twenty-five murders?"

Without hesitation and nervousness, the accused responded, "No, not even one." Nesset also asserted innocence to charges of false documentation and embezzlement.

"This is a big case," the prosecutor said, turning to the jury, "and may be drawn out. It's up to you if you want each part of the accusations fully explained; tell me. Reach a decision on the basis of what you hear in court. Do not let yourselves be affected by the publicity in the case. Disregard what you think, believe, or have heard outside of this court." Two of the twelve jurors were excused before the end of the first day.

From the start, the court focused on Nesset's ability to get his hands on curacit and why the home and staff never suspected Nesset or, if they did, follow up on these suspicions during a four-year period.

A supervisor at Orkdal Hospital told the court on the first day of the proceedings that he suspected Nesset. When he confronted him, Nesset took some bottles from his pocket and explained, "I have to put my dog to sleep." But at the time he had no dog.

That corroborated what Nesset himself had told the police investigation. Moreover, he said that he needed to kill the neighbor's dog with curacit. But in the courtroom, the neighbor testified, "Neither I nor my husband has ever talked with Nesset about putting our beloved dog to sleep. Lucy, our dog, is like family, and we would never put our family to sleep. In fact, we eventually took our fourteen-year-old poodle to the veterinarian."

Prosecutor Jaghelin asked the witness, "Did you have any other conversations with the accused about the killing of dogs?"

"Yes," responded the witness. "His own. He told me he killed his own dog. I can not recall if he described how. But he did say that he did it in a very good and humane manner and he was very 'pleased' with the process."

Presently, a medical health officer in Trondelag and then a nurse at Orkdal hospital, another witness recalled an incident in 1975 to prove that Nesset had long thought about curacit.

"On one occasion, without being asked," the witness said, "Arnfinn Nesset showed me two glasses of curacit that he was carrying in his pocket. There was always an open and cordial relation between us, so I asked him why he needed the curacit. 'I have to put a dog to sleep,' he said.

"I am familiar with dogs and happen to like dogs, so I asked him, 'Wouldn't it be better to go to a veterinarian?'

"'No, I am a nurse educated in anesthesia. Therefore, I am equipped to do it.'"

How did the accused get hold of the curacit? An Orkdal pharmacy called the home in 1980 to inquire why there had been a large order of curacit, since it was used only in difficult surgical procedures for the temporary inhibition of motor nerves. The pharmacy had sold enough curacit to kill about two hundred fifty healthy people.

The query was followed up by a local journalist. Why were there so many deaths at the nursing home? The journalist linked the deaths to curacit. Attorney General Magnar Flores was dispatched to the nursing home to help the local police. Between 1977–80, some forty deaths had occurred in the Orkdal home. "Those numbers in themselves were not alarming," Dr. John Dalseth, the District Physician representing Trondheim, had told police. "Other nursing homes had comparable numbers during that period. We had one hundred ten patients; forty deaths were not unusual."

According to Dalseth, "There was nothing then suspicious about the situation. We did learn that Nesset first got nine thousand milligrams of curacit in 1980 and was sent twenty-eight hundred milligrams also in 1980. Nesset said that he needed the first order to put a dog to sleep. The second order was needed for the same reason."

Police investigations showed that Nesset regularly received the curacit by ordering, or adding, the curacit on a list after a physician had signed the list.

The police did not accept Nesset's dog story. Police Inspector Arne S. Karoliussen told the court that Nesset claimed that when he didn't need the second package of curacit, he returned the curacit to the pharmacy with the instructions "marked for destruction." He claimed the pharmacist destroyed the medicine in a fire and never opened the package. "Therefore, we didn't know whether curacit was returned or how much, if any, was returned," said Karoliussen.

The police queried Nesset. "Where are the requisitions for the prescriptions?" At first, Nesset denied any knowledge of the order. Later, he admitted he faked prescriptions to buy the drug. The police found prescriptions and curacit in a drawer in his home. Nesset was arrested in February and charged in March 1981. The charges grew from one to twenty-five in July 1981.

Those at the home should have taken more notice, according to the supervisor, because Nesset was giving medicine intravenously to patients without the procedure being prescribed.

In 1977, one nurse was convinced something was not right at the home. She saw some connection between mysterious deaths at the home. The nurse posted a sign at the home that all injections that were not prescribed by a physician had to note the date and time of the procedure and permission had to be signed by someone other than the patient.

All Nesset's killings occurred between 1977–80. One physician voiced suspicion in 1977 about the number of unusual deaths, but the home did not act on these suspicions. In the fall of 1980, the home did not respond to the report of a woman employee at Orkdal, who noticed needle marks in the arm of a dead resident. She had been on the alert before because she wondered why there were so many deaths at the home. "Curacit is only used for surgery," she told her supervisor, "and has no place in a home for sick people." Her concerns were disregarded, as was her appeal to the chief medical officer in Orkdal.

In fact, it was not difficult for Nesset to get his hands on curacit. "In the winter of 1977–78 I gave Nesset curacit," a nurse told the court. "I knew that curacit had been previously used in the home, so I gave it to him. Obviously, Nesset knew that I was a nurse assigned to the operating room, and he looked me up.

"He came up in the corridor outside the ward and rang the bell. I can still see him standing in front of me."

That witness also testified that later, in 1978, that another nurse told her that Nesset had come to her for curacit, and she also gave him the drug.

Because one nurse had previously used curacit to kill cats in the home, the witness did not find Nesset's request unusual.

The witness continued: "Once given the curacit, Nesset approached the second nurse again. That was in 1978 or 1979. This time she refused. The first time I had given him two glasses. Both times he said that he needed the medicine to put a dog to sleep, but he didn't say which dog. I was not convinced that he was telling the truth."

Nesset was quite "clever," the witness said.

> In 1977, a dying patient had been seen eight to ten times every hour. Just before the patient died, I had been with her to take her pulse. I went back into the hall to prepare dinner when Nesset poked his head from the room and said, 'Well, now she is dead.'
>
> 'What are you saying? I was just in the room.'
>
> Nesset responded, 'That's what I thought. You were the last one in there.'
>
> I saw his comment as being critical of me and an accusation that I was responsible for her death.
>
> I discussed this incident with the nurses on the ward. It was

strange that Nesset had discovered this death because Nesset was seldom seen on the wards.

Another witness related the suspicions she had of Nesset. The nurse placed the time frame in 1980.

Once, Nesset demanded the painkilling medicine fortralin with a syringe, for a very sick person. I stood up to Nesset and told him that without a physician's prescription he could not have the medicine. But then he demanded the keys to the medicine cabinet.

He obviously got the medicine and used the syringe. The patient later died that year. He was never charged with murder. But because he took too many liberties as manager of the home, I resolved to have little to say or do with him.

I kept a close watch on the manager. I found an empty box that had contained curacit. The box had been locked in the lab. I put the box back and went to speak with department head Dr. Noa. Why was there curacit in the nursing home? I immediately returned to the lab with Dr. Noa, but Nesset got there before us. The box had been removed.

After this incident, Dr. Noa and I were both looking for the chance to catch Nesset in the act.

The defense attorney interrupted the testimony. "But wasn't this watch at the risk of more deaths? Why didn't you bring charges against the accused?"

Responded the witness, "We talked about bringing charges, but that would have only been based on what we had seen. We felt that it was not enough, and if our charges were unsuccessful, we would have alerted Nesset, and all the evidence would have disappeared."

Many witnesses knew or had strong suspicions about Nesset and the curacit deaths. Only two witnesses expressed strong grief and guilt about not stepping forward with more vigor and correcting the situation. The two were both formerly in the home's employ: a nurse and supervising physician. The nurse testified:

In 1979, I found a syringe and its tip in a room where a patient had just died. The deceased had a prickmark in her left armpit, covered with cotton and a Band-Aid. The tip of the syringe was in the bed of the patient.

I had heard about other mysterious deaths at the home but said nothing to the home's administration. When the case came to light against Nesset, I felt depressed. I knew that he was in the room and had given the injection, but the word "murder" was never in my mind.

As more details were in the press, I started to cry. I decided to come forward on my own as witness. It has been a relief, although sad, to relate what I saw.

The former supervising physician, Dr. Kari Noer, was described as the principal prosecution witness. She was grilled for three days by counsel Nordhaus. "I have not been happy about this description," Dr. Noer said. "This is a very sad case. I have cried a lot in thinking about all the deaths. And it has not been pleasant to be personally associated with these sad events."

Noer had responsibility for the care of the twenty-five patients listed in the accusations against Nesset. "What especially concerns me," she said, "is that people who worked with me and around me didn't come forward with their experiences and feelings earlier in this story. Had they done so, this sad story would have been different. When I became suspicious, I proceeded as quickly as I could. Could I have done more? I am saddened by the answer."

Where was the administration of the home? The laxity of the home in acting on the suspicions led to the resignation of the entire board of directors in 1981. The board chairman, Olav Metilaas, told the court, "We decided that maybe we had been too lax and decided to resign.

"Before Christmas of 1989, we had information about the ordering of curacit for the nursing home. We decided to wait. We wanted to protect the patients and the staff during the holiday season. We didn't discuss the case until the end of January.

Depravity

"In reflection, this was a stupid mistake. It was done out of naivete and humane reasons."

The long drawn-out proceedings spotlighted the explanation and defense of Nesset. The court also was able to piece together a profile of the accused, both from testimony and the presentation of police reports.

The accused was on the stand October 22. The state attorney wanted to know why the accused had confessed to the police and now had withdrawn the admissions.

"When I learned about the suspicions against me, I was sure that I had never killed anyone. I may be confused in my head, but I remember everything that happened in the home and I know I never killed anyone.

"But I became scared when the police questioned me, so I admitted crimes I never committed. What could I do when the police intimidated me and told me that they had proof, and, if necessary, they would dig up the dead?" In fact, the police had permission to exhume the dead but abandoned the plan because curacit would not show up.

The state attorney asked, "Can you tell us more about the police hearings? What actually happened? The police wrote down what you said. Is there doubt that the police did it honestly? And in their report, you confessed many premeditated murders. What do you say to that?"

Responded Nesset, "Maybe that's the way I explained it, but I never killed anyone."

"Now, we are talking about police hearings on the seventh, eighth, ninth, and tenth of April 1981." The defense attorney questioned Nesset: "Were you asked about one murder or were you asked about more? Were there more hearings? How many hours were you interrogated?

"Nesset, you have to help us here in the court. Did you break down at the hearings?"

"That is what happened," Nesset said.

"During one of the hearings," continued the defense, "you said,

'I am confused in my head.' And you said about the confession, 'I confessed so that I could get done with it.' What did you mean when you said that, Nesset? What did you have to finish? Was it your conscience that made you feel bad? Did you realize the consequences of your confession?

"The police report said you cried when the talk was about the details of the third death. Was it because you had done something horrible? The report also noted that you 'cried because of the battle of good and evil within me.'"

Nesset only responded to the last question. "When I told about the evil and good inside me, it was because the policemen from the criminal division asked if I had evil and good within me."

The defense resumed, "I have to dig a little deeper inside you, Nesset, even if it is unpleasant for you. We still have to know a little more why you reacted to the police the way you did."

Nesset quickly answered, "I know for sure that I never used curacit on anyone to kill them."

Having fully maintained his innocence, Nesset then faced prosecutor Solberg. The defendant heard the murder charge number four, an eighty-eight-year-old female patient. "I remember that patient very well," he said. "I never gave her any injection and never did I give her any medicine."

"Then," asked the prosecutor, "how do you explain that in the room of the deceased, a syringe was found in the sink, and in her bed a container and tip of a syringe? The deceased had a prick in her armpit with a Band-Aid on it."

"I don't know a thing about that," answered Nesset.

"Of course not!" returned Solberg. "But someone must have done it."

During another round of interrogations that day, both defense and prosecution asked about police reports that Nesset had "seen himself" in the halls of the nursing home and next to the dying patient.

"Is that the way your memory works?" asked defense counsel Nordhaus.

"No. When being questioned by the police, they asked if I could see myself in those situations, and I answered, 'Yes.' When I got back to my cell in Tunga prison, I thought more about this."

"How have you slept?" asked the defense attorney.

"I slept very little during this period."

Nordhaus continued, "Now, you have come to a situation where your job is destroyed. Your family has gone. The future is uncertain. Doesn't that bother you during the night?"

"I dreamt about all this," said Nesset. "I dreamt that I was home with my family."

Nordhaus continued, "But did you also dream about the deceased, of whom you talked about, that you were standing next to their bed?"

"No, I only dreamt that I was driving around in wheelchairs!" answered Nesset.

During his questioning of the accused, state attorney Olaf Jakhelln tried to deflate Nesset's self-portrait that he was an agreeable "yes" person who always was anxious to satisfy the police and agreed to crimes he never committed.

In his report, Dag Pedersen quoted an incredulous Jakhelln: "I can not merely accept Nesset's 'yes' on questions of guilt because he was psychologically broken down or he was ready to please.

"He doesn't want to please all the time. There are many instances at the hearings, when time after time, he resists when asked about deaths in the nursing home."

The prosecution stood by the police reports, which said, among other things, "I've killed so many I can't remember them all."

After that statement, Nesset then requested a list of all the patients at the facilities where he worked since 1962 so that he could "sharpen" his memory.

As slides were shown in court about the application of syringes with curacit, Jakhelln asked Nesset to explain how the drug worked. He did this very willingly and professionally. "It is very possible to give the patient an intravenous liquid through a needle without removing the tube," he said.

How does one put together a mental profile of the balding, mild-mannered Nesset? What were the motives for administering curacit: mercy killings, need for pleasure, thirst for power, or other reasons? Criminal behavior specialists in Norway added reasons of schizophrenia, self-assertion, and sadism.

Dag Pedersen commented on the "favorable public image" of Nesset. "He enjoyed an excellent local reputation as a dedicated member of the Salvation Army and a strong opponent of abortion."

Nesset's neighbor was very complimentary about the accused. He was a "good and helpful man. Whenever we needed help with anything, he came quickly. Often, he came without asking, and after he came, he would follow up to see that everything was in order."

The court also heard praise from Nesset's former colleagues. "I have only good things to say about Arnfinn Nesset from the time I first met him," said a midwife who knew the accused as far back as the summer of 1962. At the time, they were students in anesthesiology at the Trondheim Hospital. The former chief physician in the Anesthesiology Department in the Hospital also thought highly of Nesset.

Said the midwife of Nesset, "He was a very kind student. He was also very skilled and could do anything on the ward. He was very good with his hands. If he could have worked in the operating room, he would have been able to accomplish that, too.

"I never saw him unwilling to help or irritable. That was remarkable since we would put in eight to twelve hours a day."

The department head described Nesset as "conscientious, pleasant, eager to learn, a student who always asked good questions during his training."

However, the puzzling side of Nesset appeared during the questioning of the physician. Asked the prosecutor, "At any time, did the accused mention in any way, even if in jest, that it was possible to kill a person with curacit?

"The only thing," the chief physician answered, "was that a nurse's aide approached me and said that Arnfinn Nesset had stood next to her with syringe and said, 'If I put this on you, then you will be dead in a moment.' But the aide took this as a joke."

The defense attorney interjected, "Did the nurse's aide tell you this at the time when Nesset was a student?"

"No," responded the physician. "That conversation took place after this case came up."

"To understand the matter clearly," said the defense attorney, "was that after this case was already well-known?"

"Yes."

Certainly, the most comprehensive and authoritative personality evaluation of the accused was given by Geirr Molde Jensen, a psychologist who interviewed Nesset while he was in police custody.

Jensen said that Nesset relished power, was not sadistic, was obsessed with death, and displayed conflicting personality traits.

"Nesset enjoyed power," he said. "He had power as manager of the home. There is power when someone is dependent on another for help."

Jensen said that Nesset insisted that he was not sadistic. The accused told him, "I never wished anything bad for a single individual. I believe that we have a need for human contact. Such contact gives a good feeling.

"I would not be sitting here today if I had been tougher and less kind. Then, I would have been sitting outside and just looked at this whole misery. I am not sadistic and am not a murderer. Try to understand."

Perhaps this is the reason that Nesset has never shown any remorse for his actions. He thinks he is the victim.

Nesset was contradictory, offered Jensen. "Nesset is a strong and determined individual. On another side, he is a timid, servile individual."

Excessive concern about death was another observation, Jensen noted. Jensen called Nesset's behavior "contraphobish," the quality of "looking for and trying to subdue that which one is most afraid of … In Nesset's case, it was death. He wished for a peaceful place in the cemetery. This was consistent with the dread he felt about death and graves."

Necrophilia formed a major focus of Dr. Noer's testimony. The court psychiatrist, Dr. Karl-Ewerth Hornemann asked Dr. Noer about Nesset's motives. "He was unable to control his desire to take away life. He was a necrophiliac. Apart from necrophilia, there was talk in the home, not proven, about sexual contact with the dead. If that were true, then his condition was worse than I realized.

"I did notice that Nesset had a desire to be present at the funerals of those from the home. And he was always eager to be with the families of the deceased."

Dr. Noer also spoke of Nesset's "variant" personalities. "While he was domineering and self-assertive, Nesset was basically good-natured, an individual who liked to be at the center and make decisions. This need was also reflected in his wanting to play doctor. He felt good playing doctor although he had no professional basis for this role."

The witness said that he sensed a defect in Nesset's personality. "I don't think," said Noer, "Nesset had a clear idea of the distinction between right and wrong. He presented reality as he saw it and felt comfortable with that."

Psychologist Halvard Tomta, who interviewed Nesset for the police, said that the accused during the confession offered three reasons for his actions: "to make room for new patients in the home," "to help the old, infirm, pain-stricken people," and "Something inside me made me do it."

In his closing defense, Nordhaus conceded that Nesset enjoyed power, but his confessions to police were given while he was depressed. "Nesset felt the power of administering mercy killings. He looked at himself as a virtual demigod who believed he possessed absolute power of life or death over the elderly patients he controlled."

However, four psychiatrists had submitted pretrial evaluations that

Nesset was sane and accountable for his actions while administering curacit.

According to Dr. Tomta, Nesset did see himself beset with problems. "Nesset compared himself to a schizophrenic patient that he had researched for his thesis to earn his nursing diploma. 'Something has to be wrong with me,' he told me, "when I could do something like that [the curacit killings]. Because of these deaths I have not had a good day in my life since 1977.'"

Was sex a factor, psychologist Dr. Per Nyhous was asked. "It was not a possibility," he answered.

Agreement was voiced that a troubled childhood and adolescence had a sharply adverse effect on Nesset. He was troubled by being an illegitimate child. He rarely spoke to his stepfather. In fact, they never spoke to each other while they worked side by side in a factory.

After their marriage, mother and stepfather moved, and Arnfinn went to live with his grandparents on a farm. "I was terribly lonely in childhood," Nesset told psychiatrists. "Often, I was told by non-family that I was born outside marriage."

Nesset remained close to his mother. During the trial, spectators noted how emotional he was in relating his mother's death in 1975.

Psychologist Jensen told the court:

> Nesset had a strong mother fixation. Because his mother was so close to him, this can be called a symbiotic fixation. On one occasion, his mother had not washed his coffee cup. That experience strongly affected the son.
>
> Because of his sufferings, Nesset identified himself with the sufferings of Christ, who Nesset focused on as hero. For Nesset, there was a sense of heroism in being a victim.
>
> Undoubtedly, the greatest effect on his behavior was the unwanted childhood in a poor, Christian home that was not always warm and loving. He had a need for being accepted in a man's world, and at times he felt he was not strong enough to achieve that acceptance.

During his testimony, Nesset related, "My childhood was very much filled with religion. God's name was often heard in our home. I had to follow a strong religious line."

Nesset studied nursing and worked at first in the anesthesia recovery ward in central Trondheim Hospital. He married in 1964, had two children, and was divorced after several years of marriage. He remarried and separated soon after the curacit killings became known. In fact, his second wife, Karen Neslo, was a surprise witness in court. She destroyed his alibi in the death of Petra Klukstad on July 13, 1979. Nesset claimed that he came to the nursing home that evening to pick up his wife. "Not true," she said. "I was on overtime that evening and never saw Arnfinn that night."

Nesset first became eligible for parole in March, 1993, after eleven years behind bars. *Aft Dag* reported in January 1994 that Nesset began a new routine. He spent his first workday in the laundry room at the Christian Center, a rehabilitation center for fourteen substance abusers and criminals. A Christian, Nesset was also given the role of social worker at the center. His sentence of preventive supervision still maintained limited furlough conditions.

According to *Aft Dag*, Nesset "has amassed excellent references to present in his favor from the prison authorities, the Public Prosecutor, as well as from Borre Husebo and Karl Ewert Hornemann, the psychiatric experts who testified in Nesset's trial."

Nesset was released in 2004, and is presumed to be living at an undisclosed location in Norway, under a new name.

Little has been written in Norway of Nesset in recent years. He has done his time, and few are anxious to write or talk of him. However, during his trial and after, any reasoned observer wondered how a professionally run nursing facility could allow such bizarre and strange behavior of Nesset to proceed at the home.

Orkdal Valley Nursing Home has refused to be open about the case. Before we visited Norway in the summer of 2000, we wrote Malfrid

Bogen, the director, so that we could interview her. She responded on August 18, 2000:

"Orkdal Sjuke-og Aldersheim has no new information in the case you referred to in your letter. The case ended in a criminal trial and the legal documents are to be found in official files. You may use these documents to find the information you seek.

"Orkdal Sjuke-og Aldersheim accordingly refuses to talk with you about this case."

Bibliography

Apsche, Jack. *Probing the Mind of a Serial Killer.* Morrisville, PA: International Information Associates, 1993.

Bardens, Dennis. *The Ladykiller.* London: P. Davies, 1973.

Bardsley, Marilyn. "Dean Corll: The Sex, Sadism, and Slaughter of Houston's Candy Man." 2001. 6 July 2002. www.trutv.com/library/crime/serial_killers/predators/corll/index_1.html.

Bellamy, Patrick. "Henry Lee Lucas: Deadly Drifter." 2001. The Crime Library. 6 July 2002. www.trutv.com/library/crime/serial_killers/predators/lucas/confess_1.html.

Benjamin, Walter. *Moscow Diary.* ed. Gary Smith. Cambridge, MA: Harvard University Press, 1986.

Boar, Roger. and Nigel Blundell. *The World's Most Infamous Murders,* New York: Simon and Schuster, 1984.

Bolitho, William. *Murder for Profit.* New York: Harper and Brothers, 1926.

Brown, Wenzell. *Introduction to Murder: The Unpublished Facts Behind the Notorious Lonely Hearts Killers, Martha Beck and Raymond Fernandez.* New York: Greenberg, 1952.

Call, Max. *Hand of Death; The Henry Lee Lucas Story.* Lafayette, LA: Prescott Press, 1985.

Cameron, Deborah. *The Lust to Kill; A Feminist Investigation of Sexual Murder.* New York: New York University Press, 1987.

Chehade, Carol. *Big Little White Lies.* New York: Nehmarche, 2001.

Cox, Mike. *The Confessions of Henry Lee Lucas.* New York: Ivy Books, 1991

Cullen, Robert. *The Killer Department: Detective Viktor Burakov's Eight-Year Search for the Most Savage Serial Killer in Russian History*. New York: Pantheon Books, 1993.

Du Clos, Bernard. *Fair Game*. New York: St. Martin's, 1993.

Egger, Steven. *The Killers Among Us: An Examination of Serial Murder and Its Investigation*. Upper Saddle River, NJ: Prentice Hall, 1998.

Everitt, David. *Human Monsters: An Illustrated Encyclopedia of the World's Most Vicious Murderers*. Chicago: Contemporary Books, 1993.

Fears, Daryl and Avis-Thomas Lester. "Stereotype Leads Down False Trail in the Sniper Case; Whacked Out Males Are Far From the Only Candidate." *Los Angeles Times*. 29 September 2002. A17.

Feurmann, George. *Houston: The Once and Future City*. Garden City, NY: Doubleday, 1971.

Frasier, David. *Murder Cases of the Twentieth Century*. Jefferson, NC: McFarland, 1996.

Gaddis, Thomas, and James Long. *Killer: A Journal of Murder*. New York: Macmillan 1970.

Gaddis, Thomas and James Long. *Killers*. New York: Macmillan, 1970.

Gerneta, M. N., ed. *The Criminal World of Moscow*. Moscow: Lukon, 1991.

Gilbert, Alexander. "Fritz Haarman: The Butcher of Hannover." 2001. The Crime Library. 6 July 2002. www.trutv.com/library/crime/serial_killers/history/haarman/killer_5.html.

Gilmour, Walter and Leland E. Hale. *Butcher, Baker: A True Account of a Serial Murderer*. New York: Onyx Books, 1991.

Grombach, John. *The Great Liquidator*. New York: Doubleday, 1980.

Hearn, Daniel A. *Legal Executions in New York State: A Comprehensive Reference, 1639-1963.* Jefferson, NC: McFarland, 1997.

Hickey, Eric W. *Serial Murderers and Their Victims.* Belmont, CA: Wadsworth, 1997.

Hoffman, Richard. "The Lonely Hearts Killers." *True Crime Detective.* 1 (Fall 1951), 3–8.

Holmes, Ronald. *Contemporary Perspective on Serial Murder.* Los Angeles: Sage Publications, 1998.

Holmes, Ronald and James De Burger. *Serial Murder.* Newbury Park, CA: Sage Publications, 1988.

Jancar, J. and Leila B. Kettle. "Hypergraphia and Mental Handicap." *Journal of Mental Deficiency Research.* 28 (June 1984), 151-58.

Jenkins, Philip. *Using Murder; The Social Construction of Serial Homicide.* New York: Aldine de Gruyter, 1994.

Kelleher, Michael and C.L. Kelleher. *Murder Most Rare; The Female Serial Killer.* Westport, CT: Praeger, 1998.

Kelly, Bill. "Charles Ng and Leonard Lake: The Motherlode Murders. 2000. 6 July 2002. www.cybersleuths.com.

Kinnell, Herbert. "Serial Homicide by Doctors: Shipman in Perspective." *British Medical Journal* 321 (December 23, 2000) 1594–97

Krivich. Mikhail and Olgert Ol'Gin. *Comrade Chikatilo.* Fort Lee, NJ: Barricade Books, 1993.

Lane, Brian and Wilfred Gregg. *Encyclopedia of Serial Killers.* London: Headline Book Publishing, 1992.

Lesser, Henry. *Killer.* New York: Harcourt, Brace & World, 1938.

Lessing, Theodore. *Monsters of the Weimar: The Story of a Werewolf.* London: Nemesis, 1993.

Lester, David. *Serial Killers.* Philadelphia: Charles Press, 1995.

Levin, Jack and James Fox. *Mass Murder; The Growing Menace*. New York: Plenum Press, 1985.

Leyton, Elliot. *Compulsive Killers; The Story of Modern Multiple Murder*. New York: New York University Press, 1986.

Leyton, Elliot. *Serial Murder: Modern Scientific Perspectives*. Burlington, VT: Ashgate, 2000

Linedecker, Clifford. *The Man Who Killed Boys*. New York: St. Martin's, 1980.

Linedecker, Clifford. *Thrill Killers*. New York: Paper Jacks, 1987.

London, Sondra. "Killer Arts With Ottis Toole: The Hands Don't Lie." 6 July 2001. www.sondralondon.com/tales/hands/lie.html.

"Lonely Hearts Crimes Skyrocket." *Mainichi Daily News*. 2 November 2001. A1

Lourie, Richard. *The Monster of Rostov: Hunting the Devil*. New York: Harper, 1993.

Menninger, Karl. *Man Against Himself*. New York: Harcourt, Brace, 1938.

Motluk, Alison. "Ezekiel's Visions May Owe as Much to Disease as to Divine Inspiration." *New Scientist*. 26 (November 17, 2001). 2020

Nash, Robert ed. "Hoch, Johann." *Encyclopedia of World Crime; Criminal Justice, Criminology, and Law Enforcement*. Wilmette, IL: Crime Books, 1990.

Newton, Michael. *Hunting Humans*. Port Townsend, WA: Loompatics Unlimited, 1992

Nickel, Steven. *Torso: The True Story of Eliot Ness and the Search for a Psychopathic Killer*. Winston-Salem, NC: J. F. Blair, 1989

Nocera, Joseph. "True Confessions." *Texas Monthly*. 17 (September 1984), 113–17.

Noe, Denise and Marilyn Bardsley. "The Crimes of Bela Kiss." TruTV Crime Library. 6 July 2002. www.trutv.com/library/crime/serial_killers/history/bela_kiss/1.html.

Norris, Joel. *Serial Killers*. New York: Anchor, 1989.

Olsen, Jack. *The Man With the Candy: The Story of the Houston Mass Murders*. New York: Simon and Schuster, 1973.

Pedersen, Dag. Reporter, *Aftenposten*. Personal interview. Oslo, 25 August 2000.

Ressler, R.K. et al. *FBI Law Enforcement Bulletin*, 54, 1985. 1–43.

Rose, David. *Violation*. London: Harper Press, 2006.

Schechter, Harold and David Everitt. *The A To Z Encyclopedia of Serial Killers*. New York: Pocket Books, 1996

Schutzer, A.J. "The Lady Killer." *American Heritage*. 15 (October 16, 1954), 35+.

Segrave, Kerry. *Women Serial and Mass Murderers*. Jefferson, NC. McFarland, 1992

Seltzer, Mark. *Serial Killers; Death and Life in America's Wound Culture*. New York: Routledge, 1998.

"Serial Murder: Multi-Disciplinary Perspectives for Investigators." Symposium, Behavioral Analysis Unit for the Analysis of Violent Crime, United States Department of Justice, Federal Bureau of Investigation. San Antonio, August 29, 2005.

Symons, Julian. "The Monster of Rostov." *New York Times Book Review*. March 14, 1993. p.6.

Tatar, Maria M. *Lustmord: Sexual Murder in Weimar Germany*. Princeton, NJ: Princeton University Press, 1995.

Tucker, Cynthia. *The Atlanta Journal Constitution*. 3 November 2002. F1.

"Vasili Komaroff Picture Poetry." *Rustlings of the Wind: Interpellation Issue: Lorien Creatives* 6/25/2001. wind.xephyrus.com/sum99/vasilikomaroffpoetry.html, 1999.

Werthan, Fredric. "Why Do They Commit Murder?" *New York Times*. 8 August 1954. A1+.

Wilson, Colin and Donald Seaman. *The Encyclopedia of Modern Murder*. London: Barker, 1983.

Wilson, Colin and Damon Wilson. *The Killers Among Us*. 2 vol. New York: Warner, 1995.

www.ingramcontent.com/pod-product-compliance
Lightning Source LLC
Chambersburg PA
CBHW031612160426
43196CB00006B/109